ABHANDLUNGEN FÜR DIE KUNDE
DES MORGENLANDES

Im Auftrag der Deutschen Morgenländischen Gesellschaft
herausgegeben von Florian C. Reiter

Band 66

2009

Harrassowitz Verlag · Wiesbaden

Silje Alvestad and Lutz Edzard

la-ḥšōḇ, but *la-ḥăzōr*? Sonority, Optimality, and the Hebrew פ״ח Forms

2009

Harrassowitz Verlag · Wiesbaden

Bibliografische Information der Deutschen Nationalbibliothek
Die Deutsche Nationalbibliothek verzeichnet diese Publikation in der Deutschen Nationalbibliografie; detaillierte bibliografische Daten sind im Internet über http://dnb.d-nb.de abrufbar.

Bibliographic information published by the Deutsche Nationalbibliothek
The Deutsche Nationalbibliothek lists this publication in the Deutsche Nationalbibliografie; detailed bibliographic data are available in the internet at http://dnb.d-nb.de.

For further information about our publishing program consult our website http://www.harrassowitz-verlag.de

Printed on permanent/durable paper.
Printing and binding: Hubert & Co., Göttingen
Printed in Germany

ISSN 0567-4980
ISBN 978-3-447-05910-7

Table of contents

Preface

This volume emerged as the result of informal discussions on various issues in Semitic linguistics that the two co-authors have had since June 2007. Some of these meetings revolved around issues in the Biblical and Modern Israeli Hebrew verbal systems as well as around various other morpho-phonological, syntactic, and lexical issues. A closer look at Modern Israeli Hebrew morpho-phonemics reveals a considerable amount of phenomena that point to an almost "diglossic" or "polyglossic" situation. In other words, one finds many discrepancies between the "normative" forms in Masoretic voweling that still prevail in fully voweled texts, notably grammars and dictionaries, but also in modern children's books on the one hand, and the reality of the various registers of spoken Hebrew on the other hand. Tiberian Hebrew itself displays a variety of forms, as we soon became aware of. The analysis of this broad variety of written and oral forms calls for a strictly descriptive approach in a modern theoretical framework.

One of the salient issues in this context is the realisation of the gutturals and their immediate phonetic environment. Most striking in this respect is the impact of the phoneme /ḥ/ on its environment. Not only can one observe a high degree of variation, when analysing relevant verbal and nominal forms as produced by native speakers. Also the modern Hebrew grammars and dictionaries continue to offer a diffuse picture, a picture that can be traced back all the way to ambiguities as reflected in the voweling of the corresponding forms in the Hebrew Bible by the Tiberian Masora.

The project soon developed a life of its own and proved to have a number of interesting ramifications, all of which were not obvious to us at the very outset. In order to give full justice to the wealth of written and acoustical data and their analysis, we thus decided to publish our work on this issue in a monograph, which allowed for the full representation of both written and oral data, including statistical tables and spectrograms of acoustical speech analysis.

Werner Arnold, Janet Watson, and a number of students at the Department of Semitic Studies at the University of Heidelberg offered useful comments after a first public presentation of the project in January 2008.

The project profited especially from a roundtable held jointly with Shmuel Bolozky, University of Massachusetts at Amherst, and Outi Bat-El, Tel Aviv University, on October 27, 2008, at the University of Oslo. The roundtable was co-sponsored by the Department of Culture Studies and Oriental Languages (IKOS) and the Department of Literature, Area Studies, and European Languages (ILOS), University of Oslo. We are most grateful for the critical input we received on this occasion and afterwards from both visiting scholars.

IKOS generously supported this project with a grant devoted to linguistic fieldwork. Shmuel Bolozky has stood by from the very beginning of our deliberations with constant encouragement and valuable critical input. Thanks also to Geoffrey Khan for a number of helpful written comments. We also wish to thank Inger Moen, Department of Linguistics and Scandinavian Languages (ILN), University of Oslo, Kathrine Asla Østby, ILOS, University of Oslo, and Helene Nordgård Andreassen, University of Tromsø, for helpful comments on various phonetic issues. Thanks also to Clàudia Pons Moll for e-mail communication on her 2008 poster, and Gjert Kristoffersen, University of Bergen, for e-mail communication on issues within lexical phonology. The project would not have been possible without the kind help of our informants (or respondents) Nava Bergman, Rikki Bliboim, Shira Bliboim, Yahel Harel Blystad, Rafi Ezratty, Charlotte Goldfarb, Nati Goldfarb, Benjamin Hary, Rachel Hasson, Yafit Marom, Ilan Sadeh, Shelley Shloush, and Yoad Winter. Matthew Monger helped with proofreading our final draft and compiled the index of authors. Last, but not least, we are greatly indebted to Barbara Krauß of Harrassowitz Verlag and Florian Reiter, the editor of the series *Abhandlungen für die Kunde des Morgenlandes*, both of whom made the publication of this volume possible.

Oslo and Jerusalem, January 2009

Silje Susanne Alvestad, ILOS   Lutz Edzard, IKOS

Abbreviations

1 The books of the Hebrew Bible (and Ben Sira)

Gen	Genesis
Ex	Exodus
Lev	Leviticus
Num	Numbers
Dt	Deuteronomium
Jos	Joshua
Judg	Judges
1 Sam	1st Samuel
2 Sam	2nd Samuel
1 K	1st Kings
2 K	2nd Kings
Is	Isaiah
Jer	Jeremiah
Ez	Ezekiel
Hos	Hosea
Joel	Joel
Amos	Amos
Ob	Obadiah
Jon	Jonah
Mic	Micah
Nah	Nahum
Hab	Habakkuk
Zeph	Zephaniah
Hag	Haggai
Zech	Zechariah
Mal	Malachi
Ps	Psalms
Prov	Proverbs
Job	Job
Ct	Song of Songs
Ruth	Ruth
Lam	Lamentations
Qoh	Ecclesiastes
Est	Esther
Dan	Daniel
Ezra	Ezra
Neh	Nehemiah
1 Chr	1st Chronicles
2 Chr	2nd Chronicles
Sir	Ben Sira

2 Other abbreviations

BHS	Biblia Hebraica Stuttgartensia
GvG	Grundriß der vergleichenden Grammatik [der semitischen Sprachen]
IH	Israeli Hebrew
LXX	Septuaginta
MH	Medieval Hebrew
TA	Tiberian Aramaic
TH	Tiberian Hebrew

Notes on transcription

With few exceptions, we make it a point to always provide both the original Hebrew script and a transcription. The transcription from Biblical Hebrew in the transmission of the Tiberian Masora is oriented toward the system which Goerwitz (1996: 496) calls "transliteration". In other words, a *phonetic* transcription of Tiberian Hebrew, especially as far as vowel *quality* is concerned, is not attempted. Even though we follow Khan (1987, 1997) in that vowel quantity was not phonemic in general (with few possible exceptions such as דֳמִי *dămī* [dɔ'mi:] 'silence' vs. דָמִי *dām-ī* [dɔ:'mi:] 'my blood'), we mark vowels in stressed closed syllables and (unreduced) vowels in unstressed open syllables as long. However, we do not mark long vowels in *scriptio plena* with a circumflex. Stress itself is only exceptionally indicated, notably in pausal forms on the penultima, e.g., in the form יַחְשֹׁ֫בוּ *yaḥšṓḇū* 'they think' (Is 13:17). Occasional possessive and object suffixes are separated by hyphen. The cantillation marks are not reproduced, but we point out their importance, where appropriate and/or necessary.

The transcription from Modern Israeli Hebrew, both written material and oral recordings, follows accepted descriptive standards (cf. Bolozky 1997), i.e. neither vowel nor consonant quantity is marked. Also, spirantised allophones are not marked as such; rather, other letters are used in the transcription (e.g., *yaxshevu* 'they will think'), since the *begadkefat*-rules are largely blurred in Modern Hebrew. When appropriate in the context of diachronic deliberations, descriptive modern and normative Masoretic transcriptions are juxtaposed.

The zero vowel and the short vowels are cited as follows:

– *šwā nāḥ*, *nāᶜ*, and *mərāḥēp̄*: *šwā quiescens*, *mobile*, and *medium*;

– *ḥăṭap̄ pattāḥ*, *sẹḡōl*, and *qāmāṣ*:[1] *ḥăṭāp̄* vowels *ă* [a], *ĕ* [ɛ], and *ŏ* [ɔ].

1 The absolute form is חֲטָף *ḥăṭāp̄*, in medieval Hebrew also חָטֵף *ḥāṭēp̄*.

1 Introduction: issues of synchronic vs. diachronic derivation in Biblical (Tiberian) Hebrew and Modern Israeli Hebrew:

1.1 The partial inadequacy of the Masoretic system for a proper description of Modern Israeli Hebrew morpho-phonology

While a good deal of Modern Israeli Hebrew morpho-phonology can be described in terms of the punctuation and voweling system elaborated by the Tiberian Masora, this does not hold across the board. Modern Hebrew adopted the morphology of Tiberian Hebrew, but not its phonology. Modern Hebrew does not display weight contrast, i.e. there is no distinction between short and long vowels or simple and geminate consonants (cf. Bat-El 2008: 39). While the second part of her statement about the synchronic loss of "geminates" is generally accepted, the implication of the first part of the statement to the effect that Tiberian Hebrew displayed weight contrast is at least controversial.[1] The bulk of Modern Hebrew morpho-phonology can and must be described in strictly synchronic terms; at the same time, Bat-El (2008: 40) concedes that some phenomena, notably the behaviour of stems *primae gutturalis*, can hardly be properly described without any historical perspective. In the following, we will briefly review some relevant phenomena in this context, which illustrate the need to distinguish between a diachronic and a synchronic analysis.

1.1.1 Geminates in Tiberian Hebrew and Modern Israeli Hebrew

In Modern Israeli Hebrew there is no phonetic evidence for gemination, except across morpheme boundaries, and this only in careful deliberate speech. Examples include שָׁבַתִּי *šavátti* 'I was on strike' and יָשַׁנּוּ *yašánnu* 'we slept'. Therefore, it is reasonable and necessary to describe the modern language without recourse to the morpho-phonemic rules stipulated by the Masoretic system.

---

1 There is an ongoing controversy about whether or not the Tiberian vowel system displayed just quality oppositions (the opinion of, e.g., Khan 1987) or quality *and* quantity oppositions (the opinion of, e.g., Morag 1962). Cf. also section 4.1.2.7 below for some illuminating minimal pairs.

As an illustration of the foregoing point consider the following pair of lemmata: whereas the lemma דָּבָר *dāḇār* 'word' (whose first syllable receives pretonic lengthening) has the plural דְּבָרִים *dəḇārīm*,[2] the (post-classical) lemma דַּוָּר *dawwār* 'postman' has the plural דַּוָּרִים *dawwārīm*, the point being that the first vowel cannot be shortened to *šwā* due to the geminated *w*. In the Tiberian Hebrew system, the opposition between these two lemmata is entirely transparent, of course. In Modern Israeli Hebrew, however, where gemination is said to be obliterated (and where spirantised *ḇ* and the glide *w* have merged as [v]), the opposition is all of a sudden opaque. Thus, one arrives at the following pairs, contrasting the morpho-phonemics of Tiberian Hebrew on the one hand and Modern Israeli Hebrew on the other:

(1) (Minimal) pairs in Tiberian Hebrew and Modern Israeli Hebrew

Singular	Plural	Singular	Plural
דָּבָר *dāḇār*	דְּבָרִים *dəḇārīm*	*davar*	*dvarim*
דַּוָּר *dawwār*	דַּוָּרִים *dawwārīm*	*davar*	*davarim*

Obviously, the strictly synchronic derivation of the minimal pair *dvarim* 'words' vs. *davarim* 'postmen' in Modern Israeli Hebrew represents a major theoretical challenge (cf. also the chart in Bat-El 2008: 42). Bat-El argues that one has to assume the selection between two lexical stems in case of the suffixation to *davar* 'word', whereas only one lexical stem exists when it comes to the suffixation to *davar* 'postman', where reduction of the first vowel is blocked for historical reasons (no *šwā* before double-consonance).

1.1.2 Gemination and post-vocalic spirantisation

Historically, geminated *bgdkpt* {ב, ג, ד, כ, פ, ת}, as marked by *dāḡēš forte* after a vowel, were never spirantised. In Modern Hebrew, this rule, which typically affects C_2, does no longer hold across the board. As an example, note the infinite form *le-rakhel* (<לְרַכֵּל>) 'to slander' in collo-

2 Here and in the following, *šwā nāᶜ* (*mobile*) is mostly transcribed as <ə> in the context of Tiberian Hebrew, irrespective of its phonetic realisation which may depend on the sonority of its consonantal environment.

quial Israeli Hebrew, where the middle radical /k/ is not de-spirantised (historically: "geminated"), as one would expect.[3]

In colloquial registers of Modern Israeli Hebrew (where the *bgdkpt*-rules are restricted to /b, k, p/ anyway), the quality of an underlying /b, k, p/ consonant ([± spirantised]) can be "transferred" from the past-form to the infinitive or *vice versa* through a process of "paradigmatic leveling", independently of whether this consonant directly follows a vowel (or a historical *šwā nāᶜ*) or not:

(2) "Transfer" of the feature [± spirantised] in colloquial registers of Israeli Hebrew ("paradigmatic leveling")

maxar	⇒	*li-mxor*	("standard": *li-mkor*)	'to sell'
šabar ("standard": *šavar*)	⇐	*li-šbor*		'to break'

Only individual lexical items seem to be affected by this process, though, which is by no means "productive". However, Bolozky (1997: 306f.) adduces many more examples of residual (non-)spirantisation in the Modern Hebrew verbal and nominal system. Thus, the standard prefix conjugation form *yikhtov* (Tiberian יִכְתֹּב *yiḵtōḇ*) 'he writes' can surface colloquially as *yiktov*, and the adjective *ratov/ratuv* 'wet' can surface in the feminine singular as *retuva* instead of standard *retuba* with non-spirantised *b* (Tiberian רְטוּבָּה *rəṭubbā*).

After the conjunction וְ *ve-* (*wə-*) as well as after the the mono-consonantal prepositions בְּ *be-* (*bə-*) and לְ *le-* (*lə-*), spirantisation is no longer active in colloquial registers of Modern Israeli Hebrew. Thus, one will always hear *be-Ber Ševa* (בְּאֵר שֶׁבַע) and *le-Ber Ševa* 'in/to Ber Sheva', not **be-Ver Ševa* and **le-Ver Ševa*. Conversely, loan words no longer have to be adapted to the phonotactic rules for spirantisation. Thus, syllable-initial *f* in a form like תִּלְפֵּן *tilfen* (instead of *tilpen*) 'he called on the phone' is nowadays perfectly grammatical. Word-initial *f* in פַּלֶסְטִינַאי *falestinai* 'Palestinian' is likewise acceptable.

3 We owe this observation to our colleague and informant Rikki Bliboim. This issue will be taken up again below under 4.1.2.3. For a sophisticated Optimality-Theoretic analysis of the stop-fricative alternations in Modern Hebrew cf. Adam 2002: 146–171.

1.1.3 Other phenomena

Some other features of Modern Israeli Hebrew deserve to be mentioned in this context as well:

The conjunction וְ *ve-* (*wə-*) no longer surfaces as [ū] before the labials /b, m, p/ or before *šwā nāʿ* in general. Thus, one will hear *ve-Baktus*, not **u-Vaktus*.[4]

The sequence of two historical *šwā nāʿ*s will no longer be automatically conflated to (long) *i*, i.e. one will hear *be-Yerušalaym* (יְרוּשָׁלַיִם), not necessarily **b-Irušalaym*.

One of the most prominent features of Modern Israeli Hebrew is the loss of the gutturals /ʾ, h, ʿ/, both word-initially and intervocally, e.g., יש לו המון בעיות *yéš lo hamón beʿayót* > *yéš lo amón beayót/baayót/ba:yót* 'he has many problems' or הוא רוצה להבין מא הולך *hu rotsé le-havin ma holékh* > *u rotsé leavin/lavín ma olékh* 'he wants to understand what is going on' (Bolozky 2008: handout). Bolozky argues that similar reduction phenomena can already be observed in Biblical Hebrew, at least as far as the omission of /ʾ/ and /h/ are concerned. Consider the following pairs (all from Bolozky 2008: handout; cf. also Blau 1993: 24):

(3) Intervocalic deletion of /ʾ/ and /h/ forms in Biblical Hebrew

Non-reduced	**Reduced**
שְׁאֵרִית *səʾērīṯ* 'rest of' (2 Chr 34:9)	שֵׁרִית *šērīṯ* (1 Chr 12:39)'
תְאוֹמִים *təʾōmīm* 'twins' (Gen 38:27)	תוֹמִם *tōmīm* (Gen 25:24)
לְהַגִּיד *lə-haggīḏ* 'to tell' (1 K 18:12)	לַגִּיד *l-aggīḏ* (2 K 9:15)
לְהֵרָאוֹת *lə-hērāʾōṯ* 'to be seen' (1 K 18:2)	לֵרָאוֹת *l-ērāʾōṯ* (Ex 34:24)

The important conclusion to be drawn from these data is that "casual speech reduction" should never be exclusively considered a modern "degenerate" phenomenon, but evidence of the "down-to-earth" reality of the Masoretic transmission of the Hebrew Bible.

4 We have seen this word in the Hebrew version of the Norwegian children's book *Karius og Baktus*, voweled in a normative way ובַּקטוּס, but the actual pronunciation is as indicated above, pointing to an almost "diglossic" situation.

1.2 פ"ח forms: an outline of the research strategy

The central theme of this study is the question as to under precisely which circumstances an epenthetic *ḥăṭāp̄* vowel is inserted after C_1 = /ḥ/ in verbal and nominal forms of the structure Cvḥ(v̆)C_2vC_3(v̄). Both historical forms found in the corpus of the Hebrew Bible and modern written and oral data will be the subject of this study. The tension between the need to refer to historical circumstances on the one hand and the need to stick as far as possible to a strictly synchronic description of the modern data will be a central *leitmotiv* of this study. Bolozky (1997: 297) makes exactly this point when he discusses the non-reduction of *a* that historically was preceded by a guttural ("low" consonant) which synchronically is no longer present, at least in informal speech registers. Bolozky observes plausibly that "[t]oday, however, with no phonetic realization of such consonants, the blocking of reduction is hard to motivate." Consider the following adjectives in Modern Hebrew, where such reduction is blocked (for comparative reference the examples are also given in the Masoretic voweling):[5]

(4) Blocked reduction of a vowel historically preceded by a guttural

m.sg.			**m.pl.**			**Gloss**
עָשִׁיר	*ᶜāšīr*	*ašir*	עֲשִׁירִים	*ᶜăsīrīm*	*aširim*	'rich'
אָבוּד	*ʾāḇūḏ*	*avud*	אֲבוּדִים	*ʾăḇūḏīm*	*avudim*	'lost'
הָרוּג	*hārūḡ*	*arug*	הֲרוּגִים	*hărūḡīm*	*arugim*	'killed'

Bolozky (1997: 302; 2008: handout) argues convincingly that the ex-gutturals or their traces still play a role as markers of consonantal slots, to give speakers clues as to *mišqal* (noun pattern) membership. At the same time, speakers appear to have "recognition strategies based on regularities observed in surface configurations". Instances of a historical *pattāḥ furtivum* are a case in point here. Synchronically, relevant forms surface with a word-final syllabic *a* (phonetically and in transcription), which is preceded by a stressed vowel in the preceding syllable:

5 Cf. also section 2.8 below.

(5) Synchronic surface forms with historical *paṭṭāḥ furtivum*

Lemma	Masoretic	Modern	Gloss
יָדוּעַ	*yāḏūᵃᶜ*	*yadúa*	'known'
גָּבוֹהַ	*gāḇōᵃh*	*gavóa*	'high'
שָׁלִיחַ	*šālīᵃḥ*	*šalíax*	'messenger'

Modern Hebrew also creates some ambiguous forms in this context, e.g., *higía* 'he/she arrived', reflecting Masoretic הִגִּיעַ *higgīᵃᶜ* (m.) and חִגִּיעָה *higgīᶜā* (f.), respectively.

Returning to the פ"ח forms, we will look more specifically at the following angles of this issue throughout this study:

1. Which role does the second root-consonant's position on the sonority scale play in determining the phonological output forms (paᶜal: non-past, infinitive; nifᶜal: past, participle, infinitive; hifᶜīl, hofᶜal/hufᶜal: past, non-past, imperative, infinitive; relevant nominal forms)?
2. What factors beyond the sonority scale, if any, influenced the voweling decisions of the Masoretes, especially in the case of conflicting forms within the paradigm of one and the same verb or pairs of verbs with one and the same second root-consonant?
3. What is the relationship between the Masora-based forms found in the "normative" description of Modern Israeli Hebrew on the one hand and the evidence of the living (casual/colloquial) language on the other? What can be inferred from "informal" transcriptions of relevant verb forms in Latin script as found on various websites (e.g., titles of Hebrew songs in transcription)? What role, if any, do rhyme and rhythm play in this context?

In order to get a reliable database, we proceeded as follows: first the relevant Biblical Hebrew (and Aramaic) verbal and nominal forms were extrapolated from Lisowsky's concordance and Gesenius' and Koehler and Baumgartner's dictionaries – cf. items **(41)** and **(42)** below. Then, the data (verbs and nouns) in various dictionaries of Modern Hebrew, both large-scale dictionaries (Even-Shoshan), medium-size school dictionaries (Langenscheidt Achiasaf), and pocket-size dictionaries (Bantam-Megiddo), as well as Bolozky's (1996/2008) *501 Hebrew*

Verbs were checked (Appendices 3–7). In addition, we tested a number of forms taken from Bolozky 1996/2008 and the modern dictionaries both in isolation and in "camouflaged" context with a number of native speakers of Israeli Hebrew in the Oslo area and in Israel (Appendices 3–8). Finally, we considered semi-popular transcriptions of relevant verb forms within Hebrew prose and poetry excerpts, as they appear on various internet sites, an important source of information, as these reflect a "naïve" descriptive approach to the issue at hand.

In order to properly display the competing strategies which can account for the spectrum of different output forms we adopt an Optimality-Theoretic approach as has witnessed meaningful applications to other phonological issues in Semitic languages, mainly Arabic,[6] but also Hebrew[7] and Ethio-Semitic[8]. The optimality-theoretical framework will then be applied to both the Masoretic and the modern Masora-based data.

In order to gain ground for further argumentation, we will begin with an overview of pertinent issues in guttural phonology as well as the role that consonantal sonority plays in gerenal and in Semitic phonology in particular.

At the end of this introductory chapter we also wish to stress that our discusssion is essentially limited to the Tiberian Masoretic textual transmission. Other traditions, notably the Babylonian one, might also shed light on the question under investigation.[9] According to Kahle (1902: 31 and 54) and Yeivin (1985, vol. 1: 454ff.), syllable-closing /h/ and /ḥ/ were treated in the Babylonian tradition exactly as other (non-guttural) consonants. Not even vowel lowering took place here.

6 Cf., for instance McCarthy 2005; an overview of meaningful applications to issues of syncope and epenthesis in Arabic dialects is provided in Edzard 2008 (cf. also section 6.2 below).

7 Cf., for instance, Bat-El 1996 for an application to Modern Hebrew compound forms or Graf and Ussishkin 2002 for stress assignment.

8 Cf., for instance, Rose & Walker 2004 for an application to co-occurrence restrictions in Amharic and Chaha.

9 Cf., for instance, Bergsträsser 1918–1929, vol. 2: 111 on the quality of the prefix-vowels of verbs *primae laryngalis* and Bauer & Leander 1922: 110–114 = § 7k'–q' and 211 = § 20 e–g on epenthetic vowels in this context.

Of interest are also observations on the status of the Hebrew gutturals in Greek transcriptions, notably the *Secunda* of Origenes. Basing his arguments on such transcriptions, Kahle (1902: 164–171), for instance, claimed that the gutturals by and large had vanished already in the pre-Masoretic pronunciation of Hebrew and that the Tiberian tradition artificially had reconstituted these gutturals. Ginsberg (1929–1930: 131–133) adduced sound arguments against this proposal, showing that it would lead to numerous internal contradictions. Also Brønno (1970) rejected this view, basing his argumentation on the pronunciation of the Hebrew gutturals according to the testimony of Jerome.

As the Hebrew Bible is only attested completely in the tradition of the Tiberian Masora, our focus will rest entirely on the relevant verbal and nominal forms handed down in this tradition.[10]

10 As Blau (1993: 9) correctly observes, the Tiberian version *a priori* has no more "authenticity" than any of the other versions.

2 The theoretical outset A: guttural phonology and the derivation of the Hebrew פ"ח forms

2.1 Gutturals as a distinct field of research: phonological processes

Phonological processes involving gutturals (laryngeals, pharyngeals, and uvulars) have elicited significant attention in linguistic literature dealing with Semitic languages (cf. notably McCarthy 1991 and 1994). In the following, we shall cast light on some notable commonalities of gutturals in Semitic.

2.1.1 Cooccurrence restrictions within the Semitic root

As already Joseph Greenberg (1950) had pointed out, cooccurrence restrictions largely rule out more than one guttural in a given Arabic or Hebrew root, disregarding reduplicated quadriliteral roots and onomatopoetic root formations. More precisely, Greenberg (1950: 178) had set up a classification hierarchy with repect to co-occurrence restrictions as follows:

(6) C-classification (cooccurrence restrictions) according to Greenberg (1950)

(a) "back" (velar, pharyngeal, uvular): *ʾ, h, ḥ, q, x (ḫ), γ (ġ), k, g*

(b) "liquid": *r, l, n*

(c) "labial": *p, b, m*

(d) "front" (except for labials) or "coronal" (except for liquids), i.e. anterior alveolar obstruents: *ḍ, š, ś, s, z, ṣ, t, d, ṭ, þ, ð, ẓ*

In formal phonology, the so-called Obligatory Contour Principle (OCP)[1] has often been invoked as a technical rationale for such co-occurrence restrictions, which disallow homorganic adjacent elements within a given structure. Well-known examples include "Grassmann's Law" for Indo-European,[2] which prohibits two aspirated stops within one stem,

1 For an overview, cf. McCarthy 1986.

2 Cf. Grassmann 1863.

and "Geers' Law" for Akkadian,[3] which forbids two "emphatic" consonants within one root. The colliding elements need not necessarily be adjacent; in Akkadian, for instance, *ma*-prefixes are dissimilated to *na*-, in case the following root contains a labial, in whatever position.[4]

McCarthy (1991: 66–69) has shown that out of 2703 triliteral roots in Wehr's dictionary and out of 1057 triliteral roots in the Hebrew Bible, only very few roots (one-digit numbers), if any, feature more than one guttural in either adjacent or non-adjacent position.

2.1.2 Vowel lowering in the Semitic verbal and nominal system

Brockelmann (1908 = *GvG* I: 194f.) argued that vowel lowering (*i* and *u*) before a guttural applied first in the apocopated verb forms and was then extended by analogy to the other (non-apocopated) verb forms. The common-Semitic root {p-t-ḥ} 'to open' is instructive in this context. One finds the following relevant forms in various kinds of prefix-conjugation: Akkadian *ipte* (< **iptaḥ*), Hebrew *yip̄taḥ*, Syriac *nep̄taḥ*, Arabic *yaftaḥu*, and Gəᶜəz *yeftāḥ*. In the nominal system, such vowel lowering is not that wide-spread (but cf. the remarks on *pattāḥ furtivum* below); however, one finds forms like *maḥrāb* (< *miḥrāb*) 'prayer niche' in modern Arabic dialects, e.g., varieties of Egyptian Arabic.

As is well known, Classical Arabic displays five different ablaut classes (a/u, a/i, i/a, a/a, and u/u), of which the u/u class is semantically determined (stative verbs), as is the i/a class (mostly intransitive/stative verbs). Looking at the total of Arabic verbal roots, it is evi-dent that the a/a ablaut class is phonologically conditioned (a/u or a/i ablaut is not attested with roots containing a guttural). Based on a root count in Wehr's dictionary, 411 of 436 a/a verbs (i.e. ca. 94%) have a guttural as second or third radical. The a/u ablaut class in Arabic, however, is not affected by vowel lowering, nor are the passive perfect (always *u–i–a*) or vowels in any other morphological context (cf. again McCarthy 1991: 70). The following chart provides an illustration:

3 Cf. Geers 1945.

4 Cf. Edzard 1992.

(7) Ablaut in Arabic

a/a	**Perfect**	**Imperfect**	**Gloss**
	صَعَقَ *ṣaᶜaqa*	يَصْعَقُ *yaṣᶜaqu*	'strike by lightning'
	قَطَعَ *qaṭaᶜa*	يَقْطَعُ *yaqṭaᶜu*	'cut off'
	فَحَصَ *faḥaṣa*	يَفْحَصُ *yafḥaṣu*	'scratch up, examine'
	سَمَحَ *samaḥa*	يَسْمَحُ *yasmaḥu*	'grant'
	سَأَلَ *saʾala*	يَسْأَلُ *yasʾalu*	'ask'
	بَدَأَ *badaʾa*	يَبْدَأُ *yabdaʾu*	'begin'
a/u	**Perfect**	**Imperfect**	**Gloss**
	صَعُبَ *ṣaᶜuba*	يَصْعُبُ *yaṣᶜubu*	'be difficult'
	سَمُحَ *samuḥa*	يَسْمُحُ *yasmuḥu*	'be generous'
Pass.	**Perfect**	**Imperfect**	**Gloss**
	قُطِعَ *quṭiᶜa*	يُقْطَعُ *yuqṭaᶜu*	'was cut off'
	سُمِحَ *sumiḥa*	يُسْمَحُ *yusmaḥu*	'was granted'

To give another example of vowel lowering: low vowels appear regulary in the context of Hebrew segolates ($/C_1vC_2C_3/ > [C_1eC_2eC_3]$) which feature a guttural in the second or third position (i.e. one finds output forms such as בַּעַל *báᶜal* 'master' as opposed to מֶלֶךְ *méleḵ* 'king'):

(8) Hebrew segolates containing a guttural in second or third position

Guttural in second position[5]	**Guttural in third position**
רַעַשׁ *ráᶜaš* 'noise'	בֶּלַע *bélaᶜ* 'swallowing'
נַחַל *náḥal* 'valley'	בֶּטַח *béṭaḥ* 'security'
בַּהַט *báhaṭ* 'alabaster'	**but:**
דַּאַב *dáʾaḇ* 'pain'	דֶּשֶׁא *déšeʾ* 'grass'

Following McCarthy 1991: 71, these output forms can be synchronically derived as follows:

5 Exceptionally, vowel lowering does not apply in some roots of the ע"ח type, as in לֶחֶם *léḥem* 'bread' and רֶחֶם *réḥem* 'uterus' (but also רַחַם *ráḥam*). Cf., e.g., Bauer & Leander 1922: 456 = § 72d.

(9) Synchronic derivation of segolate output forms with gutturals

underlying representation	/malk/	/naḥl/	/batḥ/
stress assignment	málk	náḥl	báth
vowel epenthesis	málek	náḥal	bátеḥ
raising of á > e	mélek	–	béteḥ
pre-guttural lowering	–	–	bétaḥ

Preguttural lowering also affects the gutturals in C3-position (except for /ʾ/), as witnessed by the Hebrew *pattāḥ furtivum*:

(10) Insertion of *pattāḥ furtivum*

נוֹעַ *nō*^{ac} 'movement'

מוֹחַ *mō*^{a}*ḥ* 'brain'

נוֹהַ *nō*^{a}*h* 'Noah'

There is some irregularity with respect to preguttural lowering in the pi^{cc}el and hitpa^{cc}el of verbs *III gutturalis*, in so far as the *paṭṭāḥ furtivum* supersedes the previous *e*-vowel in the finite verb forms and can do so in the infinitive forms:

(11) Preguttural lowering in verbs *III gutturalis*

	III /ḥ/		**III /^{c}/**	
pi^{cc}el	שִׁלַּח	*šillaḥ* 'he sent'	קֵרַע	*qēra*^{c} 'he tore to pieces' (MH)
	מְשַׁלֵּחַ	*məšallē*^{a}*ḥ*	מְקָרֵעַ	*məqārē*^{ac}
	יְשַׁלַּח	*yəšallaḥ*	יְקָרַע	*yəqāra*^{c}
	לְשַׁלֵּחַ	*lə-šallē*^{a}*ḥ*[6]	לְקָרֵעַ	*lə-qārē*^{ac}
hitpa^{cc}el	הִשְׁתַּלַּח	*hištallaḥ* 'he was sent'	הִתְקָרַע	*hiṯqāra*^{c} 'he was torn to pieces' (MH)
	מִשְׁתַּלֵּחַ	*mištallē*^{a}*ḥ*	מִתְקָרֵעַ	*miṯqārē*^{ac}
	יִשְׁתַּלַּח	*yištallaḥ*	יִתְקָרַע	*yiṯqāra*^{c}
	לְהִשְׁתַּלֵּחַ	*lə-hištallē*^{a}*ḥ*	לְהִתְקָרֵעַ	*lə-hiṯqārē*^{ac}

6 Also לְשַׁלַּח *lə-šallaḥ*, לְקָרַע *lə-qāra*^{c}, לְהִשְׁתַּלַּח *lə-hištallaḥ*, and לְהִתְקָרַע *lə-hiṯqāra*^{c}.

2.1.3 Cross-guttural vowel assimilation in Classical Ethiopic (Gəᶜəz)

A further phenomenon, which clearly establishes the set of gutturals as a natural class, is cross-guttural vowel assimilation as occurring in Classical Ethiopic (Gəᶜəz).[7] In the case of verbs *I gutturalis* the prefix-vowel in the imperfect is *a* instead of *ə*. In the case of verbs *II gutturalis*, the sequence **aGGə* in the verb stem turns *əGGə* in the imperfect and the sequence **əGa* turns *aGa* in the imperative. In other words, by way of regressive assimilation of the feature [high] across gutturals, but not across other consonants, one arrives at the following forms:

(12) Vocalic cross-guttural assimilation in Gəᶜəz

Non-guttural C_1	**Guttural C_1**
ይናብር *yənabbər* 'he sits'	ያኣምን *yaʾammən* 'he believes'
	ያሓንጽ *yaḥannəṣ* 'he builds'
	ያኃብር *yaxabbər* 'he connects'
	ያዓቅብ *yaᶜaqqəb* 'he guards'
Non-guttural C_2	**Guttural C_2**
ይናብር *yənabbər* 'he sits'	ይልእክ *yələʾʾək* 'he sends'
	ይልህቅ *yələhhəq* 'he grows up'
	ይስሕት *yəsəḥḥət* 'he gets lost'
	ይብዕል *yəbəᶜᶜəl* 'he is rich'
ንባር *nəbar* 'sit!'	ላኣክ *laʾak* 'send!'
	ላሃቅ *lahaq* 'grow up!'
	ሳሓት *saḥat* 'get lost'
	ባዓል *baᶜal* 'be rich!'

2.1.4 Degemination of gutturals in Hebrew

Unlike Arabic and Classical Ethiopic, Hebrew does not allow for the gemination of gutturals (and not either for the gemination of *r*[8]). Degemination of a guttural in C_2-position tends to entail "compensatory leng-

7 Cf. Lambdin 1978: 174 and 180 as well as McCarthy 1991: 75f.

8 Note that word-initial Greek *rho* always carries the *spiritus asper* (phonetically corresponding to the laryngeal fricative *h*).

thening" of the preceding vowel. There is, however, lexical variation which escapes an exact phonological analysis. Thus one finds אִחֵד *ʾiḥēḏ* 'he united' (no compensatory lengthening) as opposed to אֵחֵר *ʾēḥēr* 'he was late' (compensatory lengthening). Here is an overview of some relevant verbal forms:[9]

(13) Degemination within Hebrew roots containing a guttural C_2

Non-guttural C_2	**Guttural C_2**	**Comp. length.**
דִּבֵּר *dibbēr* 'he spoke'	בֵּאֵר *bēʾēr* 'he explained'	+
	נִאֲפָה *niʾăfā* 'she was unfaithful'	–
	מְתוֹאָר *mətōʾār* 'stretched'	+
	נֵהַלְתָּ *nēhalta* 'you led the herd'	+
	מִהַר *mihar* 'he hastened'	–
	מְבוֹהָל *məbōhāl* 'frightened'	+
	נִחֵשׁ *niḥēš* 'he divined'	–
	נֻחַם *nuḥam* 'he was consolated'	–
	שִׁעֵר *šiʿēr* 'he supposed' (MH)	–
	שׁוֹעַר *šōʿar* 'it was supposed' (MH)	–
	בֵּרַךְ *bēraḵ* 'he kneeled'	+

Degemination also takes place when the structural gemination is the result of regressive assimilation, as in the following two examples:

(14) Degemination within Hebrew roots containing a guttural C_2

Non-guttural C_2	**Guttural C_2**	**Comp. length.**
יִתֵּן *yitten* 'he will give' (< **yinten*)	יֵחַת *yēḥat* 'he will descend' (< **yinḥat*)	+
נִתַּן *nittan* 'he was given' (< **nintan*)	נִחַם *niḥam* 'he consolated himself' (< **ninḥam*)	–

9 For a comprehensive overview cf. Bauer & Leander 1922: 353–358 = § 50.

Similar doublets can also occur across morpheme boundaries, notably in connection with the definite article, the *wāw consecutivum*, the preposition מִן *min* (as a prefix), and the preclitic interrogative (or exclamatory) pronoun מָה *mā*; in cases where the noun begins with laryngeal/pharyngeal plus *qāmāṣ*, the lengthened vowel *ā* is additionally dissimilated to *ē*.[10]

(15) Degemination within Hebrew roots containing a guttural C_1

Non-guttural C_1	**Guttural C_1**	**Comp. length.**
הַסֵּפֶר *has-sēfer* 'the book'	הָאִישׁ *hā-ʾīš* 'the man'	+
	הָהַר *hā-har* 'the mountain'	+
	הֶחָבֵר *hē-ḥāḇer* 'the friend'	+
	הָעָם *hā-ʿām* 'the people'	+
וַיּוֹמַר *way-yōmar* 'and he said'	וָאוֹמַר *wā-ʾōmar* 'and I said'	+
מִשָּׁם *miš-šam* 'from there'	מֵרֹאשׁ *mē-rō(ʾ)š* 'from beforehand'	+
מַזֹּאת *maz-zō(ṯ)* 'what is this'	מֶה חָדָשׁ *mē ḥāḏāš* 'what's new'	+

2.2 Historical mergers of gutturals

The last point McCarthy (1991: 77) raises, regarding the status of the gutturals as a distinct class, is processes of historical mergers of such gutturals *within* the class. Whereas the Epigraphic South Arabian languages and Ugaritic are said to have preserved the "Proto-Semitic" set of six gutturals, (/ʾ/, /h/, /ḥ/, /ḫ/, /ʿ/, and /ġ/[11]), as has Classical Arabic, other ancient and modern Semitic languages feature only subgroups of the whole set. Akkadian witnessed the strongest reduction of the guttural inventory. In Old Akkadian, /ḥ/ and /ʿ/ may still have preserved their phonemic status, as can be inferred from the relevant signs containing a <ḫ>-element, e.g., <ḫapārum> representing *ḥapārum* 'to dig' and

10 For a modern analysis of the phenomenon cf. Lowenstamm & Kaye 1985: 104ff.

11 The "Proto-Semitic" character of /ġ/ has been challenged by Ružička (1954).

<raḫābum> representing *raʿābum* 'to be terrified'.[12] In later stages of Assyrian and Babylonian, however, probably due to Sumerian substratum, only /ḫ/ survived, while the other gutturals and inter-vocalic glides (ʾ = ʾ$_1$; *h* = ʾ$_2$; *ḥ* = ʾ$_3$; ʿ = ʾ$_4$; *ġ* = ʾ$_5$; *w* = ʾ$_6$; *y* = ʾ$_7$) were neutralised and, in the case of *ḥ* = ʾ$_3$; ʿ = ʾ$_4$; *ġ* = ʾ$_5$ left traces in the vocalic appearance of a word (**ḥaqlum* > *eqlum* 'field; **baʿlum* > *bēlum* 'lord'; **taġrub* > *tērub* 'you (m.s.) entered').[13] The fact that Akkadian /ḫ/ can also mirror West-Semitic /ḥ/ (or *vice versa*) is noteworthy and puzzling. Tropper (1995) has argued for the etymological connection of Akkadian *nuḫḫutu(m)* 'to trim, clip' with Arabic *naḥata* 'to cut hew', among other examples, thus contradicting traditional wisdom about Akkadian laryngeals. Huehnergard (2003) has shown in addition that no phonologically conditioning factors can be held responsible for these "skewed correspondences" (to use a term by Patrick Bennett), neither from East Semitic (Akkadian) towards West Semitic or the other way round. Therefore, he (2003: 114ff.) suggests a third "Proto-Semitic" consonant phoneme */x̣/, which "unifies" the phonetic features of /ḫ/ and /ḥ/ and which also is attested as a spirantised allophone of /ḳ/ in Tigrinya (e.g., *ḳäräba* 'he approached > *yəx̣ärrəb* 'he approaches'). In concord with accepted methodology in Indo-European linguistics, Huehnergard (2003: 116) then arranges the new "proto-phoneme" within a system of "triads" of consonant phonemes (the following chart only represents triads for the articulation areas "dental plosive" and "velar fricative"):

(16) Huehnergard's (2003) suggestion for an "emphatic"[14] velar fricative

	Voiced	**Voiceless**	**"Emphatic"**
dental plosive	/d/	/t/	/ṭ/
…			
velar fricative	/ġ/ (γ)	/ḫ/ (x)	/x̣/

12 Cf. Buccellati 1997: 18 and Lipiński 2001: 151.

13 Cf., e.g., Huehnergard 2000: 40.

14 According to common Semiticist practice, "emphatic" can designate both velarised ([+ATR]) and post-glottalised phonemes.

With the help of this assumed proto-phoneme /x̣/, one is able, in principle, to derive both East-Semitic (Akkadian) *nuḫḫutu(m)* 'to trim, clip' and West-Semitic (Arabic) *naḥata* 'to cut, hew' from a "Proto-Semitic" root *√NX̣T, without having to worry about phonological factors conditioning a skewed correspondence. Both the Akkadian and the Arabic lemma would then have lost one feature of /x̣/, to wit the features "emphasis" ([Advanced Tongue Root = ATR]) and [+velar], respectively.

Both Hebrew, Aramaic, and, as a more recently attested language, Maltese have witnessed a merger of /ġ/ and /ᶜ/ to /ᶜ/ and of /ḫ/ and /ḥ/ to /ḥ/. Some Modern South Arabian languages and some Yemeni dialects have merged /ᶜ/ and /ᵓ/ to /ᵓ/. In Soqoṭrī and varieties of Arabic spoken in Chad, /ḥ/ and /h/ have collapsed in /h/.

The mentioned consonant mergers, which serve as an additional argument for establishing the group of gutturals as a natural class, should not make one forget that sound correspondences do exist *beyond* this group, e.g., in the Semitic word for 'earth': the /ᶜ/ in Aramaic *ᵓarᶜā* (also *ᵓarqā*) is mirrored by /ṣ/ in Hebrew *ᵓāreṣ* and /ḍ/in Arabic *ᵓarḍ*.

2.3 Case study: the *gaháwa*-syndrome

An interesting case in point is the "*gaháwa*-syndrome" found in Arabic dialects (cf. Fischer & Jastrow 1980: 145; McCarthy 1991: 73f.; de Jong 2007), deriving from the word for "coffee", *qahwa*, which winds up as *gaháwa* through a process of vowel epenthesis with subsequent stress shift (disregarding the changed quality of /q/). While the phenomenon *per se* has been known since the 19th century (cf., e.g., Wetzstein 1868), it was Haim Blanc (1970) who coined the term itself. This process also applies to non-past verb forms *primae gutturalis* ("G"):

(17) The "*gaháwa*-syndrome" found in dialectal Arabic verb forms

underlying:	/yáGC_2iC_2/	*yaḫdim* 'he serves'
post-guttural epenthesis:	yaGaC_2iC_3	*yaḫádim*
a-deletion:	yGáC_2iC_3	*yḫádim*

Examples of nominal forms involving several gutturals include the following (cf. Fischer & Jastrow 1980: 145 and de Jong 2007: 251):

(18) Examples of the "*gaháwa*-syndrome" in nouns

/naᶜja/	→	*naᶜája*	'ewe'
/ˀaḥmar/	→	*ˀaḥámar*	'red'
/ˀaẖḍar/	→	*ˀaẖáḍar*	'green'
/qahwa/	→	*gaháwa*	'coffee'
/baġla/	→	*baġála*	'female mule'

The quality of the epenthetic vowel may vary depending on whether the phonetic environment is velarised or not; in non-velarised environment, the vowel approaches a front [a], whereas in velarised environment its quality is closer to a back [a].

Many Arabic dialects then reduce the first vowel in such forms (as in **(18)** above), thus yielding a structure which informally can be described as "vowel-metathesis", e.g., *(i)mẖázūn* instead of *maẖzūn* 'stored'.

2.4 The historical quality of Hebrew /ḥ/

Before we turn to our research subject proper, it is important to reflect a moment on the (assumed) historical quality of Hebrew /ḥ/. Its "traditional" pronunciation as a pharyngeal fricative stands in marked contrast to its quality as a velar fricative in Modern Standard Israeli Hebrew. According to Rendsburg (1977: 73f.), the Semitic phonemes /ḥ/ and /ẖ/ = /x/ merged in Hebrew ca. 200 BC, presumably to [ḥ]. Accordingly, later generations could not distinguish synchronically between homophone roots, which historically constituted minimal pairs (e.g., חלק (*ḥ-l-q*) 'to be smooth' vs. חלק (*ẖ-l-q*) 'to distribute' or חמר (*ḥ-m-r*) 'to pitch with resin' vs. חמר (*ẖ-m-r*) 'to ferment'), to give just two examples.[15] However, transcriptions of Hebrew proper names in the Septuaginta from around 250 BC show that the distinction between /ḥ/ and /x/ must still have been audible at the time when the two phonemes had already graphically collapsed: *grosso modo*, /ḥ/ was ignored in the transcription and

15 Cf. Koehler & Baumgartner 1994 and Gesenius 1995, s.v.

/ḫ/ was rendered as <χ>, e.g., Ενωχ (חֲנוֹךְ) vs. Χεβρων (חֶבְרוֹן) in the Septuaginta (cf., e.g., Wevers 1970).

2.5 Hebrew verbs *primae gutturalis*, epenthetic *ḥăṭāp̄* vowels, and synchronic derivation

In this study, we will look specifically at the phonological behaviour of Hebrew verbs of the פ״ח type,[16] i.e. a subgroup of the verbs *primae gutturalis*.[17] One aim of this study is to find out whether the historical distribution of *ḥăṭap̄ pattāḥ, sẹḡōl*, or *qāmāṣ* after the /ḥ/ in פ״ח verbs follows some principle(s), which are not obvious at first sight, at least as a tendency. Generally speaking, verbs *primae gutturalis* are characterised by the tendency to insert a short vowel after a (non-stressed-)syllable-final guttural; in other words: "syllable-final gutturals [in a non-stressed syllable] are made syllable-initial by inserting after them a copy of the preceding vowel" (cf. McCarthy 1991: 73):

(19) Epenthesis of a copied vowel

Ø ---> V / V [pharyngeal] __]σ
[– str]

Thus, one arrives, for instance, at the following forms (loc. cit.):[18]

(20) Example surface forms: verbs *I* {א, ה, ח, ע}

Root	**Non-past ("imperf.")**	**Infinitive**	**Gloss**
עמד	יַעֲמֹד *yaʿămōḏ*	לַעֲמֹד *la-ʿămōḏ*	'to stand'
חלם	יַחֲלֹם *yaḥălōm*	לַחֲלֹם *la-ḥălōm*	'to dream'
הפך	יַהֲפֹךְ *yahăp̄ōḵ*	לַהֲפֹךְ *la-hăp̄ōḵ*	'to turn'
אהב	יֶאֱהֹב *yeʾĕhōḇ*	לֶאֱהֹב *le-ʾĕhōḇ*	'to love'

16 Again, Hebrew <ח> can be the historical reflex of Semitic /ḥ/ or /ḫ/ (see above section 2.4 and below section 4.1.2.8), but this distinction is synchronically irrelevant for our investigation.

17 Ginsberg's (1929–1930), LaSor's (1956), and DeCaen's (2003) studies offer important insights here (cf. chapter 4 below).

18 In modern times, the prevalent non-past form is יֹאהַב *yohav*.

A tentative synchronic derivation (which later may have to be modified) of Tiberian Hebrew *primae gutturalis* ("G") forms with *o* as theme vowel is the following (3. m. sg. non-past):

(21) Synchronic derivation of surface verbs forms *primae gutturalis*

underlying	/yiGC_2ōC_3/
preguttural lowering[19]	yaGC_2ōC_3
post-guttural epenthesis	yaGăC_2ōC_3
post-vocalic spirantisation of C_2 (if $C_2 \in$ {ב, ג, ד, כ, פ, ת})	yaGă$\underline{C}_2$ōC_3

An underlying /yiGC_2aC_3/ verb form would, according to a comparable derivational process, surface as *yeGĕC_2aC_3* (*yeGĕ$\underline{C}_2$aC_3*). According to conventional wisdom, the preguttural lowering "stops" at *e* here due to a dissimilatory effect (cf. also the vowel dissimilation in Tiberian Hebrew הֶעָרִים *hē-ʿārīm* 'the cities' or מֶה חָדָשׁ *mē ḥādāš* 'what is new?').

2.6 Hebrew פ"ח forms in conflict: an initial assessment

The issue of variation one finds with the Masoretic treatment of syllable final *ḥ* in the case of a non-stressed syllable is intriguing.[20] Looking at the totality of פ"ח verbs attested from Biblical Hebrew all the way up to (the more elevated registers of) Modern Israeli Hebrew, the stem of these

19 Diachronically, one can argue that the /a/ is "retained" before a guttural, rather than "lowered" (cf., e.g., Gesenius 1910: 164–168 = §§ 62–63 and Bauer & Leander 1922: 347 = § 49).

20 Stressed syllables, however, e.g., the second syllable in שָׁלַחְתִּי *šālaḥtī* 'I sent', do not show such variation, i.e. hypothetical forms such as שָׁלַחֲתִי **šālaḥăṯī* are not attested. Cf., however, the suffixed form בִּלַּעֲנוּהוּ *billaʿănū-hū* 'we annihilated him' (Ps 35:25), in which the stress lies on the penultimate (*nū*) and thus does not block the insertion of an epenthetic *ḥăṭap̄ pattāḥ* (cf. also McCarthy 1985: 69). Verbs III {ʿ, ḥ, h} show the additional peculiarity that the second person feminine of the suffix conjugation, where the guttural is part of a complex syllable coda, undergo anaptyxis, however without spirantising the final *t*, i.e. שָׁכַחַתְּ *šāḵáḥat* 'you (f.sg.) forgot' (Jer 13:25) (cf., e.g., Blau 1993: 56 (= § 30.2) and 213, as well as Benua 1997: 105). With pronominal suffixes carrying ultima-stress one finds forms with epenthetic *ḥăṭāp̄* such as אֶשְׁלָחֲךָ *ʾešlāḥăḵā* 'I shall send you' (Ex 3:10 and 1 Sam 16:1). Cf. also Ben-David 1994–1995.

verbs exhibit a *prima facie* surprising phonotactic alternation between a CCvC and a Cv̆CvC structure in both the past ("perfect"), non-past ("imperfect"), imperative, infinitive, and participle forms.[21] As far as the past forms are concerned, the relevant binyanim are nifᶜal and hifᶜīl (and occasionally hofᶜal/hufᶜal); as far as the future forms are concerned, the relevant binyanim are paᶜal and hifᶜīl (and again occasionally hofᶜal/hufᶜal); relevant imperative forms occur only in hifᶜīl, relevant infinite forms in paᶜal and hifᶜīl. In addition, a sizable number of nominal forms is relevant in this context, notably such forms with an *m*-, a *t*-, or an *h*-prefix, e.g., מַחֲשָׁבָה *maḥăšāḇā* 'thought', תַּחֲנָה *taḥănā* 'station', and הַחְיָאָה *haḥyāʾā* 'revitalisation', to give just three examples.[22] In addition, one also finds rare occurrences of nouns and proper names (nominalised verbs/"Satznamen") with a *y*-prefix: יַחְנוּף *yaḥnūp̄* (a certain plant), יַחְנוּק *yaḥnūq* (another plant), יַחְדִּיאֵל *yaḥdī-ʾēl* (a proper name), and יַחְמוּר *yaḥmūr* (an antilope-like animal). What is more, a number of Aramaic forms are relevant in this context: concerned are both causative verbal nouns such as אַחְזָקָה *ʾaḥzāqā* 'maintenance', אַחְלָמָה *ʾaḥlāmā* 'healing' (or: 'amethyst'), and *ʾaḥsānā* אַחְסָנָה 'storage', as well as a number of adverbs, לַחֲזוּרִין *la-ḥăzūrīn* 'by rotation', לַחֲלוּטִין *la-ḥălūṭīn* 'absolutely', לַחֲלוּפִין *la-ḥălūp̄īn* 'alternatively', and לַחֲצָאִין *la-ḥăṣāʾīn* 'in half'.

Here is the pair of lemmata of the פ״ח type, which gave rise to our study, and which, as we will see, can be accounted for in systematic terms. While the former verb (root חשב) does not feature epenthesis (the "unmarked" case), the latter (root חזר) does (the "marked" case):

21 A comparable alternation with ע״ח verbs cannot be observed. For instance, the Masoretes always voweled שָׁחֲטוּ *šaḥăṭū* (instead of שָׁחְטוּ* *šaḥṭū*), as compared to "regular" קָטְלוּ *qaṭlū* (cf., e.g., Joüon & Muraoka 1993: 182 = § 69). Cf. also lexicalised forms such as אַחֲרוֹן *ʾaḥărōn* 'the last (one)' or מָחֳרָת *moḥŏraṯ* 'the next day', where the *ḥăṭap̄ pattāḥ* and *ḥăṭap̄ qāmāṣ*, respectively, are stable (or rather full-fledged vowels) also in Modern Israeli Hebrew. See, however, section 2.9 and chapter 5 below for oral data, in which such *ḥăṭāp̄* vowels are dropped anyway.

22 Only מַחֲשָׁבָה is attested in Biblical Hebrew. The latter form is also attested as הַחֲיָאָה.

(22) Forms without (unmarked) and with (marked) epenthetic *ḥăṭāp̄*

Root	Imperfect	Infinitive	Gloss
חשב	יַחשֹׁב *yaḥšōḇ*	לַחשֹׁב *la-ḥšōḇ*	'to think'
חזר	יַחֲזֹר *yaḥăzōr*	לַחֲזֹר *la-ḥăzōr*	'to return'

We will see that a lot of complicating factors (or "constraints") work together when it comes to the determination of the variety of output forms one can observe in this context. The following short list shows two Biblical Hebrew examples within one and the same root, which exhibit an internally "contradictory" voweling, once within the non-past (imperfect) paradigm and once in comparison of an imperfect form with the infinitive form belonging to the same root (cf., for instance, Gesenius and Koehler & Baumgartner, s.v. חבל and s.v. חגר):

(23) Forms without and with epenthetic *ḥăṭāp̄* within one root

Root	Form without *ḥăṭāp̄*	Form with *ḥăṭāp̄*	Gloss
חבל	תַחְבּוֹל *taḥbōl*	יַחֲבֹל *yaḥăḇōl*	'to impound'
חגר	יַחְגֹּר *yaḥgōr*	לַחֲגֹר *la-ḥăḡōr*	'to buckle up'

Comparable examples can also be found in the grammatical documentation of Modern Israeli Hebrew. In Bolozky 1996/2008, s.v. חסך, one finds, for instance the opposition between יַחְסֹךְ *yaḥsōḵ* (*yachsokh*) 'he will save money' on the one hand and לַחֲסֹךְ *la-ḥăsōḵ* (*la-chasokh*) 'to save money' on the other hand (the root חסך is not attested in Biblical Hebrew), to give just one example.

As can be seen, even within this arbitrary and very limited set of three פ"ח verbs in Biblical and Modern Hebrew, *ḥăṭap̄ pattāḥ* (ֲ) is not regularly distributed in the future and infinitive forms (indeed, one might expect יַחֲגֹר *yaḥăḡōr* and יַחֲסֹךְ *yaḥăsōḵ*, respectively).[23] What is more, one can easily find doublets for one and the same verb form in Biblical Hebrew, e.g., יַחְשֹׁב *yaḥšōḇ* ("unmarked") vs. יַחֲשָׁב־ *yaḥăšoḇ* ("marked", e.g., 2 Sam 19:20 and Ps 40:18). It remains to be seen whether

23 For an overview, including partially conflicting forms, cf. Gesenius 1910: 164–169 = §§ 62–63, Bauer & Leander 1922: 347–353 = § 49, Beer & Meyer 1955, vol. 2: 38–41 = § 73, Blau 1993: 54–55 = § 28, and Joüon & Muraoka 1993: 179–181 = § 68.

poetic language registers or stress patterns in general are more likely to retain (viz. to produce) the forms with *ḥăṭap̄ pattāḥ, sęḡōl,* or *qāmāṣ* than non-poetic prose texts.

The grammars of Biblical Hebrew list a number of ambiguous forms, but do not give any satisfactory account of the alternations and propose at best *ad hoc* solutions.[24] Bauer & Leander (1922: 348 = § 49h), for instance, while stating that *la*-$GC_2\bar{o}C_3$ is the statistically unmarked bound infinitive of $G\bar{a}C_2aC_3$, argue that the infinite form with *l*-prefix *la*-$G\breve{a}C_2\bar{o}C_3$ is formed in analogy to the "free" infinitive $G\breve{a}C_2\bar{o}C_3$ in the cases where this is not true.

At first glance, not even the second root consonant's position on the sonority scale can automatically account for the forms with *ḥăṭap̄ pattāḥ* cited above,[25] as it is not difficult to find doublets with one and the same *second* root consonant such as יַחְבֹּט *yaḥbōṭ* 'he cuts off' (Is 27:12) vs. יַחֲבֹל *yaḥăḇōl* 'he takes a collateral' (Dt 24:6). It remains to be seen, though, whether there is a stronger *tendency* to insert an epenthetic vowel (*ḥăṭap̄ pattāḥ, sęḡōl,* or *qāmāṣ*) before the second root consonant of the relevant forms, depending on how high the latter's position on the sonority scale is.

There is not much to say about Rabbinical Hebrew in this context, given the lack of a reliable voweling system for Mishnaic texts (cf. Segal 1958: 74 = §§ 158 and 159). Later Hebrew texts up to the *haskala*-period display a "classicising" voweling oriented at the Masoretic system and thus can be disregarded here. Of course, the vocabulary coined in this period plays an important role for the database.

Modern Israeli Hebrew, however, is all the more interesting in this respect, as one can observe a tension between a historically oriented "normative" voweling, based on the Tiberian Masora, in official context, and a "casual" voweling in everyday speech, which calls for a strictly descriptive (as opposed to a normative) approach. Of crucial importance

24 The same holds for some observations relating to *ḥăṭap̄* vowels in already older articles dealing with "irregularities" in the Tiberian Hebrew punctuation (voweling) system; cf., e.g., Nöldeke 1912: 9 and Blake 1926: 337f.

25 Joüon & Muraoka (1993: 90 = § 22) mention at least that the quality of the second root consonant "may or may not favour the use of the ḥaṭef".

is the "new" quality of /ḥ/ as a velar fricative ([x]), which *synchronically* undermines the need for epenthetic *ḥăṭāp̄* vowels. Bolozky (1997: 301) argues: "in the case of *ḥ*, for instance, the merger with *x* has indeed resulted in some degree of regularisation, particularly in dispensing with the need for *a*-epenthesis to avoid syllable-final *ḥ*". According to Bolozky (loc. cit.), *saxăqan* 'actor' is now an almost "hypercorrect" artificial variant (in formal speech) of regular *saxqan*. Coffin & Bolozky (2005: 62) claim that the forms with *ḥăṭap̄ pattāḥ* are still acceptable, but that the pronunciation with *zero šwā* is more common in speech. As examples, they list לַחְשֹׁב *la-xshov* 'to think', לַחְצֹב *la-xtsov* 'to hue stones', and לַחְתֹּר *la-xtor*'to undermine' on the one hand and לַחֲשֹׁב *la-xashov*, לַחֲצֹב *la-xatsov*, לַחֲתֹר *la-xator*, on the other hand as true alternatives. Both Glinert (1989: 477, 566) and Schwarzwald (2001: 17), however, go one step further in maintaining that the insertion of *ḥăṭap̄ pattāḥ, sẹḡōl,* or *qāmāṣ* ("vowel copying") does not occur *at all* in colloquial speech, as far as the immediate environment of /ḥ/ ([x]) is concerned.

As stated above, the obvious reason for this circumstance is the phonetic merger of /ḥ/ with the spirantised allophone of /k/, [ḵ]. One way to test this phenomenon is to oppose quasi-minimal pairs of roots which share the same C_2 (preferably of high sonority), but which feature /k/ vs. /ḥ/ as C_1 (no such pairs with equal C_3 are found, but this disparity does not influence the data here):

(24) Quasi-minimal pairs (C_1 = /k/ vs. C_1 = /ḥ/) in Modern Hebrew[26]

להכזיב *le-hakhziv* 'to disappoint'	להחזיק *le-haxzik* 'to grab'
להכליא *le-hakhli* 'to cross' (tr.)	להחלות *le-haxlot* 'to sicken'
להכניס *le-hakhnis* 'to introduce'	להחניף *le-haxnif* 'to flatter'
להכריח *le-hakhriax* 'to force'	להחריב *le-haxriv* 'to destroy'

Our comparing of [ḵ] and [x] in the first pair of item **(24)** (cf. chapter 5 below) showed no striking differences in the relevant spectrograms.

26 <kh> and <x> are both realised as [x]. Cf. already pairs such as לִכְלוּךְ *liḵlūḵ* and לִחְלוּחַ *liḥlūaḥ* 'soiling' (from לַח *laḥ* 'wet') – Segal 1958: 28 = § 43.

2.7 The special status of פ״ח verbs within the group of verbs *primae gutturalis*

While verbs *primae gutturalis* in general already have received monographic atttention – cf. notably the articles by LaSor (1956) and DeCaen (2003), which we will discuss below in chapter 4 – the special status of פ״ח verbs (and nouns) has so far not caught the attention it deserves.

As a last introductory remark, let it therefore be stated that the alternation phenomenon in Biblical Hebrew (epenthetic *ḥăṭāp̄* vowel or not) in question *can* occur also with other verbs *primae gutturalis* such as פ״ע verbs (e.g., יַעְקֹב *yaᶜqōḇ* 'he deceives', Jer 9:3, vs. יַעֲקֹב *yaᶜăqōḇ* as a proper name). As a salient feature, however, this alternation appears to be restricted in Biblical Hebrew to פ״ח verbs.[27] In Modern Hebrew (dictionaries), the scenario is regularised for א, ה, and ע, all of which always take *ḥăṭāp̄* vowels in the discussed environments.

2.8 Blocked vowel reduction or epenthesis of *ḥăṭap̄ pattāḥ*?

So far we have been concerned with epenthetic *ḥăṭāp̄* vowels (underlying $CvGC_2vC_3$ environments). Gutturals ("G"), however, also can have the effect of blocking vowel reduction in environments where a vowel would otherwise be reduced to zero or *šwā* (unspecified short vowel), depending on the sonority of the root consonant (cf. section 4.1.2.1 below). While the singular pattern $C_1\bar{a}C_2\bar{v}C_3$ is mapped onto the regular plural pattern $C_1(ə)C_2\bar{v}C_3\bar{ı}m$ (or $C_1(ə)C_2\bar{v}C_3\bar{o}t$)[28] in the case of a non-guttural C_1,[29] the reduction of the first vowel is blocked in the case of a guttural C_1. Alternatively, one can say that in forms with an initial guttural, the *šwā* surfaces as reduced *a* (*ă*) via the phonetic assimilation to the feature [low] of the guttural. The following chart illustrates this point:

27 Cf., for instance, Bauer & Leander 1922: 349 = § 49. Joüon & Muraoka (1993: 89 = § 22) state that "א and ע readily take the ḥaṭef; ה and ח readily go without it."

28 The notation "*(ə)*" designates *šwā nāᶜ*, i.e. a *swā* which may be phonetically zero but still keeps the spirantisation of a following *bgdkpt*-consonant intact.

29 For the modern language, one can state that the first *a* vowel (deletable *qāmāṣ*) is reduced to [e] (/ə/), if the first root consonant has high sonority (י, ל, מ, נ, ר) or the second root consonant is a guttural (cf. Coffin & Bolozky 2005: 420).

(25) Blocked vowel reduction/insertion of an epenthetic *ḥăṭap̄ pattāḥ*/*swā* assimilation in case of a guttural C_1 (in nouns)

Non-guttural C_1			**Guttural C_1**		
sg.	**pl.**	**Gloss**	**sg.**	**pl.**	**Gloss**
קָטָן	קְטַנִּים	'small'	עָנָו *ᶜānāw*	עֲנָוִים *ᶜănāwīm*	'humble'
qāṭān	*q(ə)ṭānīm*		חָזָק *ḥāzāq*	חֲזָקִים *ḥăzāqīm*	'strong'
			הָרוּג *hārūḡ*	הֲרוּגִים *hărūḡīm*	'killed'
			אָשָׁם *ʾāšām*	אֲשָׁמִים *ʾăšāmīm*	'sin'

In the verbal system, comparable cases can be found throughout the various binyanim. The difference, though, is that the underlying vowel to be reduced is mostly /e/ in this context (e.g., **gōmerīm* > **gōm(ə)rīm* '(they (m.) are) finishing'. Therefore, one can argue in two directions in terms of a synchronic derivation (cf. Coffin & Bolozky 2005: 412f.): either the underlying vowel is first deleted and then replaced by an epenthetic *ḥăṭap̄ pattāḥ*; or the underlying vowel is not deleted, but rather directly assimilated to the guttural, i.e. the vowel deletion is "blocked". Coffin & Bolozky (2005: 413) favour the last option when the underlying vowel is *a* (as is the case in some forms of the paᶜal past and non-past, the nifᶜal past, the puᶜᶜal past and non-past, as well as the hufᶜal past and non-past), but they also allow for the first option as an alternative in principle. Here are some relevant forms:[30]

(26) Blocked vowel reduction (C_2 = /ḥ/)

paᶜal:	*bāḥan* 'he tested'	*baḥănā*/*baḥănū* 'she/they tested'
	yiḇḥan 'he will test'	*tiḇḥănī*/*yiḇḥănū*/*tiḇḥănū* 'you (f.sg./pl.)/they will test'
	b(ə)ḥan 'test! (m.sg.)'	*baḥănī*/*baḥănū* 'test! (f.sg./m.pl.)'
nifᶜal:	*niḇḥar* 'he was elected'	*niḇḥărā*/*niḇḥărū* 'she/they was/were elected'

30 In the following three items, the forms are transcribed slightly anachronistically in a classical fashion (without, however, spirantising postvocalic /g, d, t/), in order to highlight the point made.

puᶜᶜal:	*nuḥam*	*nuḥămā / nuḥămū*
	'he was consolated'	'she / they was / were consolated'[31]
	yənuḥam	*tənuḥămī / yənuḥămū / tənuḥămū*
	'he will be consolated'	'you (f.sg. / pl.) / they will be consol.'
hufᶜal:	*hub̲ḥan*	*hub̲ḥănā / hub̲ḥănū*
	'he was discerned'	'she / they was / were discerned'
	yub̲ḥan	*tub̲ḥănī / yub̲ḥănū / tub̲ḥănū*
	'he will be discerned'	'you (f.sg. / m.pl.) / they will be discerned'

The same scenario applies to verbs *primae gutturalis* in the second person plural as well as in the infinitive sing. masc. and fem. pl.:

(27) Blocked vowel reduction/insertion of an epenthetic *ḥăṭap̄ pattāḥ / šwā* assimilation in case of a guttural C_1 (in verbs)

Non-guttural C_1		**Guttural C_1**	
gəmartem	'you (m.pl.) finished'[32]	*ʾămartem*	'you (m.pl.) said'
		hălak̲tem	'you (m.pl.) went'
		ḥăšab̲tem	'you (m.pl.) thought'
		ᶜăb̲adtem	'you (m.pl.) worked'
g(ə)mōr/nā	'finish! (m.sg. / f.pl.)'	*ʾĕsōp̄ / nā*[33]	'gather! (m.sg. / f.pl.)'
		hărōg / nā	'kill! (m.sg. / f.pl.)'
		ḥăzōr/nā	'return! (m.sg. / f.pl.)'
		ᶜăzōr/nā	'help! (m.sg. / f.pl.)'

In the following list, an attempt is made to present a picture that is as complete as possible of the relevant finite verb forms, where reduc-

31 Note that no "compensatory lengthening" takes place here in front of the pharyngeal /ḥ/, unlike in front of the other gutturals (cf. section 2.1.4 above).

32 In Modern Hebrew, this form (with stress on the last syllable) has been largely replaced by *gamártem*, a typical example of paradigmatic leveling.

33 In Modern Hebrew, the imperative fem. pl. (just as the 2./3. ps. fem. pl. future tense) is, of course, largely obsolete.

tion is blocked (restricted though to C_2 = /ḥ/), including the examples already given:

(28) Blocked vowel reduction/insertion of an epenthetic *ḥăṭap̄ pattāḥ*/*šwā* assimilation in case of a guttural C_2

Non-guttural C_2	**Guttural C_2**
paᶜal:	
gām(ə)rā / *gām(ə)rū* 'she/they finished'	*bāḥănā* / *bāḥănū* 'she/they tested'
tigm(ə)rī / *yigm(ə)rū* / *tigm(ə)rū* 'you (f.sg./pl.)/they will finish'	*tiḇḥănī* / *yiḇḥănū* / *tiḇḥănū* 'you (f.sg./pl.)/they will test'
gim(ə)rī / *gim(ə)rū* 'finish! (f.sg./pl.)	*baḥănī* / *baḥănū* 'test! (f.sg./m.pl.)'
gōm(ə)rīm / *gōm(ə)rōt* '(they (m./f.) are) finishing'	*bōḥănīm* / *bōḥănōt* 'testing (m./f.pl.)'
nifᶜal:	
nip̄g(ə)šā / *nip̄g(ə)šū* 'she/they met'	*niḇḥărā* / *niḇḥărū* 'she/they was/were elected'
tippāg(ə)šī / *yippāg(ə)šū* / *tippāg(ə)šū* 'you (f.sg./pl.)/they will meet'	*tibbāḥărī* / *yibbāḥărū* / *tibbāḥărū* 'you (f.sg./pl.)/they will be elected'
hippāg(ə)šī / *hippāg(ə)šū* 'meet! (f.sg./pl.)'	*hibbāḥărī* / *hibbāḥărū* 'get elected! (f.sg./pl.)'
piᶜᶜel:	
dibb(ə)rā / *dibb(ə)rū* 'she/they spoke'	*śiḥăqā* / *śiḥăqū* 'she/they played'
mədabb(ə)rīm / *mədabb(ə)rōt* '(they (m./f.) are) speaking'	*məśāḥăqīm* / *məśāḥăqōt* '(they (m./f.) are) playing'
tədabb(ə)rī / *yədabb(ə)rū* / *tədabb(ə)rū* 'you (f.sg./m.pl.)/they will speak'	*təśāḥăqī* / *yəśāḥăqū* / *təśāḥăqū* 'you (f.sg./pl.)/they will play'
dabb(ə)rī / *dabb(ə)rū* 'speak!' (f.sg./pl.)'	*śāḥăqī* / *śāḥăqū* 'play! (f.sg./pl.)'

pu^{cc}al:

dubb(ə)rā / dubb(ə)rū	*nuḥămā / nuḥămū*
'she / they was / were spoken'	'she / they was / were consolated'
tədubb(ə)rī / yədubb(ə)rū / tədubb(ə)rū	*tənuḥămī / yənuḥămū / tənuḥămū*
'you (f.sg. / m.pl.) / they will be spoken'	'you (f.sg. / pl.) / they will be consolated'

hitpa^{cc}el:

hitlabb(ə)šā / hitlabb(ə)šū	*hitnāḥălā / hitnāḥălū*
'she / they dressed'	'she / they settled'
mitlabb(ə)šīm / mitlabb(ə)šōt	*mitnāḥălīm / mitnāḥălōt*
'(they (m. / f.) are) dressing'	'(they (m. / f.) are) settling'
titlabb(ə)šī / yitlabb(ə)šū / titlabb(ə)šū	*titnāḥălī / yitnāḥălū / titnāḥălū*
'you / they (f.sg. / m.pl.) will dress'	'you (f.sg. / pl.) / they will settle'
hitlabb(ə)šī / hitlabb(ə)šū	*hitnāḥălī / hitnāḥălū*
'dress (f.sg. / pl.)'	'settle! (f.sg. / pl.)'
hufr(ə)dā / hufr(ə)dū	*hubḥ̱ănā / hubḥ̱ănū*
'she / they was / were separated'	'she / they was / were discerned'
tufr(ə)dī / yufr(ə)dū / tufr(ə)dū	*tubḥ̱ănī / yubḥ̱ănū / tubḥ̱ănū*
'you (f.sg. / m.pl.) / they will be separated'	'you (f.sg. / m.pl.) / they will be discerned'

2.9 The role of the ח"ע forms

The forms listed in section 2.8 show clearly that there is no variation in the Masoretic and Masora-based *verbal* ח"ע forms, as far as the insertion of epenthetic *ḥăṭāp* vowels is concerned. We will see below (sections 4.1.3.4.4 and 4.2.2.3.4) that there exists variation, though, in the Masoretic and Masora-based *nominal* ח"ע forms, in which /ḥ/ is the coda of an underlyingly closed unstressed syllable.

As far as the oral data are concerned, variation exists also in the verbal ח"ע forms (cf. section 5 below). Glinert (1989: 477) suggests that the insertion of *a* between a guttural and the next consonant is entirely optional in the case of C_2 = /ḥ/ in colloquial registers of Israeli Hebrew: "casually, H in mid-word needs no such support: ... בוחרים *boH(a)rim* '[they] elect', שיחקו *siH(a)ku* '[they] played' ...". This is also the opinion of Bolozky (1997: 301), who gives the examples "*sixka* 'she played' (rarely *sixaka*)" and "*maxku* 'they erased' (rarely *maxaku*)", in addition to the already mentioned "*saxkan* 'actor' (*saxakan* only in a very formal register)".

2.10 Excursus: the free infinitive, the bound infinitive, the imperative forms, and synchronic derivation

An intricate issue in connection with the free and the bound infinitive (construct) is the following. Regardless of forms *primae gutturalis*, one finds two types of bound infinitive forms, both with a firmly closed first syllable, in case $C_2 \in$ {ב, ג, ד, כ, פ, ת}: one, where the second *bgdkpt*-consonant carries a *dāḡēš*, and one in which the second *bgdkpt*-consonant is spirantised. While the first type is (statistically) typical with the preposition לְ *lə-* 'for, to', the second type is (statistically) typical with the prepositions בְּ *bə-* 'in' and כְּ *kə-* 'as', but exceptions (*vice versa*) exist in both cases.[34] Here are some relevant "typical" and "untypical" forms:

(29) Bound infinitives (construct) with the prepositions לְ *lə-*, בְּ *bə-*, כְּ *kə-*

Non-spirantised C_2	**Spirantised C_2**
לִקְבֹּר *li-qbōr* 'to bury' (Gen 50:14)	
לִשְׁכַּב *li-škab* 'to lie' (Gen 34:7)	
לִנְפֹּל *li-npōl* 'to fall' (Ps 118:13)	בִּנְפֹל *bi-np̄ōl* (Job 4:13)
	כִּנְפוֹל *ki-np̄ōl* (2 Sam 3:34)
לִכְתֹּב *li-ktōḇ* 'to write' (Jos 18:8)	בִּכְתוֹב *bi-ḵṯōḇ* (Ps 87:6)
but ("atypical"):	לִצְבֹא *li-ṣḇō(ʾ)* 'to wage war' (Num 4:23)
בִּשְׁכֹּן *bi-škōn* 'in residing' (Gen 35:22)	לִשְׁדוֹד *li-šḏōḏ* 'to be violent' (Jer 47:4)
כִּזְכֹּר *ki-zkōr* 'because of thinking' (Jer 17:2)	לִנְתוֹץ *li-nṯōṣ* 'to destroy' (Jer 1:10)

34 Cf. Gesenius 1910: 124 = § 45g and Bauer & Leander 1922: 210 = § 19f.

If the situation were indeed as uniform (לְ *lə-* on the one hand vs. בְּ *bə-* and כְּ *kə-* on the other hand) as claimed, e.g., by Idsardi (1998: 68) and McCarthy (2003: 34f.), then an analysis in terms of Lexical Phonology would be attractive. One would then say that the preposition לְ *lə-* was [+cyclic] and the prepositions בְּ *bə-* and כְּ *kə-* [–cyclic], i.e. לִכְתֹּב *li-ḵtōḇ* would be derived at an earlier stratum, where epenthesis with subsequent post-vocalic spirantisation and syncope does not apply, as it does in בִּכְתוֹב *bi-ḵṯōḇ*. As diffuse as the situation is (given the counter-examples), however, an analysis in terms of free variation is more appropriate.[35]

Towards the end of this other introductory chapter, let us have a look at the issue of the synchronic and diachronic derivation of the Hebrew פ"ח forms in connection with the morphological overlap of the (construct) infinitive forms and the imperative forms (cf., e.g., Bergsträsser 1918–1929, vol. 2: 54 = § 11b). As is the common opinion (and in the words of Bergsträsser, loc. cit.), the $C_1C_2vC_3$-form constitutes the nominal-verbal basis of the Semitic verbal system.

Beyond the morphological overlap, one can possibly also discern a semantic connection between the infinitive and the imperative, insofar as the former can be used formally in the sense of the latter. Glinert (1989: 287), for instance, formulates as follows: "An infinitive has no person, number or gender; nor has it a subject. Aptly, a main clause infinitive expresses a request more remote in tone than the future tense or imperative – and appropriate to persons of authority or written instructions". Examples adduced by Glinert (loc. cit.) include לעבור בבקשה *la-avor be-vakasha* 'to move along please' = 'move along, please!' and כולם לקום *kulam la-kum* 'everyone to stand up' = 'all stand!'

This morphological (and semantic) connection was exploited in the following letter which appeared in a net-based discussion group on February 10, 2008.[36] The letter raises the issue that there is – synchronically speaking – no need to lower the prefix-vowel *i* in the preposition *li-* before the infinite construct of a root beginning with /ḥ/. More importantly, the author motivates the epenthesis of the *ḥăṭāp̄* vowel in the

35 Cf. also Beer & Meyer 1952, vol. 1: 37, and item **(2)** in section 1.1.2 above.

36 http://forum.wordreference.com/showthread.php?t=825437 (cfu507).

bound infinitive (gerund) *lv-$C_1C_2vC_3$* with the circumstance that the isolated infinitive (which overlaps morphologically with the imperative – the category that the author cites) cannot be pronounced without an epenthetic vowel in case C_1 = /ḥ/. This line of argument is reminiscent of Bauer & Leander's (1922: 348 = § 49) *ad hoc* argument to the effect that, while *la-ḥC_2ōC_3* is the statistically unmarked bound infinitive of *ḥāC_2aC_3*, the infinite form with *l*-prefix *la-ḥăC_2ōC_3* is formed in analogy to the "free" infinitive *ḥăC_2ōC_3* in the cases where this is not true. Neither Bauer & Leander nor the author of the letter under consideration refer to the circumstance that the resulting syllable structure in the bound infinitive does *not* necessitate the insertion of an epenthetic *ḥăṭāp̄* vowel (at least not in the case of a strong C_2) in the same way as the isolated infinitive (or imperative) does.

As the letter is so interesting in both form and content, and since it documents the wider relevance of our investigation, also from a "popular" perspective, we reproduce the letter here in its entirety:[37]

(30) פ"ח blog

שלום, שתי שאלות לי אליכם:

Hello, I have two questions to [ask] you.

האחת, מדוע בשם הפועל בבנין קל, כאשר אות ראשונה של השורש היא א', ה-א' מקבלת חטף סגול ולכן גם הל' של שם הפועל מקבלת סגול, ואילו, כאשר האות הראשונה בשורש היא ע' או ה', אותיות אלו מקבלות חטף פתח ולכן הל' מקבלת פתח. מדוע הא' "מקבלת יחס שונה" מהאחרות?

First, why is it so in the binyan qal [paᶜal], when the first root consonant is *ᵓālep̄*, that this *ᵓālep̄* carries a *ḥăṭap̄ sẹ̄gōl* [e-vowel], and likewise the *lāmed* [which precedes the infinitive, as, e.g., in *le-'ekhol*]? However, when the first root consonant is *ᶜayn* or *hē*, [why do] these consonants carry *ḥăṭap̄ pattāḥ* and likewise the *lāmed* [as, e.g., in *la-'avod* or *la-hafokh*]? Why does the *ᵓālep̄* carry a different "connection [vowel]" than the other ones [guttural letters]?

שנית, מדוע האות ח' מצטרפת לחבורת המיוחדים האלו? למה יש קושי

37 The citations in Latin script within the Hebrew script appear exactly like this in the blog. Comments in angled brackets ("[ ]") are ours.

שהאות ח' תקבל שווא ולפניה הל' תהיה עם חיריק כמו כל שאר האותיות הרגילות? לדוגמה, אומרים לשמור *lishmor* למה אומרים לחשוב *lachshov* ואי אפשר לומר *lichshov* כאילו היתה זו אות אחרת?

Second, why is the letter *ḥēt* part of the group of these particular ones [phonemes]? Why is it difficult for the letter *ḥēt* to carry a *šwā* [i.e. to be vowelless] and why is it difficult for the *lāmed* in front of it to carry a *ḥīriq* [i-vowel], as in [the case of] the other letters? For example, one says *li-shmor*; so why does one say *la-chshov* and why can't one say *li-chshov*, as it would be [correct] with another [non-guttural] letter?

לי קשה לומר *lichshov*, אבל סתם כי זה נשמע מוזר. האם יש סיבה שלא כך אומרים את שם הפועל של ח.ש.ב. למשל?

For me, it is difficult to say *li-chshov*, but only because this [latter form] sounds strange. Is there a reason for the fact that one does not pronounce the infinitive of, e.g., [the root] *ch-sh-v* like that [i.e. like *li-chshov*]?

ההשערה שלי היא:

אני יודעת ששם הפועל הוא צורת ציווי + ל. ברור לי שאומר לאדם שצריך לפתור תרגיל חשבון: חשוב *chashov* ולא *chshov* (ח' עם שווא). אני מניחה כי קשה לומר ח' עם שווא בתחילת מילה, ולכן אם כך גם צריכים לומר *lachashov* לחשוב, *lachasoch* לחסוך, *lachapor* לחפור. אם כך, כולנו טועים באומרנו לחפור *lachpor* ולא *lachapor*.

My hypothesis is the following:

I know that the infinitive consists (has the shape) of the imperative + *lāmed* [e.g., *l* + *ktov* > *li-chtov*]. It is clear to me that one says to someone, who must solve a thinking exercise, *chashov* and not *chshov* (*ḥēt* with *šwā*). I suppose [this is so] because it is difficult to pronounce *ḥēt* with a *šwā* [i.e. vowelless] at the beginning of a word. If this is the case, then one must [indeed] say *la-chashov, la-chasokh, la-chapor*. If so, we are all wrong when we say *la-chpor* and not *la-chapor*.

אשמח לשמוע האם אני צודקת או טועה בעניין הזה. (מעדיפה לשמוע צודקת **:)**).

I am looking forward to hearing whether I am right or wrong in this matter (I prefer to hear that I am right **:)**).[38]

38 The sign ":)" at the end of this document is a "smiley".

3 The theoretical outset B: the sonority scale and preference laws for syllable structure

3.1 The sonority scale

3.1.1 Universal vs. language-specific characteristics

The sonority scale was explicitly described more than one-hundred years ago by Otto Jespersen (1897–1899: 523f.; 1904/1920: 190ff.) and Eduard Sievers (1901). While Jespersen's (1904/1920) classification glides > rhotics > laterals > nasals > voiced fricatives > voiced stops > voiceless fricatives > voiceless stops is generally accepted, there subsists a variety of opinions regarding the relative sonority of laterals/rhotics, voiced/voiceless stops, stops/fricatives/affricatives and the place of glottals (cf. Gouskova 2004: 208), not to mention the relative position of "emphatic" consonants and gutturals.[1] Pons Moll (2008, poster) gives an overview of the problems associated with issues of relative sonority, pointing out that one should rather speak of a gradient sonority hierarchy than a categorical one. What is more, different languages and language groups have different sonority "thresholds", as far as the contact laws affecting syllable structure are concerned.

In sections 3.1.2 and 3.1.3 as well as 4.1.2.1 the gutturals are ignored, since they never occur in C_2-position due to cooccurrence restrictions. If they were included, /ḥ/ in its "traditional" pronunciation would be assigned a medium degree of sonority (e.g., |5|),[2] whereas the gutturals /ᶜ/, /h/, and /ʾ/ would be placed relatively at the bottom of the sonority scale, i.e. would be assigned high consonantal strength (e.g., |7|; cf., for instance, Angoujard 1997: 28 and DeCaen 2003: 46). /ḥ/ in its modern pronunciation [x] is also of low sonority, i.e. high consonantal strenth.

1 Cf. Parker 2002 for a recent comprehensive overview. Cf. also Vennemann 1988: 9, where the voiced stops directly follow the voiceless stops in the hierarchy.

2 Cf., for instance, Al-Ani 2008: 599, where /ḥ/ is described as a "voiceless pharyngeal constricted fricative [..., which] is produced with a constriction formed at the dorsum of the tongue against the posterior wall of the pharynx".

3.1.2 The sonority scale as applied to Biblical (Tiberian) Hebrew

Basing the likely phonetic values of the Tiberian Hebrew consonant inventory on presentations as found in Goerwitz 1996: 490 and Khan 1997: 86–89, one arrives at a tentative representation of the Tiberian Hebrew sonority hierarchy as the following:[3]

(31) A tentative sonority scale for Tiberian Hebrew

Consonantal strength / Sonority		Consonantal strength / Sonority classes	Hebrew consonants
most sonorous (weakest consonantality)	0	low (open) vowels	NA
	0	mid vowels	NA
	1	high (close) vowels/glides	ו י
	2	central liquids (*r*-sounds)	ר
	3	lateral liquids (*l*-sounds)	ל
↑	4	nasals	מ נ
↓	5	voiced fricatives	ב ג ד ז
	6	voiceless velarised fricative	צ
	7	voiceless plain fricatives	כ ס פ שׂ שׁ ת
	8	voiced plosives	בּ גּ דּ
least sonorous (strongest consonantality)	9	voiceless velarised plosive	ט
	10	voiceless plosives	כּ פּ ק תּ

3 Gutturals are excluded from the list, as they do not occur in C_2 position (in the context of this research). We will conclude below (section 4.1.3.3.6) that the phonemes /ṭ/ and /ś/ "behave" as much more sonorous consonants (almost as if the ancient Hebrew values for these consonant phonemes had been the basis for the Tiberian Masora), as far as the processes of *ḥăṭāp̄* epenthesis investigated in this study are concerned. This observation would be in line with the supposedly voiced quality of /ṭ/ in medieval Arabic. The ancient lateral quality of /ś/, or at least of one of its allophones, is well-established (cf. Hebrew כַּשְׂדִּים *kaśdīm* 'Chaldeans' corresponding to Greek χαλδαίοι). Cf. also Steiner 1977. We will also see that /n/ "behaves" as a more sonorous consonant in comparison with /m/, which serves more frequently as a syllable onset than /n/.

3.1.3 The sonority scale as applied to Modern Israeli Hebrew

For Modern Israeli Hebrew, the corresponding sonority scale looks somewhat different, taking into consideration that the difference between the velarised ("emphatic") and the non-velarised ("plain") consonants is obliterated and that /ṣ/ is by now a voiceless affricate ([t^s]). The gutturals are/ʾ/, /h/, and /ʿ/ tend to be reduced in Modern Israeli Hebrew, whereas /ḥ/ now surfaces as [x].[4]

(32) A sonority scale for Modern Israeli Hebrew

Consonantal strength / Sonority		**Consonantal strength / Sonority classes**	**Hebrew consonants**
most sonorous (weakest consonantality)	1	low (open) vowels	NA
	1	mid vowels	NA
	2	high (close) vowels/glides	ו י
	3	central liquids (*r*-sounds)	ר
	4	lateral liquids (*l*-sounds)	ל
↑	5	nasals	מ נ
↓	6	voiced fricatives	ב ז
	7	voiceless fricatives	כ ס פ שׂ שׁ
	8	voiced plosives	בּ גּ דּ
least sonorous (strongest consonantality)	9	voiceless plosives	ט כּ פּ ק תּ
	10	complex plosives	צ

3.2 The universal character of the preference laws

Preference laws in natural generative phonology have been implicitly recognised for a long time (cf. notably Hooper 1976 and Vennemann 1988) and thus represent a conceptual forerunner of Optimality Theory. They represent a graded concept of linguistic quality relative to one or more

4 Again, the gutturals are excluded from the list for the reasons given above.

linguistic parameters. As an example, let us consider the interplay of two relevant laws, the "Strength Assimilation Law" (cf. Vennemann 1988: 35):

> "If Consonantal Strength is assimilated in a syllable contact, the Consonantal Strength of the stronger speech sound decreases."

and the "Contact Law" (cf. Vennemann 1988: 40):

> "A syllable contact A$^{\$}$B is the more preferred, the less the Consonantal Strength of the offset A and the greater the Consonantal Strength of the onset B; more precisely – the greater the characteristic difference CS(B)–CS(A) between the Consonantal Strength of B and that of A."

As is well known, the *t* of the prefix *hit-* in the Hebrew binyan *hitpa*^{cc}*el* undergoes metathesis with a following sibilant and partial assimilation with respect to voicedness and emphasis (velarisation) takes place. Here are relevant Modern Hebrew examples ("$^{\$}$" marks the relevant syllable boundary):[5]

(33) Strength assimilation and syllable contact in Hebrew

Root	Past in hitpa^{cc}el	Gloss
שׁדל	הִשְׁתַּדֵּל *hish*$^{\$}$*tadel* (*hiš*$^{\$}$*taddēl*)	'make an effort'
סכל	הִסְתַּכֵּל *his*$^{\$}$*takel* (*his*$^{\$}$*takkēl*)	'look at'
צרף	הִצְטָרֵף *hits*$^{\$}$*taref* (*hiṣ*$^{\$}$*ṭārēp̄*)	'join (intr.)'
זמן	הִזְדַּמֵּן *hiz*$^{\$}$*damen* (*hiz*$^{\$}$*dammēn*)	'meet accidentally'

A comparable scenario has been found, for instance, in the Highland East Cushitic language Sidamo (cf. Murray & Vennemann 1982, Edzard 1991: 405, and Gouskova 2004: 225–232). Here the last consonant of the stem undergoes strength and place assimilation as well as metathesis, where appropriate, i.e. in order to improve the syllable contact. Consider the following four examples, in all of which metathesis applies in order to remedy the unfortunate syllable onset *n* in the suffix. In addition, the second and fourth instances exhibit partial place assimilation to the labial *b* and the velar *k*, respectively:

---

5 As usual, gemination is not marked in the modern transcription of these forms.

(34) Strength assimilation and syllable contact in Sidamo

Stem	Suffix	Output form	Gloss
haš-	-nemmo	*han$šemmo*	'we look for'
hab-	-nemmo	*ham$bemmo*	'we forget'
it-	-nanni	*in$tanni*	'they eat'
duk-	-nanni	*dung$kanni*	'they carry'

Generally speaking, the sonority scale plays an important role in Semitic phonology in general and in Hebrew phonology in particular. Speiser 1926 was a seminal paper in this context, in which both secondary vowels and secondary gemination are explained by recourse to the sonority scale (and, implicitly, optimised syllable structure).[6] Again, the conceptual ancestry to Optimality Theory is obvious.

3.3 Specific processes in Tiberian and Modern Israeli Hebrew

3.3.1 Processes involving the syllable onset

As an illustration, consider the plural formation of nouns beginning with a C_1*ā*-syllable (*qāmāṣ*). Structurally, the *a*-vowel of the first open syllable is reduced to *šwā nāᶜ* in the Masoretic system, as in the following nouns (comparable examples with guttural C_1, which were treated already in section 1.2 above, are excluded for consideration at the moment):

(35) Vowel reduction in the plural formation of $C_1āC_2āC_3$ nouns

Singular	Plural	Gloss
זָקָן *zāqān*	זְקָנִים *zəqānīm*	'beard'
כָּזָב *kāzāḇ*	כְּזָבִים *kəzāḇīm*	'lie'
מָלָח *mālāḥ*	מְלָחִים *məlāḥīm*	'rag'
רָבִיד *rāḇīḏ*	רְבִידִים *rəḇīḏīm*	'necklace'

6 Further less recent attempts in this direction include Greenstein 1984 for Akkadian, Abu-Mansour 1991 for Meccan Arabic, and Edzard 1991 for Semitic in general (and the above-mentioned Cushitic example).

In the pronunciation of Modern Israeli Hebrew, the structurally present *šwā nāʿ* is reduced to zero depending on the strength of the onset C_1. If the C_1 preceding the deletable *qāmāṣ* is one of the following weak consonants {י, ל, מ, נ, ר}, i.e., one of the consonants with especially high sonority, the *a*-vowel will be reduced to *e*; otherwise, it tends to be deleted altogether.[7] Taking the two above-mentioned examples, the output forms will be *zqanim* and *kzavim* on the one hand (phonetically [skanim] and [ksavim] as a result of partial assimilation with respect to devoicedness), and *melaxim* and *revidim* on the other hand.

This observation perfectly matches Vennemann's (1988: 13f.) "Head Law":

> "A syllable head is the more preferred: (a) the closer the number of speech sounds in the head is to one, (b) the greater the Consonantal Strength value of its onset, and (c) the more sharply the Consonantal Strength drops from the onset toward the Consonantal Strength of the following syllable nucleus."

As in other Semitic languages, word initial clusters are disallowed in principle in classical Hebrew. Thus, loanwords beginning with two consonants are often incorporated by adding a prosthetic *ʾālep̄* / *ʾalif*, e.g., (medieval) Hebrew *ʾaplaton* and Arabic *ʾiflaṭūn* 'Plato' from Greek Πλάτων. Among the very few inner-Semitic exceptions to this rule, said to be attested as such already in "Proto-Semitic", are the lemmata for "two" in Hebrew and Aramaic, *šnáy(i)m* / *štáy(i)m* and *trēn*, respectively, as well as the Aramaic lemma for "six", *štā*. Hoberman (1989) argues that these forms should indeed be interpreted as starting with a sibilant-stop onset cluster, as is in tune with the mentioned "Head Law". What is more, Hoberman (1989: 27) shows that the sound shift *n* > *r* in **θnayn* > *trēn* 'two' (just as in the definite form *brā* 'son') can be accounted for as the product of a better onset creation, as *r* has a slightly higher degree of sonority than *n*.

Bolozky (2006) summarises the discussion on initial clusters in Israeli Hebrew. In his words (2006: 227) "constraints on initial consonant clusters are essentially due to the difficulty of effecting articulatory transitions that are either too extreme or too minute, whereas ease-of-articulation favors assimilation, gradual transition, or cluster splitting so

---

7 Cf., for instance, Coffin & Bolozky 2005: 420.

as to avoid such transitions". Some of Bolozky's examples lend themselves in an ideal way to an Optimality-Theoretic treatment (cf. section 6 below). Consider the two nouns בְּטִיחוּת /btixut/ 'safety' (cf. the adjective בָּטִיחַ /batiax/ 'safe') and בְּטֵלִים /btelim/ 'idle, annulled (m.pl.)' (cf. m.sg. בָּטֵל /batel/). In both cases, the consonantal onset is unfortunate due to its decreasing sonority; indeed, all three parameters (a),(b), and (c) in the above-mentioned onset law are violated. In principle, this situation can be remedied in two ways: either the initial consonant clusters are broken up by an epenthetic *e*, or the first *b* is devoiced, thus yielding a structurally better syllable onset. In general, the second solution is preferred, at least in normal every-day speech. In the case of the first noun, however, devoicing of the *b* would entail semantic confusion, as a homonym to פְּתִיחוּת /ptixut/ 'openness' would arise. Therefore, according to Bolozky (2006: 233), the first solution (epenthesis) is preferred in the case of the noun /btixut/, whereas the second solution is warranted in the case of /btulim/, where no such semantic confusion can arise:

(36) Improvement of syllable onset in two comparable cases

Underlying	Possible phonetic output	Preferred solution
בְּטִיחוּת /btixut/	[betixut] ~[ptixut]	[betixut]
בְּטֵלִים /btelim/	[betelim] ~[ptelim]	[ptelim]

3.3.2 Processes involving the syllable coda

Comparable observations can be made for syllable codas, which present the mirror image as to their optimal structure. Accordingly, Vennemann (1988: 21) has formulated a "Coda Law" as follows:

> "A syllable coda is the more preferred: (a) the smaller the number of speech sounds in the coda, (b) the lesser the Consonantal Strength of its offset, and (c) the more sharply the Consonantal Strength drops from the offset toward the Consonantal Strength of the preceding syllable nucleus."

Many Arabic dialects exhibit epenthetic vowels in $C_1vC_2C_3$-structures, depending on the sonority relationship of C_2 and C_3. The surfacing forms have justly been compared to Hebrew segolates, which feature precisely such epenthetic vowels (as has even been claimed for the Standard Arabic form *malik* 'king' as compared with the Hebrew *mélek̲*).

The following (quasi-minimal) pairs illustrate the situation:[8]

(37) Epenthesis in Arabic $C_1vC_2C_3$-structures

Falling sonority (syllable coda)	**Rising sonority (syllable coda)**
/bard/ > [bard] 'cold'	/badr/ > [badir] 'full moon'
/širk/ > [širk] 'disbelief'	/šukr/ > [šukur] 'thanks'
/qalb/ > [ʾalb] 'heart'	/qabl/ > [ʾabil] 'before'
/bint/ > [bint] 'girl'	/baṭn/ > [baṭin] 'stomach'

Among others, Speiser (1926: 161) and DeCaen (2003: 40) account for the acceptance of the final clusters in the unusual Biblical Hebrew lemmata (*hapax legomena*) קֹשְׁטְ *qōšṭ* 'truth' and נֵרְדְּ *nērd* 'nard' (a certain oil) in terms of the falling sonority in the syllable codas of those words.

The apocopated consecutive verb forms of the ל״ה type are especially instructive in this context: epenthetic vowels set in regularly before a liquid or nasal C_2, but not otherwise. As is well established, these forms clearly demonstrate the historical relationship of the Hebrew "consecutive" *way-yiqṭol* to the Akkadian preterite *iprus* and the Arabic apocopate (not to be confounded with the jussive) found in the negation of the perfect *lam yaqtul*. Here are examples with falling and rising sonority in the syllable coda, respectively:[9]

(38) Epenthesis in apocopated consecutive verb forms of the ל״ה type

Root Falling sonority ($C_1 \rightarrow C_2$)

שבה וַיִּשְׁבְּ *way-yišb* 'and he took captive' (Num 21:1)

שתה וַיֵּשְׁתְּ *way-yešt* 'and he drank' (Gen 9:21)

Root Rising sonority ($C_1 \rightarrow C_2$)

מרה וַתֶּמֶר *wat-témer* 'and it [Jerusalem] was reluctant' (Ez 5:6)

גלה וַיֶּגֶל *way-yígel* 'and he uncovered' (2 K 17:23)

8 Cf. Edzard 1991: 402 (using examples furnished by Samira Farwaneh) and Abu-Mansour 1991: 139 and 143, cited in DeCaen 2003: 37.

9 Cf. Speiser 1926: 161 and Benua 1997: 99f.

In some Ethio-Semitic languages (notably Chaha), the form of the jussive is either *yä*C_1C_2*ə*C_2 or *yä*C_1*ə*C_2C_3, depending on the sonority relationship of C_2 and C_3.[10] The first alternative occurs in case of rising sonority ($C_2 \rightarrow C_3$) in order to avoid an unfortunate syllable coda, even though the syllable contact may not be ideal. The second alternative occurs in case of falling sonority ($C_2 \rightarrow C_3$), which guarantees a fortunate syllable coda and, incidentally avoids an unfortunate syllable contact between C_1 and C_2. Here is an illustration:

(39) Jussive forms in Chaha

Root	**Rising sonority ($C_2 \rightarrow C_3$)**
g-f-r	*yägfər* 'let him release'
k'-ß-r	*yäk'ßər* 'let him plant'
f-t'-m	*yäft'əm* 'let him block'
Root	**Falling sonority ($C_2 \rightarrow C_3$)**
s-r-t	*yäsərt* 'let him cauterise'
t-r-x	*yätərx* 'let him make an incision'
g-m-t	*yägəmt'* 'let him chew off'

3.3.3 Processes involving syllable contact

The most important applications of the sonority principle concerns the contact between two syllables.

In Akkadian, as also in Northwest Semitic, there is a strong tendency to avoid sequences of two or more consecutive open syllables. Whenever possible (i.e. unless morphological confusion arises), syncope takes place with a view of getting rid of the second vowel in such sequences. If, however, the third consonant in an underlying $C_1vC_2vC_3(v)$-sequence is a liquid (*r* or *l*), there is a tendency (stronger for *r* than for *l*) not to apply syncope; in other words: syncope is "blocked" in the non-reduced variant of the possible surface forms:[11]

10 Cf. McCarthy & Prince: 1995: 330f.

11 Cf. Greenstein 1984: 27 and Huehnergard 2000: 24.

(40) Possible blocking of syncope in Akkadian $C_1vC_2vC_3(v)$-structures

Non-reduced form	**Reduced form**
zikaru(m) 'male'	*zikrum*
nakiru(m) 'hostile'	*nakrum*
akalu(m) 'food'	*aklum*
ubilū 'they (m.) brought'	*ublū*

These examples clearly illustrate the conflict between the constraint to minimise the number of consecutive open (and light) syllables on the one hand and the constraint to avoid disfavoured syllable contacts, such as k$r ("$" marks the syllable boundary) on the other hand.

Taking another example from the realm of Modern Hebrew compound formations, Bat-El (1996: 309) has suggested that the lemma *ram-kol* 'loudspeaker', which is composed of the elements *ram* (*rām*) 'loud' and *kol* (*qōl*) 'sound', surfaces precisely in this sequence, as the otherwise expected order of constituents **kolram* (= *kol* + *ram*) would yield an unfortunate syllable contact l$r (cf. section 6.2.3 below).

Turning again to the main issue at hand, a more thorough glance at the data supports the impression that the insertion of a *ḥăṭāp̄* after the first root consonant *ḥ* is not an entirely arbitrary matter, but rather dependent to a certain degree on the strength of the second root consonant. The point is that a better syllable contact results when the onset of the second syllable is stronger than the offset (coda) of the preceding syllable. Taking again the symbol "$" as a marker for a syllable boundary, one arrives, for instance, at the notation yvG$$C_2vC_3 (3rd ps. m.s. impf.), where G constitutes the coda of the first syllable and C_2 the onset of the second, typically a C_2 with low sonority (i.e. high consonantal strength). In the case of an epenthetic *ḥăṭāp̄*, the two notations ya$Gă$$C_2ōC_3 and ye$Gă$$C_2āC_3 represent the resulting syllabification, typically in case of a C_2 with high sonority (i.e. low consonantal strength). The analysis of this issue in the following chapters makes up the core of this study.

3.4 Alternatives to the sonority scale and preference laws?

For the sake of completeness, let us also mention that the very validity of the concept "sonority scale" has at times been challenged. Ohala (1992) presented (unconvincing and polemically formulated) arguments to the effect that there was no empirically verifiable definition of "sonority" and that hence all explanations for syllable shape were circular. His own alternative proposal (1992: 325f.) includes three main points: (1) attention on acoustical parameters such as "amplitude, periodicity, spectral shape, and fundamental frequency (F0)"; (2) concentration on "modulations in the relevant parameters created by concatenating one speech sound with another"; and (3) definition of the quality of acoustic modulations "as proportional to the length of the trajectory it makes through the acoustic 'space' whose dimensions are the acoustic parameters listed above". Except for a few CV-sequences (Ohala 1992: 327), no examples are given, however, that would illustrate a meaningful application of these acoustic parameters. What is more, Ohala does not even refrain from calling the syllable *per se* a "perceptual construct" (1992: 331), thus undermining all further discussion on the subject.

As Parker (2002) has shown, a better procedure consists in refining the sonority scale and to align it with measurable physical (acoustical) properties, such as "intensity, peak intraoral air pressure, F[ormant] 1, peak air flow, and duration" (cf. Pons Moll 2008, poster). Indeed, all available evidence supports the position that the sonority scale *is* empirically verifiable.

4 The evidence of the written language: the פ״ח forms in the Hebrew Bible and the modern dictionaries

4.1 The Biblical (Tiberian) Hebrew and Aramaic forms

4.1.1 Overview of the data

In sections 4.1.1 through 4.1.2.10 we will present some of the issues that will be thoroughly accounted for quantitatively and qualitatively in the rest of the chapter. We begin this section with an overview of the relevant Hebrew and Aramaic verbal and nominal forms in the Hebrew Bible (the Aramaic forms are so few, though, that they are neglected in the further analysis). The following two charts contain only פ״ח roots with *attested* finite and non-finite verb forms in the relevant binyanim as well as nominal forms that are relevant to the issue under investigation, i.e. forms which feature an underlyingly closed and unstressed syllable with the coda ח (forms with a $Cvḥ C_2 ə C_3 \bar{v}$-structure are included, when these are the only attestations for a given root, but they do not "count", as a *ḥăṭāp̄* cannot be inserted here for phonotactic reasons in the first place). If a third-person form is attested (including a few nominalised verbphrases functioning as "Satznamen"), second- and first-person forms are only listed in addition when voweled differently with respect to an epenthetic *ḥăṭāp̄*. Participles and infinitives, as far as attested, are added under the corresponding finite forms in the respective binyan, in exactly this order. Relevant nominal forms ("n.f.") are also included in the list. In the case of doublets ("/"), forms without *ḥăṭāp̄* are listed before the corresponding forms with *ḥăṭāp̄*).

The charts also contain information about the historical value of C_1 (i.e. /ḥ/ or /ḫ/), mark whether the root is III-weak (*tertiae infirmae*) or not (Boolean), whether C_2 can be spirantised or not (Boolean), and whether there is variation as to the insertion of epenthetic *ḥăṭāp̄* vowels or not (Boolean). Additionally, the charts provide the approximate percentage of forms with epenthetic *ḥăṭāp̄* as well as a numerical value of the consonantal strength (CS) of C_2.

(41) Hebrew פ״ח verbs and nouns, as listed in Lisowsky (1993) as well as in Gesenius' (1995) and Koehler & Baumgartner's (1994) Hebrew and Aramaic dictionaries of the Old Testament

Var. *ḥăṭāp̄*	**CS(C_2) =**	**$\underline{C}_2$**	**Root**	**IIIw.**	**C_1 =**	**paʿal**	**nifʿal**	**hifʿīl/ hofʿal**	**Nominal form**	**Gloss (paʿal)**
NO 0% (only n.f.)	(5) 8	+	חבא	+	/ḫ/	---	נֶחְבָּא	הֶחְבִּיאָה	מַחֲבֵא מַחֲבֹאִים	hide
NO 0%	8	+	חבה	+	/ḫ/	---	נֶחְבָּה	---	---	hide
NO 0%	8	+	חבט	–	/ḫ/	יַחְבֹּט	---	---	---	beat off
YES 40%	(5) 8	+	חבל	–	/ḫ/	יַחֲבֹל תַחְבּוֹל	---	---	---	impound
NO 0%	8	+	חבל	–	/ḫ/	אֶחְבֹּל	---	---	תַחְבֻּלוֹת	act corruptly
NO 100%	(5) 8	+	חבק	–	/ḥ/	לַחֲבֹק	---	---	---	embrace
NO 0%	8	+	חבר	–	/ḥ/	---	---	אַחְבִּירָה	---	talk elegantly
NO 0%	8	+	חבר	–	/ḥ/	---	---	---	מַחְבֶּרֶת	bind together
YES 91%	(5) 8	+	חבשׁ	–	/ḥ/	וַיַּחֲבֹשׁ וְיֶחְבָּשׁ לַחֲבֹשׁ	---	---	---	wrap
NO 100% (only n.f.)	(5) 8	+	חב?	–	?	---	---	---	מַחֲבַת	bake bread

Var. *ḥăṭāp*	$CS(C_2)$ =	$\underline{C}_2$	Root	IIIw.	C_1 =	paʿal	nifʿal	hifʿīl/ hofʿal	Nominal form	Gloss (paʿal)
YES 9% (only inf., n.f.)	(5) 8	+	חגר	–	/ḥ/	יַחְגֹּר יַחְגְּרוּ? לַחֲגֹר	---	---	מַחֲגֹרֶת	gird, buckle on
NO 0%	8	+	חדה	+	/ḫ/	יַחְדִּיאֵל יֶחְדְּיָהוּ	---	---	---	rejoice
NO 0%	8	+	חדל	–	/ḫ/	יֶחְדַּל	---	---	---	stop
NO 100%	1	–	חוה	+	/ḥ/	הִשְׁתַּחֲוָה יִשְׁתַּחֲוֶה מִשְׁתַּחֲוֶה	---	---	---	bow down
NO 100%	1	–	חוה	+	/ḥ/	---	---	---	אַחֲוָה	declare
NO 100%	1	–	חור	–	/ḥ/	יֶחֱוָרוּ	---	---	---	grow pale
NO 100%	5	–	חזה	+	/ḥ/	יֶחֱזֶה יַחֲזִיאֵל	---	---	מַחֲזֶה	see
YES 99%	5	–	חזק	–	/ḥ/	יֶחְזַק / יֶחֱזַק יֶחְזְקוּ	---	הֶחֱזִיק יַחֲזִיק/יַחְזֵק הַחֲזֵק וְאַחְזֵק מַחֲזִיק לְהַחֲזִיק	---	be(come) strong

Var. *ḥăṭāp*	CS(C_2) =	$\underline{C}_2$	Root	IIIw.	C_1 =	paʿal	nifʿal	hifʿīl/ hofʿal	Nominal form	Gloss (paʿal)
NO 100%	9	–	חטא	+	/ḫ/	יֶחֱטָא לַחֲטֹא	---	הֶחֱטִיא יַחֲטִא מַחֲטִאֵי לַחֲטִיא		sin
NO 0%	9	–	חטב	–	/ḥ/	יַחְטְבוּ לַחְטֹב	---	---	---	cut wood
NO 100%	9	–	חטם	–	/ḫ/	אֶחֱטָם־	---	---	---	rein in anger
YES 50%	9	–	חטף	–	/ḫ/	יַחְטֹף לַחֲטוֹף	---	---	---	rob
YES 25% (only hifʿīl)	1	–	חיה	+	/ḥ/	יִחְיֶה אֶחְיֶה לִחְיוֹת	---	הֶחֱיָה הַחֲיוּ לְהַחֲיוֹת	מִחְיָה	live
NO 0%	10	+	חכם	–	/ḥ/	יֶחְכַּם	---	מַחְכִּימַת	תַּחְכְּמֹנִי	be prudent
NO 100%	3	–	חלא	+	/ḫ/	וַיֶּחֱלֶא	---	הֶחֱלִי	תַּחֲלֻאִים	be weak / sick
? ?	3	–	חלט	+	/?/	וַיַּחְלְטוּ	---	וַיַּחְלְטוּ		consider irrevocable

Var. *ḥăṭāp̄*	CS(C_2) =	$\underline{C}_2$	Root	IIIw.	C_1 =	paʿal	nifʿal	hifʿīl/ hofʿal	Nominal form	Gloss (paʿal)
YES 67%	3	–	חלה	+	/ḫ/	---	נֶחֱלֵיתִי נֶחְלוּ נַחְלָה/ נַחֲלָה	הֶחֱלֵתִי הֶחֱלוּ הָחֳלֵיתִי מַחֲלָה	מַחֲלָה נַחֲלָה	be weak/sick
NO 100% (only n.f.)	3	–	חל?	–	/ḥ/	---	---	---	מַחֲלַת	play the flute
YES 100%	3	–	חלם	–	/ḥ/	יַחְלְמוּ	---	וְתַחֲלִמֵינִי	---	become strong
YES 100%	3	–	חלם	–	/ḥ/	יַחֲלֹם	---	--- מַחְלְמִים	---	dream
NO 100%	3	–	חלף	–	/ḫ/	יַחֲלֹף לַחֲלֹף	---	הֶחֱלִף יַחֲלִיף הַחֲלִיפוּ	מַחְלְפוֹת	pass by
NO ?	3	–	חלף	–	/ḥ/	תַחְלְפֵהוּ	---	---	מַחֲלַפִים	cut through
NO 100%	3	–	חלץ	–	/ḫ/	תַחֲלֹץ	נֶחֱלָץ	יַחֲלִיץ	מַחֲלָצוֹת	/undress /pull back gird
NO 100%	3	–	חלק	–	/ḥ/	---	---	הֶחֱלִיק יַחֲלִיקוּן מַחֲלִיק	---	be smooth

Var. *ḥăṭāp̄*	CS(C_2) =	$\underline{C}_2$	Root	IIIw.	C_1 =	paʿal	nifʿal	hifʿīl/ hofʿal	Nominal form	Gloss (paʿal)
YES 100%	3	–	חלק	–	/ḫ/	יַחֲלֹק יַחְלְקוּ	---	לַחֲלִק (<לְהַחֲלִק*)	מַחֲלֹקֶת	distribute
NO 100%	3	–	חלשׁ	–	/ḫ/	וַיַּחֲלֹשׁ	---	---	---	gain victory
NO 100%	3	–	חלשׁ	–	/ḥ/	וַיֶּחֱלָשׁ				be weakened
NO 100% (only n.f.)	4	+	חמא	–	/ḫ/	---	---	---	מַחֲמָאֹת	milk
NO 10% (only one participle)	4	–	חמד	–	/ḥ/	יַחְמֹד	נֶחְמָד נֶחֱמָדִים	---	מַחְמָד מַחֲמַדֶּיהָ	desire
NO 0%	4	–	חמל	–	/ḥ/	יַחְמֹל	---	---	מַחְמָל	have pity
NO 0%	4	–	חמס	–	/ḥ/	יַחְמֹס	נֶחְמְסוּ	---	תַּחְמָס	be violent
NO 0%	4	–	חמץ	–	/ḥ/	יֶחְמָץ	---	מַחְמֶצֶת	מַחְמֶצֶת	be sour
NO 0%	4	–	חמר	–	/ḫ/	יֶחְמְרוּ	---	---	---	ferment
NO 0%	4	–	חמר	–	/ḥ/	וַתַּחְמְרָה	---	---	יַחְמוּר	pitch with resin
NO 100%	4	–	חנה	+	/ḥ/	תַּחֲנֶה	---	---	מַחֲנֶה תַּחֲנוֹתִי	bend, settle
NO 100%	4	–	חנט	–	/ḥ/	וַיַּחַנְטוּ לַחֲנֹט	---	---	---	enbalm

Var. *ḥăṭāp*	CS(C_2) =	$\underline{C}_2$	Root	IIIw.	C_1 =	paʿal	nifʿal	hifʿīl/ hofʿal	Nominal form	Gloss (paʿal)
NO ?	4	–	חנך	–	/ḥ/	וַיַּחְנְכוּ	---	---	---	inaugurate
NO 100%	4	–	חנן	–	/ḥ/	יֶחֱנַן לַחֲנַנְכֶם	---	---	תַּחֲנוּנִים	be clement
NO 100%	4	–	חנף	–	?	תֶּחֱנַף	---	יַחֲנִיף	---	be impious
NO 100% (only n.f.)	4	–	חנק	–	/ḫ/	---	---	---	מַחֲנָק	throttle
YES 73%	7	–	חסה	+	/ḫ/	יֶחְסֶה / יֶחֱסֶה אֶחְסֶה / אֶחֱסֶה לַחְסוֹת / לַחֲסוֹת	---	---	מַחְסֶה / מַחֲסֶה	seek refuge
NO ?	7	–	חסל	–	?	יַחְסְלֶנּוּ	---	יַחְסְלֶנּוּ	---	eat away
NO 0%	7	–	חסם	–	/ḥ/	תַחְסֹם	---	---	מַחְסוֹם	tie up the mouth
NO 0%	7	–	חסר	–	/ḫ/	יֶחְסָר	---	הֶחְסִיר יַחְסִיר	מַחְסוֹר	be deficient
NO 0%	10	–	חפה	+	/ḫ/	---	נֶחְפָּה	---	---	cover
NO 0%	10	+	חפז	–	/ḥ/	יַחְפּוֹז	נֶחְפָּזוּ	---	---	run frightened

Var.	*ḥăṭāp̄*	CS(C_2) =	$\underline{C}_2$	Root	IIIw.	C_1 =	paʿal	nifʿal	hifʿīl/ hofʿal	Nominal form	Gloss (paʿal)
NO	0%	10	+	חפץ	–	/ḥ/	יַחְפֹּץ	---	---	---	be pleased
NO	0%	10	+	חפץ	–	/ḥ/	יַחְפֹּץ	---	---	---	hang, stretch
NO	0%	10	+	חפר	–	/ḥ/	וַיַּחְפֹּר לַחְפֹּר	---	---	---	dig / investigate
NO	0%	10	+	חפר	–	/ḫ/	יַחְפְּרוּ / יֶחְפְּרוּ	---	הֶחְפִּר יַחְפִּר מַחְפִּיר	---	be ashamed
NO	0%	10	+	חפשׂ	–	/ḥ/	יַחְפְּשׂוּ	נֶחְפְּשׂוּ	---	---	investigate
NO	0%	6	–	חצב	–	/ḫ/	תַּחְצֹב לַחְצֹב	---	מַחְצֶבֶת	מַחְצֵב	split
NO	100%	6	–	חצה	+	/ḫ/	יֶחֱצֶה יַחְצְאֵל יַחֲצִיאֵל	---	---	מַחֲצִית מֶחֱצָה	divide
NO	11%	10	–	חקר	–	?	יַחְקֹר יַחֲקָר־	נֶחְקַר	---	מֶחְקְרֵי	research
NO	100% (only n.f.)	2	+	חרא	–	/ḫ/	---	---	---	מַחֲרָאוֹת	defecate

Var. *ḥăṭāp*	CS(C_2) =	<u>C_2</u>	Root	IIIw.	C_1 =	paᶜal	nifᶜal	hifᶜīl/ hofᶜal	Nominal form	Gloss (paᶜal)
YES 78%	2	–	חרב	–	/ḫ/	יֶחֱרַב	---	הֶחֱרִיב אַחְרִב / אַחֲרִיב מַחֲרֶבֶת	---	dry
NO 100%	2	–	חרב	–	/ḫ/	תֶּחֱרַב	נֶחֶרְבוּ נֶחֱרֶבֶת	הֶחֱרִיב מַחֲרִיב הָחֳרָבָה מָחֳרָבוֹת	---	be devastated
NO 100%	2	–	חרב	–	/ḥ/	---	נֶחֶרְבוּ	---	---	massacre
NO ?	2	–	חרג	–	?	וַיֶּחְרְגוּ	---	---	---	tremble
NO 100%	2	–	חרד	–	/ḥ/	יֶחֱרַד	---	הֶחֱרִיד מַחֲרִיד הַחֲרִיד	---	tremble
NO 100%	2	–	חרה	+	/ḥ/	יֶחֱרֶה	נֶחֱרִים	הֶחֱרָה תְּתַחֲרֶה (tifᶜīl)	תַּחֲרָה	be enraged
NO 100%	2	–	חרך	–	/ḥ/	יַחֲרֹךְ	---	---	---	fry?

Var. *ḥăṭāp̄*	CS(C_2) =	$\underline{C}_2$	Root	IIIw.	C_1 =	paʿal	nifʿal	hifʿīl/ hofʿal	Nominal form	Gloss (paʿal)
NO 100%	2	–	חרם	–	/ḥ/	---	---	הֶחֱרִים יַחֲרִים הַחֲרֵם יָחֳרַם	---	ban; devote to annihilation
NO 100%	2	–	חרף	–	/ḫ/	תֶּחֱרַף	נֶחֱרֶפֶת	---	---	spend the fall
NO 100%	2	–	חרף	–	/ḥ/	יֶחֱרַף	---	---	---	insult
NO 100%	2	–	חרף	–	?	---	נֶחֱרֶפֶת	---	---	be intended for marriage
NO 100%	2	–	חרץ	–	/ḥ/	יֶחֱרַץ	נֶחֱרָצָה	---	---	sharpen, decide
NO 100%	2	–	חרק	–	/ḥ/	יַחֲרֹק	---	---	---	gnash
NO 100%	2	–	חרשׁ	–	/ḥ/	יַחֲרֹשׁ לַחֲרֹשׁ	---	מַחֲרִישׁ	מַחֲרֵשָׁה	plough, engrave
NO 100%	2	–	חרשׁ	–	/ḫ/	תֶּחֱרַשׁ	---	הֶחֱרִישׁ יַחֲרִישׁ מַחֲרִישׁ הַחֲרֵשׁ	---	be silent/ deaf
NO 13%	7	–	חשׂך	–	?	יַחְשֹׂךְ אֶחֱשָׂךְ	---	---	---	hold back

Var. *ḥăṭāp*	$CS(C_2) =$	$\underline{C}_2$	Root	IIIw.	$C_1 =$	paʿal	nifʿal	hifʿīl/ hofʿal	Nominal form	Gloss (paʿal)
NO 100% (not n.f.)	7	–	חשׂף	–	/ḫ/	וַיֶּחֱשֹׂף	---	---	מַחְשֹׂף	peel
NO 0%	7	–	חשׂף	–	/ḥ/	לַחְשֹׂף	---	---	---	decant
YES 11%	7	–	חשׁב	–	/ḥ/	יַחְשֹׁב / יַחֲשֹׁב לַחְשֹׁב	נֶחְשַׁב	---	מַחֲשָׁבָה	deem, think
YES 67%	7	–	חשׁה	+	/ḥ/	תֶּחֱשֶׁה לַחֲשׁוֹת	---	הֶחֱשֵׁיתִי הֶחֱשׁוּ מַחְשֶׁה	---	be silent
YES 11%	7	–	חשׁך	–	?	תֶּחְשַׁךְ	---	הֶחְשִׁיךְ וְהַחֲשַׁכְתִּי יַחְשִׁיךְ מַכְשִׁיךְ	מַחְשָׁךְ מַחֲשַׁכִּים	be dark
NO 100%	7	–	חשׁל	–	?	---	נֶחֱשָׁלִים	---	---	be worn out
NO 0%	10	+	חתה	+	/ḫ/	יַחְתֶּה לַחְתּוֹת	---	---	מַחְתָּה	kindle, strike
NO 0%	10	+	חתך	–	/ḥ/	---	נֶחְתַּךְ	---	---	decide
NO 0%	10	+	חתל	–	/ḥ/	---	---	הָחְתֵּל	---	be swathed

Var.	*ḥăṭāp̄*	CS(C_2) =	$\underline{C}_2$	Root	IIIw.	C_1 =	paʿal	nifʿal	hifʿīl/ hofʿal	Nominal form	Gloss (paʿal)
NO	0%	10	+	חתם	–	/ḫ/	יַחְתֹּם לַחְתֹּם	נֶחְתָּם נַחְתּוֹם	הֶחְתִּים	---	seal
NO	0%	10	+	חתף	–	/ḫ/	יַחְתֹּף	---	---	---	tear away
NO	0%	10	+	חתר	–	/ḥ/	יַחְתְּרוּ	---	---	מַחְתֶּרֶת	break through
NO	0%	10	+	חתת	–	/ḥ/	---	---	הַחְתַּתִּי	---	break through

Ad ?חב : Some modern dictionaries (notably Even-Shoshan 2003) point to a (fictituous) root *ḥbt*. Gesenius (1962: 213, 412) suggests to connect מַחֲבַת *maḥăḇaṯ* with the root *ḫ-b-z*, as in Arabic *ḫubz* 'bread'. In Gəʿəz one finds both a root *ḫ-b-y* and a root *ḫ-b-b*, both revolving around "to be a vessel for food".

Ad חוה : This is at least the root (in a rare binyan "hištafʿal") assigned to הִשְׁתַּחֲוָה by Koehler & Baumgartner (1994: 295f.). Cf. also Hasselbach & Huehnergard 2008: 417. Gesenius (1962: 817f.) derives הִשְׁתַּחֲוָה from a root שחה in a binyan "hitpaʿlel".

Ad חלט : Koehler & Baumgartner (1994: 317) treat the only extant form as paʿal, Gesenius (1995: 354) as hifʿīl.

Ad ?חל : Gesenius (1962: 414) suggests an etymological connection with either a root *ḫ-l-l* or a root *ḫ-l-y*, the latter of which ("to sing") is attested in Gəʿəz.

Ad חלם : Koehler & Baumgartner (1994: 320) treat these two as one and the same root.

Ad חרב : Koehler & Baumgartner (1994: 349) treat these two as one and the same root.

(42) Aramaic פ״ח verbs, as listed in Lisowsky (1993: 1547–1550) as well as in Gesenius' (1995) and Koehler & Baumgartner's (1994) Hebrew and Aramaic dictionaries of the Old Testament

Var.	***ḥăṭāp̄***	**CS(C_2) =**	**$\underline{C}_2$**	**Root**	**IIIw.**	**C_1 =**	**pəʿal**	**hafʿel**	**Gloss (pəʿal)**
NO	100%	1	–	חוא/ה	+	/ḥ/	---	יְהַחֲוֵה תְהַחֲוֹן הַחֲוֹנִי הַחֲוָיָה	announce
NO	100%	5	–	חזה	+	/ḫ/	מֶחֱזֵא	---	see
?	?	3	–	חלף	–	/ḫ/	יַחְלְפוּן	---	pass
?	50%(?)	7	–	חסן	–	/ḥ/	---	הֶחֱסִנוּ יַחְסְנוּן	possess
?	?	6	–	חצף	–	?	---	מְהַחְצְפָה מַחְצְפָה	be severe

4.1.2 Factors determining the insertion of epenthetic *ḥăṭāp̄*-vowels

While the position of the second root-consonant C_2 on the sonority scale is a crucial factor bearing on the epenthesis of a *ḥăṭāp̄* vowel in the פ״ח forms under investigation – for a precise analysis cf. section 4.1.3 below, it does by no means account for all the complications and internally conflicting forms one encounters within the Masoretic corpus. In the following, the relevance of the sonority scale with respect to C_2 will be highlighted and a tentative typology of such opposing forms will be developed and subsequently checked for its pertinence.

4.1.2.1 The position of the second root-consonant on the sonority scale

With the empirical and theoretical background developed so far, we will now investigate specifically the distribution of epenthetic *ḥăṭāp̄* vowels in Hebrew פ״ח forms.

Item **(43)** again represents an attempt at placing the inventory of available C_2 in Hebrew verbal and nominal roots on the sonority scale. Due to cooccurrence restrictions, the laryngeals/pharyngeals/uvulars {א, ה, ח, ע} do not occur in the C_2-position of verbs of the פ״ח type, and are therefore absent in items **(41)** and **(42)** above. /ḥ/ in its likely historical realisation as pharyngeal fricative ([ḥ]) can be assigned the consonantal strength value |5|; its modern realisation as a velar (voiceless) fricative ([x]) can be assigned the consonantal strength |7|. We already stated that only the (assumed) historical pronunciation of /ḥ/ can account for the insertion of a vowel in the first place, as witnessed also by the *pattāḥ furtivum* before a word-final /ḥ/, which is preceded by a vowel other than *a* (e.g., *kōᵃḥ* 'strength').

Here is again the chart introduced in section 3.1.2 above:[1]

1 DeCaen (2003), following Angoujard (1986, 1997), ascribes a higher sonority to the (historical realisation of the) "emphatic" consonant phonemes /ṭ/ (<ט>) and /ṣ/ (<צ>), as well as to the historical lateral /ś/ (<שׂ>). As mentioned earlier, we suppose that the historical value of these consonants (or rather a "ghost" thereof) was somehow still present in the Masoretic tradition, even though the contemporary phonetic values of these consonants had already changed.

(43) A tentative sonority scale for Tiberian Hebrew

Consonantal strength / Sonority		**Consonantal strength / Sonority classes**	**Hebrew consonants**
most sonorous (weakest consonantality)	0	low (open) vowels	NA
	0	mid vowels	NA
	1	high (close) vowels/glides	ו י
	2	central liquids (*r*-sounds)	ר
	3	lateral liquids (*l*-sounds)	ל
↑	4	nasals	מ נ
↓	5	voiced fricatives	ב ג ד ז
	6	voiceless velarised fricative	צ
	7	voiceless plain fricatives	כ ס פ שׁ שׂ ת
	8	voiced plosives	בּ גּ דּ
least sonorous	9	voiceless velarised plosive	ט
(strongest consonantality)	10	voiceless plosives	כּ פּ ק תּ

4.1.2.2 The relevance of the prefix vowel in the פ"ח forms

In addition, we will have to check whether the prefix-vowel in a given verbal form, e.g., *a*- vs. *e*- has any impact on the likelihood of an epenthetic *ḥăṭāp̄* vowel.[2] Also, we will have to investigate why, as we will see in sections 4.1.2.7 and 4.1.3.4 below, nominal forms appear to have a slightly higher tendency to insert *ḥăṭāp̄* vowels (typically *a*), as compared with verbal forms, notably participles, belonging to the same root (e.g., מַחֲבֵא *maḥăḇē* 'hiding place' as compared with נֶחְבָּא *neḥbā* 'hidden').

2 Indeed, this is an assumption put forward by DeCaen (2003: 43), who argues with the contrast in the pair מַחְשֶׁה *maḥšē* 'silencing' vs. תֶּחֱשֶׁה *teḥĕšē* 'you (m.) are silent'. This argument, however, can be countered with the contrast in the pair מַחֲבֵא *maḥăḇē* 'hiding place' as compared with נֶחְבָּא *neḥbā* 'hidden'. Correctly, DeCaen only accounts for verbal forms, but there is no *a priori* reason why the argument should not apply to nominal forms as well.

4.1.2.3 Alternations between two forms belonging to different roots which share one and the same *bgdkpt* C_2

Residual (non-)spirantisation is a theoretical possibility to consider in Tiberian Hebrew. In Modern Israeli Hebrew, post-vocalic spirantisation longer applies across the board and is "opaque" due to a number of factors, notably de-gemination (cf., for instance, Kapeliuk 1997: 540). In colloquial registers, the quality of an underlying /b, k, p/ consonant ([± spirantised]) can be "transferred" from the past-form to the infinitive or *vice versa* through a process of "paradigmatic leveling", disregarding the question of whether this consonant directly follows a vowel (or a historical *šwā nāᶜ*) or not. We repeat here item **(2)** from section 1.1.2:

(44) "Transfer" of the feature [± spirantised] in colloquial Israeli Hebrew ("paradigmatic leveling")

makhar	⇒	*li-mkhor*	("standard": *li-mkor)*	'to sell'
šabar ("standard": *šavar*)	⇐	*li-šbor*		'to break'

In section 2.10 above (item **(29)**), we saw that certain bound infinitive forms, e.g., לִצְבֹא *li-ṣḇō(ʾ)* 'to wage war' (Num 4:23), בִּכְתוֹב *bi-ḵṯōḇ* 'in writing' (Ps 87:6), כִּנְפוֹל *ki-np̄ōl* 'because of falling' (2 Sam 3:34), surface exactly as *li-mkhor* does, without there being any stringent rule to that effect. So the phenomenon may be much older than generally assumed.

There is no *a priori* reason to restrict such analogical leveling processes to the modern time. Indeed, the phenomen referred to by the problematic concept of the "*šwā medium*" in the grammars of Biblical Hebrew (e.g., Blau 1993: 15) might be more easily explained by referring to residual spirantisation of the *befadkefat*-letter in question. The best-known example is the plural construct form מַלְכֵי *malḵē* 'kings-of', in which the /k/ after the closed syllable *mal*$ is spirantised. While there exist attempts to account for this circumstance by invoking a blocking rule, one might simply argue that the feature [+spirantised] is preserved throughout the whole plural paradigm, even after a closed syllable.[3]

3 Cf. also Beer & Meyer 1952, vol. 1: 37. Admittedly, Blau's (1993: 15) other example in this context, כּוֹתֶבְךָ *kōṯeḇḵā* 'your writer', is harder to explain along these lines.

When variation between similar or near-similar פ"ח verbs exists, one may therefore trace it to the way the Tiberian scholars heard the forms, and hence misrepresented some pronunciation to do away with exceptions and prevent surface exceptions to their rules.[4] Let us again consider the pair יַחְבֹּט *yaḥbōṭ* (Is 27:12) vs. יַחֲבֹל *yaḥăḇōl* (Dt 24:6). The Tiberian Masoretes may not have realised that spirantisation was no longer fully productive at some time during the Biblical period, and they could not accept surface counterexamples such as יַחְבֹל ([yaḥḇōl]) and יַחֲבֹּט ([yaḥăbōṭ]). As a result, they may have distorted the vocalic representation, arbitrarily deciding whether to represent it or not as long as the result fit their spirantisation model, without exceptions. Taking the above-mentioned example with the roots {š-b-r} and {m-k-r} as a model, one can envisage an "analogical" process as follows (here, we assume that the past form is the basis of the "transfer" in all cases):

(45) Assumed transfer of the feature [± spirantised] in Tiberian Hebrew ("paradigmatic leveling")

ḥaḇal	⇒	*yaḥḇol*	("standard": *yaḥbol*)	'to take a collateral'
ḥabaṭ ("standard": *ḥaḇaṭ*)	⇒	*yaḥboṭ / yaḥăboṭ*		'to cut off'

The problem remains that the second radical in $C_2 = b$ or *g* verbs is never systematically spirantised or non-spirantised in any of the relevant verb forms of this type. As we saw in item **(41)**, the other four "begadkefat" *d*, *k*, *p*, and *t* are never spirantised after /ḥ/ within the Biblical Hebrew corpus and thus cannot support this line of argument in the first place. We will revisit this issue in section 6.3.

Blau (1993: 213) notes that the allophone [ṯ] of /t/ can be considered (re-)phonemised in such minimal pairs as לָקַחַתְּ *lāqáḥat* 'you (f.sg.) took' (with non-spirantised *t*) vs. לָקַחַת *lā-qáḥaṯ* 'to take' (with spirantised *t*). Khan (1997: 90), citing Harris (1941: 143–167), adduces the hypothetical (unattested) minimal pair אַלְפֵּי *ʾalpē* 'two thousand [of]' vs. אַלְפֵי *ʾalp̄ē* 'thousands [of]'.

4 We owe this suggestion to Shmuel Bolozky (e-mail communication from July 26, 2007).

4.1.2.4 Alternations between two forms belonging to different roots which share one and the same second root-consonant, and of which one is of the ל״ה or ל״א type

As will become evident in section 4.1.3.3.3 below, verbs and nouns of the ל״ה and ל״א type (*tertiae infirmae*) have a higher tendency to insert a *ḥăṭāp̄* as compared with strong verbs and nouns, also (and especially) in the case of a relatively high consonantal strength (low sonority) of C_2. In most of the 15 (out of a total of 88) verbs belonging to ל״ה roots a *ḥăṭāp̄* is inserted, while this is often not the case in strong verbs with the same second root-consonant. The following list presents four relevant examples:[5]

(46) Strong verbs vs. ל״ה and ל״א verbs with the same C_2

Form without *ḥăṭāp̄*		Form with *ḥăṭāp̄*
לַחְטֹב *la-ḥṭōḇ* (Dt 19:5)	vs.	לַחֲטֹא *la-ḥăṭō(ʾ)* (Hos 8:11)[6]
יֶחְסַר *yeḥsar* (Dt 15:8)	vs.	יֶחֱסֶה *yeḥĕsē* (Ps 34:9)
תַּחְצֹב *taḥṣōḇ* (Dt 8:9)	vs.	יֶחֱצֶה *yeḥĕṣē* (Is 30:28)
תֶּחְשַׁךְ *teḥšak̠* (Qoh 12:2)	vs.	תֶּחֱשֶׁה *teḥĕšē* (Is 6:11)

It is remarkable that nearly all nominal forms of the ל״ה type (phonologically plausible exceptions: מִחְיָה *miḥyā* 'preservation of life' (Gen 45:5) and מַחְתָּה *maḥtā* 'fire pan' (Lev 16:12)[7]) feature a *ḥăṭāp̄*, as can still be observed in Modern Israeli Hebrew (where otherwise nearly all *ḥăṭāp̄* vowels after /ḥ/ have vanished). The Biblical Hebrew corpus of *m*- and *t*-prefixed forms – cf. items **(64)** and **(65)** below – comprises מַחֲבֵא *maḥăḇē* 'hiding place' (Is 32:2), מַחֲבֹאִים *maḥăḇōʾīm* 'hiding places' (1 Sam 23:23), מַחֲזֶה *maḥăzē* 'vision' (Gen 15:1), מֶחֱזָה *meḥĕzā* 'window' (1 K 7:14), תַּחֲלֻאִים *taḥălūʾīm* 'diseases' (Jer 14:18), מַחֲלָה *maḥălā* 'disease' (1 K 8:37), מַחֲנֶה *maḥănē* 'camp' (Gen 32:2), תַּחֲנוֹת *taḥănōṯ* 'camping place' (2 K 6:8),

5 In this and the following charts, the indication of a Biblical reference does not imply that this is the only occurrence of a given form.

6 While לַחֲטֹא is, of course, a ל״א verb, the relevant forms "behave" phonologically entirely like ל״ה forms.

7 Cf., for instance, Joüon & Muraoka 1993: 211 = § 79s.

מַחֲסֶה *maḥăsē* (but also: מַחְסֶה *maḥsē*) 'refuge' (Is 4:6), מַחֲצִית *maḥăṣīṯ* and מֶחֱצָה *meḥĕṣā* 'half' (Ex 30:13 and Ruth 31:36), מַחֲרָאוֹת *maḥărāʾōṯ* 'privies' (2 K 10:27), and תַּחֲרָה *taḥărā* 'quarrel' (Sir 31/34:29, 40:5).[8]

The underlying reason behind the regular insertion of a *ḥăṭāp̄* in these cases may be an inclination to restitute a strong triconsonantal structure (as is present, for instance, in קַבָּלָה *qabbāla* = *kabala* 'receipt'); synchronically the prefix may even be re-analysed as part of the root (cf. also the roots חלל and תחל in the sense "to start": in the latter form, a historical prefix was integrated in the root as surfacing in the hifʿīl form התחיל). Even in colloquial registers of Israeli Hebrew, nominal forms of the ל"ה type such as מַחֲלָה *maḥălā* 'disease' or מַחֲנֶה *maḥănē* 'camp' never lose their historical *ḥăṭāp̄* vowel – cf. also section 5.4.3.

Alternatively, one could try to argue in terms of a synchronic analysis that the *ḥăṭāp̄* vowel compensates for the "missing" mora in the final open syllable: while an open light syllable is mono-moraic, a closed syllable is bi-moraic (cf. section 6.3.2 below).

The opposition adduced by DeCaen (2003: 43), מַחְשֶׁה *maḥšē* 'silencing' (hifʿīl, m.sg.) vs. תֶּחֱשֶׁה *teḥĕšē* 'you (paʿal, m.sg.) are silent' cannot (only) be attributed to the *a*-vowel in the first syllable and the sibilant in the C_2-position, as claimed by the author, as other examples (מַחֲזֶה *maḥăzē* 'vision', מַחֲסֶה *maḥăsē* 'refuge', and מַחֲצִית *maḥăṣīt* 'half' on the one hand, and *yeḥsē* / *ʾeḥsē* 'he/I seek(s) refuge' on the other hand) devalidate such a generalisation. If at all, this opposition can be attributed to the clearly detectable tendency that nouns (and in the case of nifʿal including some nominalised participles) more often exhibit anaptyxis than regular participles, let alone finite verbal forms (cf. also section 4.1.2.7 below).

4.1.2.5 Alternations between different forms within the paradigm of one and the same verb

Looking at alternations between different forms within the paradigm of one and the same verb, one can distinguish between two constellations:

8 The book *Ben Sira* is, of course, not part of the canonical Hebrew Bible ("Old Testament"), and the voweling is supplied *ex post* here.

(1) Alternations with an (underlyingly) identical syllable structure, e.g., תַּחְבֹּל *taḥbōl* (Ex 22:25) 'you (m.s.) take a collateral' vs. יַחֲבֹל *yaḥăḇōl* (Dt 24:6) 'he takes a collateral' (cf., for instance, Blau 1993: 55). Such alternations also occur in phonotactically comparable forms as the third person sg. masc. imperfect and the infinite (with *l*-prefix), e.g., יַחְגֹּר *yaḥgōr* (Lev 8:7) 'he girds' vs. לַחֲגֹר *la-ḥăḡōr* (Is 22:12) 'to gird. We will return to the case of /b/ and /g/ (residual spirantisation) in section 4.1.3.3 below.

(2) Alternations with an (underlyingly) different syllable structure, e.g., וַיַּחֲבֹשׁ *way-yaḥăḇōš* (Gen 22:3) 'and he bound' vs. וַיַּחְבְּשׁוּ *way-yaḥbəšū* 'and they bound' (1 K 13:13). Here, two competing strategies (or constraints in Optimality-Theoretic terms) seem to be at work. On the one hand, the syllable contact "ḥ$^{\$}$b" is not ideal due to the relatively high sonority of the voiced labial, hence anaptyxis/epenthesis takes place. On the other hand, a sequence of too many adjacent open syllables is to be avoided. While the surface form *yaḥăḇōš* features a "tolerable" number of two adjacent open syllables and thus is acceptable, a form **yaḥăḇəšū* would be prosodically inacceptable (four adjacent open syllables), unless it were to surface as *yaḥaḇšū* (cf., e.g., *yeḥrəḏū* (Ez 26:18) and *yeḥerḏū* (Hos 11:10) 'they tremble').[9] This circumstance is what DeCaen (2003: 42) labels [the constraint] "SHEWA EXEMPTION". Consequently, the non-anaptyctic form *yaḥbəšū* "wins" in this case.[10] Here is an overview of the relevant forms ending in a vowel, contrasting the opposition between the forms CvḥC_2v̌C_3v̄/Cvḥ(v)C_2v́C_3v̄ on the one hand and CvḥvC_2C_3v̄ on the other hand.[11] Only the forms in the leftmost column allow for pausal forms (at least only such forms are attested in pause), and only the pausal forms allow for an epenthetic *ḥăṭāp* vowel:

9 Extremely rare exceptions to this rule (no *šwā* directly after a *ḥăṭāp* vowel) in the Masoretic text include the possibly "hybrid" form נֶאֶסְפוּ *neʾĕsəpū* 'they were gathered' (Judg 16:23 and 1 Chr 11:13). Cf. Churchyard 1999: 80.

10 For an Optimality-Theoretic analysis, cf. section 6.3 below.

11 Besides the plural forms in the prefix conjugation, the list also contains one form in the second person singular feminine and three forms with *hē cohortativum*.

(47) Distribution of *ḥăṭāp*-vowels in prefix-conjugation forms (paᶜal) and suffix-conjugation forms (nifᶜal) ending in a vowel

Root	**CvḥC_2əC_3v̄ / Cvḥ(v̆)C_2v́C_2v̄(n)**		**CvḥvC_2C_2v̄**		**Gloss**
חבא	נֶחְבְּאוּ	*neḥbəʾū*			'they were hidden'
חבל	יַחְבְּלוּ	*yaḥbəlū*			'they impound'
	יַחְבֹּ֫לוּ	*yaḥbṓlū* (P)[12]			'they impound'
חבשׁ	וַיַּחְבְּשׁוּ	*way-yaḥbəšū*			'and they bound'
	וַיַּחֲבֹ֫שׁוּ	*way-yaḥăḇṓšū* (P)			'and they bound'
	אֶחְבְּשָׁה	*ʾeḥbəš-ā(h)*			'let me bind'
חגר	יַחְגְּרוּ	*yaḥgərū*			'they gird'
חדל	וַיַּחְדְּלוּ	*way-yaḥdəlū*			'and they stopped'
	אַחְדְּלָה	*ʾaḥdəl-ā(h)*			'let me stop'
חור	יֶחֱוָ֫רוּ	*yeḥĕwā́rū* (P)			'they grow pale'
חזק	יֶחְזְקוּ	*yeḥzəqū*	יֶחֶזְקוּ	*yeḥezqū*	'they are strong'
חטא			יֶחֶטְאוּ	*yeḥeṭʾū*	'they sin'
חטב	יַחְטְבוּ	*yaḥṭəḇū*			'they cut wood'
חכם	יֶחְכָּ֫מוּ	*yeḥkā́mū* (P)			'they are prudent'
	אֶחְכָּ֫מָה	*ʾeḥkā́m-ā(h)* (P)			'let me be prudent'
חלט	וַיַּחְלְטוּ	*way-yaḥləṭū*			'and they considered irrevocable'
חלם	יַחְלְמוּ	*yaḥləmū*			'they become strong'
חלם			וַיַּחַלְמוּ	*way-yaḥalmū*	'and they dreamt'
	וַיַּחֲלֹ֫מוּן	*way-yaḥălṓmūn* (P)			'and they dreamt'
חלף	יַחֲלֹ֫פוּ	*yaḥălṓp̄ū* (P)			'they pass'
חלק	וַיַּחְלְקוּ	*way-yaḥləqū*			'and they dealt'
	יַחֲלֹ֫קוּ	*way-yaḥălṓqū* (P)			'and they dealt'
חמל	יַחְמֹ֫לוּ	*yaḥmṓlū* (P)			'they have pity'
	תַּחְמְלוּ	*taḥməlū*			'you (pl.) have pity'

12 "(P)" denotes pausal forms, in which the stress shifts to the penultimate syllable (cf., e.g., Blau 1993: 40).

Root	$CvḥC_2əC_3v̄$ / $Cvḥ(v̆)C_2v́C_2v̄(n)$		$CvḥvC_2C_2v̄$		Gloss
חמס	תַּחְמֹסוּ	*taḥmṓsū* (P)			'you (pl.) are violent'
חמר	יֶחְמְרוּ	*yeḥmərū*			'they ferment'
חמר	וַתַּחְמְרָה	*wat-taḥmər-ā(h)*			'and she should pitch with resin'
חנט	וַיַּחְנְטוּ	*way-yaḥnəṭū*	וַיַּחַנְטוּ	*way-yaḥanṭū*	'and they embalmed'
חנך	וַיַּחְנְכוּ	*way-yaḥnəḵū*			'and they inaugurated'
חסר	יַחְסְרוּ	*yaḥsərū*			'they are deficient'
חפז	נֶחְפָּזוּ	*neḥpā́zū* (P)			'they were frightened'
חפץ	יַחְפְּצוּ	*yaḥpəṣū*			'they are pleased'
	יֶחְפָּצוּ	*yeḥpā́ṣū* (P)			'they are pleased'
חפר	יַחְפְּרוּ	*yaḥpərū*			'they dig'
חפר	יַחְפְּרוּ	*yaḥpərū*			'they are ashamed'
	יֶחְפָּרוּ	*yeḥpā́rū* (P)			'they are ashamed'
חפשׂ	יַחְפְּשׂוּ	*yaḥpəśū*			'they investigate'
	נֶחְפְּשׂוּ	*neḥpəśū*			'they w. investigated'
חקר	יַחְקֹרוּ	*yaḥqṓrū* (P)			'they research'
	תַּחְקְרוּן	*taḥqərūn*			'you (pl.) research'
חרב	יֶחֱרָבוּ	*yeḥĕrā́ḇū* (P)	יֶחֶרְבוּ	*yeḥerḇū*	'they are devastated'
			נֶחֶרְבוּ	*neḥerḇū*	'they were massacred'
חרג	וַיַּחְרְגוּ	*way-yaḥrəḡū*			'and they came out frightened'[13]
חרד	יֶחְרְדוּ	*yeḥrəḏū*	יֶחֶרְדוּ	*yeḥerḏū*	'they tremble'
	יֶחֱרָדוּ	*yeḥĕrā́ḏū* (P)			
חרק			וַיַּחַרְקוּ	*way-yaḥarqū*	'and they gnashed [teeth]'
חשׂך	תַּחְשְׂכִי	*taḥśəḵī*			'you (f. sg.) hold back'

13 According to the *BHS*, the correct reading in Ps 18:46 is יַחְגְּרוּ *yaḥgərū* 'they gird', though (cf. also DeCaen 2003: 43).

Root	**CvḥC_2əC_3v̄ / Cvḥ(v̆)C_2v́C_2v̄(n)**	**CvḥvC_2C_2v̄**	**Gloss**
חשב	יַחְשְׁבוּ *yaḥšəḇū*		'they think'
	יַחְשֹׁבוּ *yaḥšṓḇū* (P)		'they think'
	יַחֲשֹׁבוּן *yaḥăšōḇūn* (P)		'they think'
	נֶחְשְׁבוּ *neḥšəḇū*		'they were counted'
חשך	יֶחְשְׁכוּ *yeḥšəḵū*		'they are dark'
חתר	יַחְתְּרוּ *yaḥtərū*		'they break through'

This list shows clearly that the marked form CvḥvC_2C_3v̄ only occurs in those instances where C_2 is of especially high sonority (liquida *l* and *r*; voiced sibilant *z*; nasal *n*; emphatic dental stop *ṭ*).[14] In addition, the evidence provided by this list undermines the additional (sub-)constraint ("ancillary rule") "LATERAL EXEMPTION" that DeCaen (2003: 42) introduces, as the forms in question are in no way restricted to laterals and as there is nothing special about the syllable sequence in the forms *yaḥləqū* and *taḥləqū*. For the sake of further illustration, here again are the anaptyctic CvḥvC_2C_3v̄ forms extrapolated from the previous list:

חזק	יֶחֶזְקוּ *yeḥezqū*
חטא	יֶחֶטְאוּ *yeḥeṭʾū*
חלם	וַיַּחַלְמוּ *way-yaḥalmū*
חנט	וַיַּחַנְטוּ *way-yaḥanṭū*
חרב	יֶחֶרְבוּ *yeḥerḇū*
	נֶחֶרְבוּ *neḥerḇū*
חרד	יֶחֶרְדוּ *yeḥerḏū*
חרק	וַיַּחַרְקוּ *way-yaḥarqū*

The modern ("Masora-based") data (extrapolated from Bolozky 1996/2008) reflect a similar situation:[15]

14 The "behaviour" of /ṭ/ points again to a historically higher sonority of this phoneme, as compared with its modern pronunciation.

15 We will return to the issue of epenthetic full vowels in section 4.1.2.3 below.

(48) Distribution of epenthetic vowels in prefix-conjugation forms (pa^cal) and suffix-conjugation forms (nif^cal) with a sonorous C_2 ending in a vowel (Bolozky 1996/2008)[16]

Root	CvḥvC₂C₃v		Gloss
חזר	יַחַזְרוּ	*yaxazru*	'they will return'
חלם	יַחַלְמוּ	*yaxalmu*	'they will dream'
חלף	יַחַלְפוּ	*yaxalfu*	'they will pass by'
חלץ	יַחַלְצוּ	*yaxaltsu*	'they will remove'
	נֶחֶלְצוּ	*nexeltsu*	'they were taken off'
חלק	נֶחֶלְקוּ	*nexelku*	'they were divided'
חנך	יַחַנְכוּ	*yaxankhu*	'they will inaugurate'
	נֶחֶנְכוּ	*nexenkhu*	'they were inaugurated'
חרט	יַחַרְטוּ	*yaxartu*	'they will engrave'

The two informants we asked accepted these forms. In a coinage test, however, they did not produce these forms, but pronounced them exactly as those forms with a low-sonority-C_2, i.e. *yaxzeru*, *yaxlemu*, etc.

4.1.2.6 Doublets of one and the same verb form in a given paradigm

Occasionally one can observe an almost "chaotic" distribution of forms without and with *ḥăṭāp̄*, e.g., יַחְשֹׁב *yaḥšōḇ* (Is 10:7) vs. יַחֲשָׁב *yaḥăšoḇ* (Ps 40:18) 'he thinks', or לַחְסוֹת *la-ḥsōṯ* (Is 30:2) vs. לַחֲסוֹת *la-ḥăsōṯ* (Ps 118:8) 'to seek refuge' (cf., for instance Joüon & Muraoka 1993: 181). Of 88 פ"ח roots in the corpus of the Hebrew Bible, 15 (i.e. ca. 17%) show ambiguities with respect to the insertion of an epenthetic *ḥăṭāp̄*, while all the others either always have *ḥăṭāp̄* or never, largely according to the position of C_2 on the sonority scale (the higher the sonority, the more likely the insertion of a vowel). More specifically, these 15 roots involve the following C_2-consonants (most of which with relatively high sonority): the voiced labial plosive /b/, the voiced velar plosive /g/, the "empha-

16 Only the $CvḥvC_2C_3\bar{v}$-type forms are listed here (of course, one could also include the second person pl. non-past of pa^cal, e.g., *taxazru*, and the third person f. sg. of nif^cal, e.g., *nexeltsa*); all other forms are of the $CvḥC_2əC_3\bar{v}$-type.

tic" alveolar plosive /ṭ/, (velarised) sibilants (the alveolar fricatives /s/ and /z/; the postveolar fricative /š/), liquids (the alveolar lateral approximant /l/ and the alveolar trill /r/), and the palatal approximant /j/ = /y/. The following list (ordered alphabetically according to the the root), extrapolated from item **(41)**, shows alternations and, wherever possible, doublets within the same root lemma:

(49) Conflicting minimal pairs (same root; if possible same form)

Form without *ḥăṭāp̄*				**Form with *ḥăṭāp̄***	
תַּחְבֹּל	*taḥbōl* (Ex 22:25)	vs.		תַּחֲבֹל	*taḥăḇōl* (Dt 24:17)
וְיֶחְבָּשׁ	*wə-yeḥbāš* (Job 5:18)	vs.		וַיַּחֲבֹשׁ	*way-yaḥăḇōš* (Gen 22:3)
יַחְגֹּר	*yaḥgōr* (Lev 16:4)	vs.		לַחֲגֹר	*la-ḥăḡōr* (Is 22:12)
יַחְטֹף	*yaḥṭōp̄* (Ps 10:9)	vs.		לַחֲטוֹף	*la-ḥăṭōp̄* (Ps 10:9)
יִחְיֶה	*yiḥyē* (Dt 8:3)	vs.		הֶחֱיָה	*heḥĕyā* (Jos 6:25)[17]
נַחְלָה	*naḥlā* (Jer 10:19)	vs.		נַחֲלָה	*naḥălā* (Is 17:11)
אֶחְסֶה	*ʾeḥsē* (Ps 57:2)	vs.		אֶחֱסֶה	*ʾeḥĕsē* (Ps 61:5)
אַחְרִב	*ʾaḥrīḇ* (2 K 19:24)	vs.		אַחֲרִיב	*ʾaḥărīḇ* (Is 42:15)
יַחְשֹׁב	*yaḥšōḇ* (Is 10:7)	vs.		יַחֲשָׁב	*yaḥăšoḇ* (Ps 40:18)
מַחְשֶׁה	*maḥšē* (Is 57:11)	vs.		הֶחֱשֵׁיתִי	*heḥĕšītī* (Ps 39:3)
יַחְשִׁיךְ	*yaḥšīḵ* (Ps 139:12)	vs.		וְהַחֲשַׁכְתִּי	*wə-haḥăšaḵtī* (Amos 8:9)

Again, forms like יַחְלְקוּ *yaḥləqū* (Jos 14:5) cannot be contrasted in this context with forms like יַחֲלֹק *yaḥălōq* (1 Sam 30:24), since the first form does not allow for the epenthesis of a *ḥăṭāp̄* vowel in the first place, due to the immediately following *lāmeḏ* carrying *šwā nāᶜ* (*mobile*) (cf. section 4.3.3 above).

In sum, it may well be the case that we are not looking at split paradigms (section 4.1.2.5) or merely arbitrary variation (section 4.1.2.6), but at a set of forms with *ḥăṭāp̄* which may be prevalent in specific con-

17 Strictly speaking, this is no alternation, since יִחְיֶה, where the *i* in the prefix never undergoes preguttural lowering, cannot attract an epenthetic copied vowel (at least not in the Masoretic orthographical system), as is the case in the corresponding hifᶜīl-forms (cf. again Joüon & Muraoka 1993: 211 = § 79s).

texts, possibly due to rhyme and/or accentuation. This issue will be discussed in sections 4.1.2.9 and 4.1.3.3.5 below.

4.1.2.7 Doublets of near-equal surface forms belonging to different grammatical categories

Phonological differentiation in the service of semantic (or categorial) differentiation is by no means an unusual phenomenon. In German, the position of the accent can bring about the differentiation between two verbs, e.g., the two verbs *´übersetzen* 'to cross (a river)' and *übersétzen* 'to translate'. Some speakers of German distinguish *'Araber* 'people from Arabia' from *Aráber* 'horses from Arabia' by the position of the accent.[18] In Standard Norwegian (*bokmål*), the form *selger* is pronounced [seller], when used as a finite verb (e.g., *hun selger* 'she sells'); as an agent noun, however, the same form is pronounced [selger] (e.g., *hun er selger* 'she is a salesperson').[19] In Syriac Aramaic, the same orthographical string is pronounced [qyāmṯā] in the meaning "resurrection" and [qyāmtā] in the meaning "share".[20]

It is uncontroversial that stress is also phonemic in Tiberian Hebrew. Blau (1993: 19) provides the examples בָּנוּ *bā́nū* 'we came' vs. בָּנוּ *bā-nū́* 'in us' as well as קָמָה *qā́mā* 'she stood up' vs. קָמָה *qāmā́* 'getting up' (fem.). As Khan (1997: 91f.) observes, vowel length is usually predictable from syllable structure and placement of stress, and the status of minimal pairs such as אָכְלָה *ʾoḵlā* ([ʔɔx'lɔ:]) 'food' vs. אָכְלָה (marked with *gaʿyā/meṯeḡ* next to the *ḥăṭāp̄*) *ʾāḵlā* ([ʔɔ:xlɔ:]) 'she ate' is doubtful. The pair וַיִּרְאוּ *way-yirʾū* 'and they saw' (Num 17:24) vs. וַיִּירְאוּ *way-yīr(ə)ʾū* 'and they feared' (Gen 20:8) – this form being marked with *gaʿyā/meṯeḡ* next to the *ḥīriq*, however, is a better case in point.[21]

In view of the foregoing observations, one can also suppose minimal pairs in Tiberian Hebrew, which are based on the (non-)insertion of *ḥăṭāp̄* vowels. According to Gesenius 1910: 165 = § 63, the *ḥăṭap̄ pattāḥ*

18 Cf. Vennemann 1986: 30f.

19 Cf. Kristoffersen 2000: 345.

20 Cf. Nöldeke 1898: 18.

21 Cf. Yeivin 1980: 251 and Khan 1987: 39.

serves in one case specifically to bring about the distinction between two semantic categories, namely between the regular participle fem. nif^cal of חלה, i.e. נַחְלָה *naḥlā* (e.g., Jer 10:19) and the noun (lexicalised participle) נַחֲלָה *naḥălā* 'wound' from the same root (e.g., Is 17:11). As a further example, Gesenius (1910: 165= § 63) adduces the distinction found between יַעְקֹב *yaᶜqōḇ* 'he deceives' (Jer 9:3) and יַעֲקֹב *yaᶜăqōḇ* (the name *Jacob*). In both cases, this seems, however, to be an *ad hoc* explanation, which need not necessarily apply across the board in the realm of gutturals. Remarkable in this context are also the forms נַחְלָה *naḥlā* 'water masses' (Ps 124:4), apparently a secondary form of נַחַל *náḥal*, and the form נַחֲלָה *naḥălā* 'possession', both belonging, of course, to the root נחל, and not the root חלה.

4.1.2.8 Alternations and doublets between forms belonging to roots with the same C_2 or even homophonous roots, which are distinguished, however, by a historically different /ḥ/ (Semitic /ḥ/ vs. /ḫ/)

The alternations and doublets between forms belonging to roots with the same C_2 or even homophonous roots, which are distinguished, however, by a historically different /ḥ/ (Semitic /ḥ/ vs. /ḫ/), do not play a role in this context, as clearly evidenced by the data presented in tables **(41)** and **(42)**. Moreover, the Masoretes operated more than one-thousand years later than the time when this historical opposition was obliterated.[22] Opposition pairs, which could be supportive, such as וַיֶּחֱלָשׁ *way-yeḥĕlāš* (I /ḥ/) 'and he was weakened' (Job 14:10) vs. וַיַּחֲלֹשׁ *way-yaḥălōš* (I /ḫ/) 'and he gained victory' (Ex 17:13) may feature a different vocalic pattern (here: stative vs. non-stative verb), but no tendency can be observed to the effect that a historical /ḥ/ would more readily trigger a *ḥăṭāp̄* as compared to a historical /ḫ/. A counterexample would be לַחְשֹׂף *laḥśōp̄* 'to decant' (Is 30:14) vs. וַיֶּחֱשֹׂף *way-yeḥĕśōp̄* 'and he peeled' (Ps 29:9).

22 Cf., for instance, Wevers 1970. However, as we have argued in connection with both /ṭ/ and /ś/, the historical quality of phonemes can possibly still affect the synchronic pronunciation, especially in the context of religious texts.

4.1.2.9 Prosodic features

Last, but not least, metrical factors (prosodic constraints) have to be taken into account for a comprehensive analysis of the Biblical Hebrew corpus. Even though metrical factors are in no way restricted to poetic context, the Psalms appear *prima facie* as a relevant source in this context. DeCaen (2003: 42) attributes the example in pause יַחֲשֹׁבוּן *yaḥăšōḇūn* (Ps 35:20) 'they (m.) think' to prosodic conditioning, in contrast to the example (also in pause) יַחְשֹׁבוּ *yaḥšṓḇū* (Is 13:17). Two other relevant examples may be נֶחֱמָדִים *neḥĕmāḏīm* (Ps 19:11) 'pleasant' (m.pl.) – as opposed to usual נֶחְמָד *neḥmāḏ* – and נֶחֱשָׁלִים *neḥĕšālīm* (Dt 25:18) 'worn out' (m.pl.). To cite one more example: whereas one finds the form without *ḥăṭāp̄*, יַחְשִׁיךְ *yaḥšīḵ* 'he darkens' in the Psalms (Ps 139:12), a corresponding example in prose context has *ḥăṭāp̄*, וְהַחֲשַׁכְתִּי *wə-haḥăšaḵtī* 'and I shall darken' (Amos 8:9), the latter example carrying stress on the ultimate syllable.

Bergsträsser (1918–1929, vol. 2: 113) makes a strong case that *ḥăṭāp̄* vowels can be triggered by distancing of the main accent.[23] In this connection he provides the following minimal pairs:

(50) Minimal pairs contrasting *ḥăṭāp̄*-less forms with forms carrying *ḥăṭāp̄* due to prosodic influence (distancing of main accent)

Form without *ḥăṭāp̄*	**Form with *ḥăṭāp̄***
יַחְקֹר *yaḥqōr* (Job 13:9)	יַחֲקָר־זֹאת *yaḥăqor-zō(ʾ)ṯ* (Ps 44:22)
יַחְשֹׁב *yaḥšōḇ* (Is 10:7)	אַל־יַחֲשָׁב־לִי *ʾal-yaḥăšoḇ-lī* (2 Sam 19:20)[24]
יַחְשֹׁבוּ *yaḥšṓḇū* (Is 13:17)	יַחֲשֹׁבוּן *yaḥăšōḇūn* (Ps 35:20)
נֶחְמָד *neḥmāḏ* (Gen 2:9)	נֶחֱמָדִים *neḥĕmāḏīm* (Ps 19:11)
מַחְמָד *maḥmāḏ* (Hos 9:6)	מַחֲמָדִים *maḥămāḏīm* (Ct 5:16)

The role of prosodic constraints in poetic contexts of the Bible will be revisited and thoroughly discussed in section 4.1.3.3.5 below.

23 "Bisweilen werden diese Formen durch den Akzent modifiziert, indem bei Enttonung oder Fortrücken des Akzents Chatef für Schwa eintritt."

24 Note that the latter two forms are also spelled with *qāmāṣ*, indicating an *o*-vowel in a closed pretonic syllable.

4.1.2.10 The special status of חיה (paᶜal)

The only Tiberian Hebrew פ״ח forms which have prefix vowels that do not undergo lowering (but cf. section 4.1.2.11 below) are the ones belonging to the root חיה, except the forms in hifᶜīl (cf., e.g., Joüon & Muraoka 1993: 211 = § 79s). What is more, the paᶜal forms belonging to the root חיה do not feature any *ḥăṭāp̄* vowel after the /ḥ/, as do all other פ״ח forms, whose second root-consonant is of high sonority (the glide /y/ is at the top of the sonority scale), and most פ״ח forms, which are at the same time of the ל״ה type (*tertiae infirmae*).[25] Here are the relevant forms (disregarding jussive forms (יְחִי *yəḥī*) and *way-yiqṭol* forms (וַיְחִי *wa-yḥī*)), some of which also hold for Modern Hebrew (cf. Bolozky 1996/2008):

(51) The paradigm of חיה (as far as attested)

	Form without *ḥăṭāp̄* (paᶜal)	Form with *ḥăṭāp̄* (hifᶜīl)
3.sg.m.	יִחְיֶה *yiḥyē* (Dt 8:3)	הֶחֱיָה *heḥĕyā* (Jos 6:25)
2.sg.m.	תִּחְיֶה *tiḥyē* (Gen 27:40)	הֶחֱיִתָנוּ *heḥĕyīṯā-nū* (Gen 47:25)
2.sg.f.	תִּחְיִי *tiḥyī* (2 K 4:7)	—
1.sg.c.	אֶחְיֶה *ʾeḥyē* (2 K 1:2)	הֶחֱיֵיתִי *heḥĕyēṯī* (Num 22:33)
3.pl.m.	יִחְיוּ *yiḥyū* (Zech 1:5)	—
2.pl.m.	וִחְיִיתֶם *wi-ḥyīṯem* (Ez 37:5)	הַחֲיִתֶם *haḥăyīṯem* (Jos 2:13)
	תִּחְיוּ *tiḥyū* (Jer 35:7)	—
	תִּחְיוּן *tiḥyūn* (Dt 8:1)	—
2.pl.f.	תִּחְיֶינָה *tiḥyēnā* (Ez 3:21)	—
1.pl.c.	נִחְיֶה *niḥyē* (Gen 43:8)	—
ipt. sg.m.	וֶחְיֵה *we-ḥyē* (Prov 7:2)	הַחֲיֵנִי *haḥăyē-nī* (Is 38:16)
ipt. pl.m.	וִחְיוּ *wi-ḥyū* (Jer 27:12)	הַחֲיוּ *haḥăyū* (Num 31:18)
inf. cs.	לִחְיוֹת *li-ḥyōṯ* (Ez 33:12)	לְהַחֲיוֹת *lə-haḥăyōṯ* (Gen 6:20)
inf. abs.	—	הַחֲיֵה *haḥăyē* (Jos 9:20)
noun	מִחְיָה *miḥyā* (Ezra 9:8) 'preservation of life'	—

25 Cf. also Gesenius 1910: 218 = §§ 76i and 77e for the additional complication that ע״ע verbs (*mediae geminatae*) can function like ל״ה verbs and *vice versa*.

These forms have already puzzled generations of Hebraists, and we can only come up with a tentative solution here. Even though the sonority of the second root-consonant in the form יִחְיֶה *yiḥyē* is maximal, no epenthesis takes place; at least, such an epenthesis is not reflected on the surface of the Masoretic system, which does not allow for a "*ḥăṭap̄ i*". Phonetically, there may well have been an output form like [yiḥĭyē] or even [yīḥĭyē], but phonologically, such a form (/yiḥĭyē/) does not conform to standard Tiberian Hebrew phonotactics. Most surprisingly, no vowel lowering takes place before the syllable coda /ḥ/ in this case. Such vowel lowering does occur, however, in the hifʿīl form הֶחֱיָה *heḥĕyā*, which consequently also features an epenthetic *ḥăṭap̄ sə̄ḡōl*.[26]

Interestingly, Khan (1994; cf. also 1997: 92ff.) shows that some Karaite manuscripts (Hebrew in Arabic characters) transcribe the first *i* in the relevant paʿal forms with a *mater lectionis* <ي> rendering the lengthened *i* in the prefix, e.g., in the form ييحيا rendering יִחְיֶה *yiḥyē*, in the form تيحيو rendering תִּחְיוּ *tiḥyū*, or in the form ميحيا rendering מִחְיָה *miḥyā*. The prefixed imperative form וֶחְיֵה *we-ḥyē* appears as واحيى , with a *mater lectionis* <ا> rendering the lengthened *e* in the prefix.[27] All these forms are clear indication of phonetic lengthening of the first vowel before /ḥ/ in the Tiberian Masoretic tradition. What is more, some manuscripts add a *gaʿyā* /*meṯeḡ* under the first *i*, which amounts to phonetic lengthening of the *i* as well (cf., e.g., Joüon & Muraoka 1993: 61 = § 14c4), thus implying a syllable structure [yīḥ.(ə).yē], in which the "(ə)" is considered a "stray element" that is to be deleted.[28] Thus, the unfortunate syllable contact "ḥ$y" remains (cf. again Vennemann (1988: 40) for the relevant syllable contact law in this context).

If one does not adhere to Bergsträsser's (1918–1929, vol. 1: 159 = § 28t) view to the effect that יִחְיֶה *yiḥyē* etc. is formed in analogy to the frequent יְחִי *yəḥī* / וַיְחִי *wa-yḥī*, or Bolozky's view (oral communication on October 27, 2008) to the effect that the non-lowering of the prefix

26 For an analysis of יִחְיֶה *yiḥyē* and הֶחֱיָה *heḥĕyā* in terms of Optimality Theory, cf. section 6.3 below.

27 For all forms cf. Khan 1994: 137.

28 Cf. Bat-El 1995 for a formal analysis in terms of prosodic structure.

vowel *i* in the relevant forms may be simply due to the high frequency of the root חיה, high frequency being a widespread cause of irregularities in the verbal system, then Khan's observations indeed offer a way out of this puzzle. According to Khan (e-mail communication on November 6, 2008), the lengthening of the first vowel may well serve as an explanation for the lack of lowering in the forms under scrutiny.

4.1.2.11 *way-yiqṭol* forms of פ״ח verbs of the ל״ה type

We mentioned above (cf. item **(38)** in section 3.3.2) that apocopated consecutive verb forms of the ל״ה type regularly feature epenthetic vowels before a liquid or nasal C_2, but not otherwise. As far as פ״ח verbs and other verbs *primae gutturalis* are concerned, the tendency to insert epenthetic vowels in such forms appears to be even stronger, in line with our observations in section 4.1.2.4 above.[29] Here is an overview of the relevant attested forms (underlyingly /waC_i-C_iiC_1C_2/ or /*wə*-C_iiC_1C_2/):

(52) Epenthesis in *way-yiqṭol* forms of פ״ח verbs of the ל״ה type

Root	Form		Gloss
חדה	וַיִּחַדְּ	*way-yíḥad*	'and he rejoiced' (Ex 18:9)[30]
חזה	וְתַחַז	*wə-táḥaz*	'and it shall look' (Mic 4:11)
חיה	וַיֶּחִי	*way-yéḥī*	'and he stayed alive' (Dt 5:26 (23))
חלה	וַיָּחַל	*way-yā́ḥal*	'and he fell sick' (2 K 1:2)
חנה	וַיִּחַן	*way-yíḥan*	'and he made a camp' (Gen 26:17)
חצה	וַיַּחַץ	*way-yáḥaṣ*	'and he divided' (Gen 32:8)
חרה	וַיִּחַר	*way-yíḥar*	'and he got angry' (Gen 4:5)

While the epenthetic vowels *per se* in these forms are predictable, it is indeed amazing that pre-guttural lowering does not take place in the case of וַיִּחַדְּ *way-yíḥad*, וַיִּחַן *way-yíḥan*, and וַיִּחַר *way-yíḥar*, and that lowering *does* unexpectedly take place in the pausal paᶜal form וַיֶּחִי *way-yéḥī*. At the moment, we have no explanation for this circumstance.

---

29 Cf. Gesenius 1910: 211 = § 75r and Bergsträsser 1918–1929, vol. 2: 163 = § 30g.

30 For the non-spirantisation of the /d/ in וַיִּחַדְּ *way-yíḥad* cf. Benua 1997: 120.

4.1.3 Unified statistical analysis

4.1.3.1 Overview

In this section we will further discuss some of the issues raised in section 4.1.2 and present a thorough quantitative analysis of the verbal and nominal forms in question. We will account for the verbal and nominal forms separately, in this order. By taking into consideration several factors that may trigger epenthetic *ḥăṭāp̄* vowels we will in the end arrive at a hierarchy of the Biblical (Tiberian) Hebrew consonants as to the frequency of which they are involved in contact anaptyxis. It will become evident that the similarities between this hierarchy and a general sonority scale, as presented, e.g., in Vennemann (1988: 9), are striking. Thus, as for the verbal forms, we will

1) present a strictly quantitative overview of our findings;
2) make clear what verbal forms we will investigate and why;
3) clarify on what kind of contact anaptyxis we will concentrate;
4) illustrate the special status of the forms with a final weak radical;
5) give a detailed account of our method; and
6) discuss whether prosodic factors have any influence on the insertion of epenthetic *ḥăṭāp̄* vowels in the poetic parts of the Hebrew Bible in particular.

In the last section we will sum up our main findings in three points.

As for the nominal forms, we will

1) account for our method;
2) present the relevant nominal forms in tables, and
3) discuss to what extent the findings conform to our hypothesis and the results for the verbal forms.

At the end of the chapter we will present the results for the nominal forms.

4.1.3.2 Introduction

Our hypothesis is that there is a connection between an epenthetic *ḥăṭāp̄* vowel after *ḥ* and the place of the second radical on a general sonority scale, as presented by, e.g., Vennemann (1988: 9): the higher the second radical is on this sonority scale, the greater the likelihood of an epenthetic *ḥăṭāp̄* vowel. In his article "Hebrew sonority and Tiberian contact anaptyxis: the case of verbs *primae gutturalis*" from 2003, DeCaen presents a similar hypothesis. As far as we are aware, this article is the most detailed account of such verbs in the Hebrew. Therefore, we will regularly refer to DeCaen's article in our analysis. Considering the fact that his primary interest probably is cross-linguistic, DeCaen has made an impressive amount of interesting observations. However, we do not always agree to his conclusions.

In order to test our hypothesis against relevant verbal and nominal forms, we investigated all the פ"ח roots in the Hebrew Bible. Unless otherwise stated, the quantitative data in the unified statistical analysis below are based on Lisowsky's concordance to the Hebrew Bible from 1993 (pp. 459-541).[31]

4.1.3.3 The verbal forms

4.1.3.3.1 A preliminary account

Having singled out the verbs in the dictionaries mentioned above, we counted, for each verbal root, the number of cases in which epenthetic *ḥăṭāp̄* vowels occurred of the total number of relevant prefixed verbal forms. As already stated in 4.1.1 above, the prefixed forms we have considered are the paᶜal infinitive and imperfect, the nifᶜal perfect, imperfect and participle, and the hifᶜīl and hofᶜal/hufᶜal perfect, imperfect, imperative, and infinitive.

In the table below we have ranked the consonants in terms of how often an epenthetic *ḥăṭāp̄* vowel obtains in the verbal forms of the roots in the corpus, in which this consonant is the second radical. The ranking is preliminary in the sense that it is strictly quantitative – essential fac-

31 The dictionaries of Gesenius (1995: 316–413) and Koehler & Baumgartner (1994: 284–365) do not always agree with Lisowsky (1993) – or with each other – as to whether or not one should classify homophonous roots (sometimes in different binyanim) as one or two. For instance, while Gesenius (1995: 357) classifies *ḥ-l-m* as two lemmata/roots, "to be healthy, strong" and "to dream", Koehler & Baumgartner (1994: 320), as Lisowsky (1993: 500), take *ḥ-l-m* as just one lemma/root, albeit with two separate subheadings. Such minor discrepancies do not affect our statistics, though.

tors such as a third weak radical are not taken into consideration, and the number of occurrences is not expressed. Thus, the ranking in the table will be thoroughly discussed and consequently adjusted throughout the chapter.[32]

(53) A first, strictly quantitative ranking

C_2	**Percentage of forms with anaptyxis**
ב, ג, ו, נ	100%
ז, ט, ר	96-99%
ל	91-95%
י	71-75%
צ	46-50%
ס	31-35%
שׂ	26-30%
שׁ	16-20%
ק	11-15%
מ	1-5%
בּ, גּ, דּ, כּ, פּ, תּ	0%

4.1.3.3.2 The special status of the *CvḥC₂əC₃ū* and *CvḥvC₂C₃ū* forms

Within the verb groups we have considered there are two forms that need some comments. One form has to be excluded from the analysis, and the other form will be treated separately.

When the second radical in a root is followed by a *šwā mobile*, as in the third person plural of paᶜal imperfect, *ḥ* takes either a *šwā quiescens* or, in exceptional cases, which we will return to shortly, an anaptyctic full vowel (Blau 1993: 39). Examples are וַיַּחְלְקוּ *way-yaḥləqū* (Jos 14:5) and וַיַּחַלְמוּ *way-yaḥalmū* (Gen 40:5), respectively. In such cases, i.e., when the second radical is followed by a *šwā mobile*, *ḥ* is never followed by a

32 The table is organised in 5% intervals, of which only the relevant ones are listed. Tentatively, we treat [ḇ] and [ḡ] as distinct units here (cf. section 4.1.2.3 above), being aware, though, that the percentage for these units is automatically 100%. The percentage for [b] and [g] is, of course, automatically 0%.

ḥăṭāp̄ vowel. DeCaen (2003: 42) calls this phenomenon "SHEWA EXEMPTION". As far as a quantitative analysis is concerned, the term "exemption" is somewhat misleading. As we will see, if the insertion of an epenthetic *ḥăṭāp̄* vowel after *ḥ* ever can be called a rule, it is only when the second radical is *n*, or *b* occurring as [v], and so to call the observation an exception is not appropriate. The phenomenon that *ḥ* in most cases is followed by *šwā quiescens* when the second radical takes *šwā mobile*, is rather a rule, a rule that (even) verbal forms of the פ״ח type adhere to. Therefore, the CvḥC$_2$əC$_3$ū forms are excluded from our analysis.

As mentioned, DeCaen's label "exemption" is misleading in morphological terms, but, as will become evident in chapter 6 below, in Optimality-Theoretic terms, the label does make sense, or is at least technically useful.

Treating the phenomenon of "SHEWA EXEMPTION", DeCaen points out the "gross violation" of וַיַּחְרְגוּ *yaḥrəḡū* (Ps 18:46) of the syllable contact law. This is a correct observation, but the form is not more of a violation than, say, יֶחְזְקוּ *yeḥzəqū* (Is 28:22) or וַיַּחַנְטוּ *way-yaḥnəṭū* (Gen 50:2). The only alternative to יַחְרְגוּ *yaḥrəḡū* would be יַחַרְגוּ *yaḥarḡū*, in which *ḥ* is followed by *pattāḥ*, which marks a full vowel. The insertion of an anaptyctic vowel compensates for the violation of the syllable contact law. This leads us to the next paragraph.

Above we mentioned that in exceptional cases where the second radical takes *šwā mobile*, *ḥ* takes a full vowel. In the case of third person plural forms of the prefix conjugation of paᶜal and the suffix conjugation of nifᶜal, this full vowel is either *a* or *e*, marked by *pattāḥ* or *sẹḡōl*. As Blau (1993: 39) refers to these vowels as "anaptyctic", the *CvḥvC$_2$C$_3$ū* forms deserve to be accounted for. But since they should be considered marked and there are so few of them – only 23 – we decided to treat them separately. The findings turned out to be highly relevant to our hypothesis, as they reflect the overall statistics.

As mentioned, in our corpus there are 23 instances of the type *CvḥvC$_2$C$_3$ū*, i.e., forms in which the second radical is followed by *šwā mobile* and *ḥ* takes a full vowel. All the forms belong to paᶜal. There are 21 imperfect forms, all plural – four second person and 17 third person.

The two last instances are *way-yiqṭol* forms.[33] The 23 forms are spread across seven different roots, each of which will be treated separately: *ḥzq, ḥṭʾ, ḥlm, ḥnṭ, ḥrb, ḥrd,* and *ḥrq.*

There are five instances to be considered as far as *ḥzq* is concerned. The second person plural of paᶜal imperfect – תֶּחֶזְקוּ *teḥezqū* – occurs twice (in Dt 11:8 and Ezra 9:12), and the third person – יֶחֶזְקוּ *yeḥezqū* – three times (2 Sam 10:11, 1 Chr 19:12, and 2 Chr 31:4). A form without epenthesis occurs only once: יֶחְזְקוּ *yeḥzəqū* in Is 28:22.

As regards *ḥṭʾ*, there are seven forms to consider. The second person plural of paᶜal imperfect – תֶּחֶטְאוּ *teḥeṭʾū* – occurs twice (Gen 42:22 and 1 Sam 14:34), and the third person – יֶחֶטְאוּ *yeḥeṭʾū* – five times (1 K 8:33, 35, and 46, and 2 Chr 6:24, 26, and 36). Corresponding forms without epenthesis do not occur.

There are two relevant manifestations of *ḥlm*, both belonging to *way-yiqṭol* (the *wāw-* + short prefix conjugation) of paᶜal. The first person plural form with *hē cohortativum* – וַנַּחַלְמָה *wan-naḥalm-ā(h)* 'and we dreamt' – occurs in Gen 41:11, and the third person plural form – וַיַּחַלְמוּ *way-yaḥalmū* 'and they dreamt' – in Gen 40:5. No form without epenthesis occurs. One does find the hifᶜīl-form מַחְלְמִים *maḥləmīm* (Jer 29:8), but this form is of course not of the type /$CvC_1C_2\breve{v}C_3\bar{v}$/, since the last syllable is closed by a consonant.

When it comes to *ḥnṭ*, there is only one relevant form in our corpus: the third person plural of paᶜal future – וַיַּחַנְטוּ *way-yaḥanṭū* (Gen 50:26). The form without epenthesis וַיַּחְנְטוּ *way-yaḥnəṭū* also occurs once (Gen 50:2).

Concerning *ḥrb,* there are two relevant forms in our corpus – the third person plural form of paᶜal imperfect, יֶחֶרְבוּ *yeḥerḇū* (Ez 6:6), and the third person plural form of nifᶜal perfect, נֶחֶרְבוּ *neḥerḇū* (2 K 3:23). No forms without epenthesis occur.

As for *ḥrd,* we find three occurrences of וַיֶּחֶרְדוּ *way-yeḥerḏū* (Gen 42:28, 1 Sam 16:4, and 1 K 1:49), one instance of וְיֶחֶרְדוּ *wə-yeḥerḏū*

33 Cf. Waltke & O'Connor 1990: 543ff. for a thorough analysis of the *wāw-* + short prefix conjugation.

(Hos 11:10) and one of יֶחֶרְדוּ *yeḥerḏū* (Hos 11:11). Only one form without epenthesis occurs, יֶחְרְדוּ *yeḥrəḏū* (Ez 26:18).

The last root to be considered is *ḥrq*, and here only one form can be found – the third person plural form of paʿal imperfect, וַיַּחַרְקוּ־שֵׁן *way-yaḥarqū-šen* 'and they gnashed [their] teeth' (Lam 2:16). No form without epenthesis occurs.

Now, let us sum up the findings concerning the 23 instances of the type /$\text{Cv}\dot{h}\text{vC}_2\text{C}_3\bar{u}$/ in which the second radical is followed by *šwā mobile* and *ḥ* takes a full vowel. We see that the second radical is *n* in one case, *z* in five, *r* in eight, *l* in two, and *ṭ* in seven cases. As far as the four first consonants are concerned, they all find themselves at the top of the quantitative ranking in item **(53)** above.

The conclusion, then, for cases where the second radical takes *šwā mobile* and *ḥ* takes a full vowel, is that the findings support our overall hypothesis: the higher the second radical is on the sonority scale, the greater the likelihood of contact anaptyxis.

In table **(47)** we presented third person plural forms of paʿal imperfect for all פ״ח roots in the Hebrew Bible. The intention was to show that what DeCaen (2003: 42) calls "SHEWA EXEMPTION", i.e. the observation that in forms where the second radical is followed by a *šwā mobile, ḥ* never takes a *ḥăṭāp̄* vowel, is not an exception at all, but a rule that the relevant פ״ח forms adhere to. We presented such unmarked forms in the left column together with pausal forms, if extant. Forms where the second radical takes *šwā mobile* and *ḥ* takes a full vowel, which are the real *exemptions*, are, if they occur in the corpus, presented in the middle column. The gloss can be found in the right column.

4.1.3.3.3 The special status of the forms *tertiae infirmae*

In this section we will show why it is important to account for forms with a final weak radical separately when considering the relation between the sonority of a given C_2 and contact anaptyxis.

The final-weak forms occurring amongst the פ״ח verbs in the Hebrew Bible are of the type ל״א (functioning in many respects like ל״ה) and ל״ה. We will return once more to the root *ḥyh* in a separate paragraph below. In our corpus, then, there are 74 and 173 instances of the ל״א and ל״ה types, respectively. 13 roots are involved: *ḥbh, ḥbʾ, ḥzh, ḥṭʾ, ḥlh, ḥlʾ, ḥnh, ḥsh, ḥph, ḥṣh, ḥrh, ḥšh,* and *ḥth*. Below we have compared the percentage values for the relevant C_2-s when the final-weak forms are excluded, with the value for the final-weak forms alone. Thus, we oppose percentage value for strong verbs vs. value for final-weak forms only, with one and the same C_2:

(54) Percentage of contact anaptyxis depending on the status of C_2

C_2	Percentage for strong verbs	Percentage for III-weak verbs
פ (*p*):	0%	0%
ת (*t*):	0%	0%
נ (*n*):	100%	100%
ז (*z*):	99%	100%
ר (*r*):	99%	100%
צ (*ṣ*):	0%	100%
ס (*s*):	0%	73%
שׁ (*š*):	13%	67%
ט (*ṭ*):	50%	97%
ב (*b*):	61%	0%
ל (*l*):	100%	56%

As we can see, the following consonants lend themselves to such a comparison: *p, t, n, z, r, ṣ, s, š, ṭ, b,* and *l*. For *p* and *t* the percentage value for *tertiae infirmae* forms equals the value for strong forms: 0%. Therefore, the inclusion of the weak forms in the total percentage value does not render the results misleading. The same is true of *n*, for which the value is 100% in both cases. For *r* and *z*, the percentage values are 99% vs. 100%, i.e. almost equal. But for *ṣ, s, š,* and *ṭ* there is a difference in percentage points of 100, 73, 54, and 47, respectively. This means that when the second radical is a voiceless sibilant, represented by *s* and *š*, or a voiceless emphatic consonant, represented by *ṭ* and *ṣ*, and the third radical is weak, represented orthographically by *ʾ* and *h*, the likelihood of contact anaptyxis between *ḥ* and the second radical increases significantly.

The results for *b* and *l* are also intriguing. These are the only cases in which the value for final-weak forms is lower than that for regular forms. The decrease is of 61 percentage points for *b* and 44 for *l*. As far as *b* is concerned, there are 14 ל"א forms and one ל"ה form. Of the 14 ל"א forms eight belong to the binyan nifᶜal, five to hifᶜīl, and one to hofᶜal. The ל"ה form belongs to nifᶜal. We do not have any explanation as to the consistent non-spirantisation of *b* in these forms, and so the issue needs further investigation.[34]

The same is true of *l*: first, both forms – one paᶜal and one hifᶜīl – of *ḥlʾ* exhibit anaptyxis. Of *ḥlh* there are 10 forms to consider. The two hifᶜīl and three hofᶜal forms exhibit anaptyxis, whereas only one of the five nifᶜal forms do. We find וְנֶחֱלֵיתִי *wə-neḥĕlēṯī* (Dan 8:27), but נֶחְלוּ *neḥlū* (Amos 6:6 and Jer 12:13), אֶת־הַנַּחְלוֹת *ʾeṯ-han-naḥlōṯ* (Ez 34:4) and כָּל־הַנַּחְלוֹת *kol-han-naḥlōṯ* (Ez 34:21). So, perhaps the binyan influences the pointing. Additionally, the categorical (syntactic) status of the word may also be relevant: when it is a noun, the nifᶜal perfect form exhibits anaptyxis: נַחֲלָה *naḥălā*. DeCaen (2003: 42) suggests that the underlying third radical *y* may be of relevance to an explanation, but it is not clear how in this context. Unless the divergences are due to prosodic factors – the form וְנֶחֱלֵיתִי *wə-neḥĕlēṯī* (Dan 8:27), for instance, carries a secondary accent on the ultimate syllable, it seems that the case of *ḥlh* needs further investigation as well.

The root *ḥyh* should be mentioned again in this connection. This is the only root in the corpus in which the second radical is *y*. Anaptyxis obtains in all cases of hifᶜīl, but never in paᶜal (cf. sections 4.1.2.10 above and 6.3.2 below).

Another point worth mentioning is that the likelihood of contact anaptyxis seems to be slightly greater when the weak radical is *h* than when it is ʾ. This is plausible, though, since ʾ is not "weak", in principle. This, however, needs further investigation, since the values may be influenced by factors such as the number of forms of each C_2.

34 Nominal forms with $C_2 = b$ often exhibit anaptyxis, though.

4.1.3.3.4 Principles underlying the statistics

Now, let us return to our method for arriving at item **(55)** below. Having counted the relevant verbal forms in the corpus and the *ḥăṭāp̄* forms amongst them we drew a table in which we plotted the following data for each root in the corpus where one or more of the relevant verbal forms occurred:

1) Total number of *a*-prefixed forms;
2) Number of *a*-prefixed forms with an anaptyctic *ḥăṭāp̄* vowel;
3) Percentage of *a*-prefixed forms with an anaptyctic *ḥăṭāp̄* vowel;
4) Total number of *e*-prefixed forms;
5) Number of *e*-prefixed forms with an anaptyctic *ḥăṭāp̄* vowel;
6) Percentage of *e*-prefixed forms with an anaptyctic *ḥăṭāp̄* vowel;
7) Percentage value for anaptyctic *ḥăṭāp̄* vowels for the *a*- and *e*-prefixed forms together.

Thus we arrived at a percentage value for each root.

An account of the choice of prefix vowels is in order. The prefix vowels in our corpus are *i*, *o*, *a*, and *e*. *i* is the prefix vowel only in the imperfect forms – except first person singular – of the root *ḥyh*. There are 72 such cases in our corpus.[35] Contact anaptyxis does not obtain in any of them, and so our hypothesis is not supported as far as the *i*-prefixed forms are concerned. As for *o*, the situation is different. In hofᶜal forms, the prefix vowel *o* is copied as *ḥăṭap̄ qāmāṣ* after *ḥ*. In our corpus there are nine such instances, belonging to the roots *ḥlh*, *ḥrb*, and *ḥrm*. The second radical is *r* in six cases, and *l* in three: הָחֳלֵיתִי *hoḥŏlēṯī* (1 K 22:34, as well as 2 Chr 18:33, and 35:23), הָחֳרֵב *hoḥŏrēḇ* (2 K 3:23)[36], הָחֳרָבָה *hoḥŏrāḇā* (Ez 26:2), מָחֳרָבוֹת *moḥŏrāḇōṯ* (Ez 29:12), and יָחֳרָם *yoḥŏrām* (Ex 22:19, Lev 27:29, and Ezra 10:8). The laterals *r* and *l* find themselves at the top of the sonority scale, and thus our hypothesis is supported.

35 The verb forms וְנִחֲלוּ *wə-niḥălū*, belonging to *ḥll*, in Ez 7:24, and נִחָרוּ *niḥārū*, belonging to *ḥrr*, in Ps 102:4, are probably analogous formations to *n-ḥ*-C3-verbs; cf. Bauer & Leander 1922: 434 = § 58k.

36 In the apparatus of the *BHS*, this absolute infinitive is emendated to *hā-ḥereḇ* 'the sword'.

Since the *i*-prefixed forms in our corpus are so special and the *o*-prefixed forms so few, we have confined ourselves just to accounting for them here in the text. The case for *a*- and *e*-prefixed forms however, is different: in our corpus these are the prefix vowels in approximately 490 and 360 cases, respectively, and thus by far the most common prefix vowels relevant to our analysis.

One might ask why we decided to distinguish between the different prefix vowels in the first place. One reason is that it has been suggested that the prefix vowel might be a trigger of contact anaptyxis. DeCaen (2003: 43) suggests the following for פ"ח roots with a sibilant as second radical and a weak consonant as third:

> "(…) since [a] can be assumed to be more sonorous than [ɛ], the *ḥ* has two phonetic realizations that differ in sonority and hence factor into the acceptability of the syllable transition."

This assumption seems plausible in principle. Thus, we decided to investigate this factor as well. We arrived at the following results:

1) There are four roots in our corpus of the פ"ח type with a sibilant as second and a weak consonant as third radical: *ḥzh, ḥsh, ḥṣh,* and *ḥšh.*[37] DeCaen's suggestion can be discussed only in the case of *ḥšh,* and then only to a limited degree. This will be done in section 4.1.3.3.3 below.

2) The percentage value for anaptyctic *ḥăṭāp* vowels for all *a*- and *e*-prefixed forms in our corpus is approximately 73% and 70%, respectively. So, the prefix vowel does not seem to have any influence on the syllable transition at all. As we will demonstrate in chapter 5, it *is* the case that /ḥ/ has more than one phonetic realisation. But the phonetic realisation of *ḥ* seems to be irrelevant as far as contact anaptyxis is concerned.

Having arrived at a percentage value for each relevant root in the corpus, we investigated roots with the same second radical as a whole. We considered the same parameters as for the single roots: number and percentage of *ḥăṭāp* forms out of the total number of *a*- and *e*-prefixed forms, and percentage value for the *a*- and *e*-prefixed forms together. But

37 Following Rendsburg (1997: 71) and Khan (1997: 88f.), we consider Tiberian Hebrew *ṣ* a voiceless emphatic (velarised or uvularised) sibilant, as does DeCaen (2003: 46). Cf. also Goerwitz (1996: 490) for a variety of reconstructions of the pre-Masoretic pronunciations of /ṣ/ ([tsˀ, tʃˀ, and tɬˀ]).

before we present the statistics in a unified chart covering all the relevant פ״ח forms in the Hebrew Bible, some comments are in order.

The chart shows the share of anaptyctic forms according to percentage of the total number of forms. The roots are presented alphabetically. For each consonant that occurs as second radical, the number of anaptyctic and non-anaptyctic forms of all the roots that share this second radical is summed up in the same way. For each second radical the results are presented in a separate row which is doubly underlined.

In the columns of *a*-prefixed forms and *e*-prefixed forms there are three numbers. The first number is the total number of forms, the second is the number of anaptyctic forms, and the third is the share of anaptyctic forms according to percentage of the total number of forms. The rightmost column shows the share of anaptyctic forms of the *a*- and *e*-prefixed forms together.

In the case of *b*, *k*, and *p*, the realisations are given in the columns of comments. In the columns of comments we have also presented forms that differ from the majority as far as anaptyxis is concerned and where these forms occur. In five cases we have presented forms of one and the same root that, contrary to expectation, differ as to whether anaptyxis does or does not obtain. An example is the root *ḥlh*, in which the nifᶜal feminine preterite form exhibits anaptyxis, whereas the third person plural form of nifᶜal does not. Thus, we have נֶחְלוּ *neḥlū*, but נַחֲלָה *naḥălā*. In line with our statistical methods, the lexicalised participle feminine form נַחֲלָה *naḥălā* 'wound' (Is 17:11), which is a noun, is not included in the percentages. On some occasions, comments are also made in the other columns.

If, for a second radical, the share of anaptyctic forms according to percentage varies significantly depending on whether a final-weak root is included or not, two different percentages are given.

(55) Unified statistical overview

Root	*a*-prefixed forms	Comments	*e*-prefixed forms	Comments	Total
חבא	7; 0; 0%	all [b]	7; 0; 0%	all [b]	0%
חבה	0		1; 0; 0%	[b]	0%
חבט	3; 0; 0%	all [b]	0		0%
חבל I	5; 2; 40%	3 [b], 2 [ḇ]	0		[b] 0% [ḇ] 100%
חבל II	0		1; 0; 0%	[b]	0%
חבק	1; 1; 100%	[ḇ]	0		100%
ברח I	1; 0; 0%	[b]	0		0%
חבשׁ	11; 10; 91%	10 [ḇ], 1 [b]	1; 1; 100%	[ḇ]	[b] 0% [ḇ] 100%
$C_2 = b$	28; 13; 46%		10; 1; 10%		37%
$C_2 =$ בּ	15; 0; 0%		9; 0; 0%		0%
$C_2 =$ ב	13; 13; 100%		1; 1; 100%		100%
חגר	10; 1; 10%	9 [g], 1 [ḡ] *la-ḥăḡōr* in Is 22:12	0		[g] 0% [ḡ] 100%
$C_2 = g$	10; 1; 10%				10%
$C_2 =$ גּ	9; 0; 0%				0%
$C_2 =$ ג	1; 1; 100%				100%
חדל	0		21; 0; 0%	all [d]	0%
$C_2 =$ דּ			21; 0; 0%		0%
חור	0		1; 1; 100%		100%
$C_2 =$ ו			1; 1; 100%		100%
חזה	1; 1; 100%		21; 21; 100%		100%
חזק	56; 55; 98%	*wə-ʾaḥzēq* in Is 42:6	69; 69; 100%		99%
$C_2 =$ ז	57; 56; 98%		90; 90; 100%		99%
חטא	17; 17; 100%		41; 41; 100%		100%
חטב	1; 0; 0%		0		0%

Root	*a*-prefixed forms	Comments	*e*-prefixed forms	Comments	Total
חטם	0		1; 1; 100%	ʾeḥĕṭam- in Is 48:9	100%
חטף	2; 1; 50%		0	*la-ḥăṭōp̄* and *yaḥṭōp̄*, both in Ps 10:9	50%
C_2 = ט	20; 18; 90%		42; 42; 100%		97% Excluding *ḥṭʾ*: 4; 2; 50%
חיה	paʿal: 0 hifʿīl: 15; 15; 100%		paʿal: 8; 0; 0% hifʿīl: 8; 8; 100%		paʿal: 0% hifʿīl: 100% Total, i.e., share of relevant hifʿīl forms in the corpus: 74%
C_2 = י	15; 15; 100%		16; 8; 50%		74% (but cf. cell above)
חכם	1; 0; 0%	[k]	8; 0; 0%	all [k]	0%
C_2 = כ	1; 0; 0%		8; 0; 0%		0%
חלא	0		2; 2; 100%		100%

Root	*a*-prefixed forms	Comments	*e*-prefixed forms	Comments	Total
חלה I	2; 0; 0%	ʾ*eṯ-han-naḥlōṯ* and *kol-han-naḥlōṯ* in Ez 34:4 and 34:21 (but nifʿal participle fem. *naḥălā* and *maḥălā-lēḇ* in Prov 13:12 – both nouns)	5; 3; 60%	*neḥlū* in Jer 12:13; *wə-lō(ʾ) neḥlū* in Amos 6:6	nifʿal: 5; 1; 20% hifʿīl + hofʿal: 5; 5; 100% Total (including hofʿal: 67%) (excluding hofʿal): 43%
חלם	10; 10; 100%		0		100%
חלף I	16; 16; 100%		1; 1; 100%		100%
חלץ	2; 2; 100%		1; 1; 100%		100%
חלק I	4; 4; 100%		3; 3; 100%		100%
חלק II	5; 5; 100%		0		100%
חלש	1; 1; 100%		1; 1; 100%		100%
C_2 = ל	40; 38; 95%		13; 11; 85%		92%
חמד	6; 0; 0%		4; 1; 25%	*neḥĕmāḏīm* in Ps 19:11	10%
חמל	20; 0; 0%		8; 0; 0%		0%
חמס	4; 0; 0%		0		0%
חמץ I	0		1; 0; 0%		0%
C_2 = מ	30; 0; 0%		13; 1; 8%		2%
חנה	100; 100; 100%		0		100%
חנט	1; 1; 100%		0		100%
חנן	1; 1; 100%		1; 1; 100%		100%

Root	*a*-prefixed forms	Comments	*e*-prefixed forms	Comments	Total
חנף	4; 4; 100%		4; 4; 100%		100%
C_2 = נ	106; 106; 100%		5; 5; 100%		100%
חסה	3; 2; 67%		8; 6; 75%		73%
חסם	1; 0; 0%		0		0%
חסר	1; 0; 0%		10; 0; 0%		0%
C_2 = ס	5; 2; 40%		18; 6; 33%		35% Excluding *ḥśh*: 0%
חפה	0		1; 0; 0%	[p] *neḥpā* in Ps 68:14	0%
חפז	1; 0; 0%	[p]	2; 0; 0%	both [p]	0%
חפץ I	9; 0; 0%	all [p]	10; 0; 0%	all [p]	0%
חפץ II	1; 0; 0%	[p]	0		0%
חפר I	5; 0; 0%	all [p]	1; 0; 0%	[p]	0%
חפר II	3; 0; 0%	all [p]	3; 0; 0%	all [p]	0%
C_2 = פ	19; 0; 0%		17; 0; 0%		0%
חצב	5; 0; 0%		0		0%
חצה	0		5; 5; 100%		100%
C_2 = צ	5; 0; 0%		5; 5; 100%		50%
חקר	6; 1; 17%	*yaḥăqor-* in Ps 44:22	3; 0; 0%		11%
C_2 = ק	6; 1; 17%		3; 0; 0%		11%
חרב I	9; 7; 78%	*wə-ʾaḥrīḇ* in 2 K 19:24 and Is 37:25 (The sentences are identical)	16; 16; 100%		92%
חרד	15; 15; 100%		7; 7; 100%		100%

Root	*a*-prefixed forms	Comments	*e*-prefixed forms	Comments	Total
חרה	3; 3; 100%		6; 6; 100%		100%
חרך	1; 1; 100%		0		100%
חרם	26; 26; 100%		14; 14; 100%		100%
חרף I	0		2; 2; 100%		100%
חרף II	0		1; 1; 100%		100%
חרץ I	0		6; 6; 100%		100%
חרץ II	0		1; 1; 100%		100%
חרק	1; 1; 100%		0		100%
חרש I	8; 8; 100%		0		100%
חרש II	24; 24; 100%		16; 16; 100%		100%
C_2 = ר	87; 85; 98%		69; 69; 100%		99%
חשך	6; 0; 0%		2; 1; 50%	*ʾeḥĕśak̲* in Job 7:11	13%
חשף	2; 0; 0%		1; 1; 100%		33%
C_2 = שׁ	8; 0; 0%		3; 2; 67%		18%
חשב	15; 3; 20%	*yaḥăšōb̲ūn* in Ps 35:20, *ʾal-yaḥăšob̲-lī* in 2 S 19:20 and *yaḥăšob̲* in Ps 40:18 (All occurring nouns exhibit anaptyxis: *maḥăšāb̲ā* or *maḥăšāb̲ōt̲* (7 times), *maḥăšā́b̲et̲* in 2 Chr 2:13, and *maḥăšéb̲et̲* in Ez 38:10)	13; 0; 0%		11%

Root	*a*-prefixed forms	Comments	*e*-prefixed forms	Comments	Total
חשה	6; 1; 17%	The five non-anaptyctic forms: *maḥšīm* in Neh 8:11, Judg 18:9, 1 K 22:3 and 2 K 7:9, and *maḥšē* in Is 57:11. The anaptyctic form: *la-ḥăšōṯ* in Qoh 3:7	9; 9; 100%		67%
חשך	5; 1; 20%	*wə-haḥăšaḵtī* in Amos 8:9	4; 0; 0%		11%
חשל	0		1; 1; 100%	*kol-han-neḥĕšālīm* (Dt 25:18)	100%
C_2 = שׁ	26; 5; 19%		27; 10; 37%		28% Excluding *ḥšh*: 13%
חתה II	2; 0; 0%	both [t] *la-ḥtōṯ* in Is 30:14; *hă-yaḥtē* in Prov 6:27	0		0%
חתך	0		1; 0; 0%	[t]	0%
חתל	2; 0; 0%	both [t]	0		0%
חתם	8; 0; 0%	all [t]	3; 0; 0%	all [t]	0%
חתף	1; 0; 0%	[t]	0		0%
חתר	0		1; 0; 0%	[t]	0%
חתת	1; 0; 0%	[t]	0		0%
C_2 = ת	14; 0; 0%		5; 0; 0%		0%

Below we have split table **(55)** into smaller ones in order to make our results more transparent. In each table we have collected roots where the second radicals for some reason are natural to compare. For each second radical, all relevant roots are mentioned. If one or more third-weak root occurs, two percentage values are given. From the first number the weak roots are excluded. In the second they are included. In the columns of *a*-prefixed forms and *e*-prefixed forms, the first number is the sum of relevant forms, the second is the sum of *ḥăṭāp̄* forms, and the third the percent value of *ḥăṭāp̄* forms of the total number of forms. In the column of and *a*- and *e*-prefixed forms together, the percentage value of *ḥăṭāp̄* forms for the radical is given. First, let us look at the *begadkefat* consonants:[38]

(56) Statistical overview: ב (*b*), ג (*g*), ד (*d*), כ (*k*), פ (*p*), ת (*t*)

C_2	**Roots**	***a*-prefixed forms**	***e*-prefixed forms**	***a*-and *e*-prefixed forms together**
b	חבט (*ḥbṭ*), חבל (*ḥbl*) I and II, חבק (*ḥbq*), חבר (*ḥbr*) I, חבשׁ (*ḥbš*):	21; 13; 62%	2; 1; 50%	61%
	Including חבא (*ḥbʾ*) and חבה (*ḥbh*):	28; 13; 46%	10; 1; 10%	37%
בּ	חבט (*ḥbṭ*), חבל (*ḥbl*) I and II, חבר I (*ḥbr*), חבשׁ (*ḥbš*):	8; 0; 0%	1; 0; 0%	0%
	Including חבא (*ḥbʾ*) and חבה (*ḥbh*):	15; 0; 0%	9; 0; 0%	0%
ב	חבל (*ḥbl*) I, חבק (*ḥbq*), חבשׁ (*ḥbš*):	13; 13; 100%	1; 1; 100%	100%

38 In line with our deliberations above (section 4.1.2.2), we allow for the theoretical possibility that the quality of individual *begadkefat* consonants may be transferred from one paradigm to the other – "residual (non-)spirantisation" in Bolozky's terms. Therefore, the phonematisation of a spirantised allophone has to be considered a theoretical option.

C_2	Roots	*a*-prefixed forms	*e*-prefixed forms	*a*-and *e*-prefixed forms together
g	חגר (*ḥgr*)	10; 1; 10%	0	10%
גּ	חגר (*ḥgr*)	9; 0; 0%	0	0%
ג	חגר (*ḥgr*)	1; 1; 100%	0	100%
דּ	חדל (*ḥdl*)	0	21; 0; 0%	0%
כּ	חכם (*ḥkm*)	1; 0; 0%	8; 0; 0%	0%
פּ	חפה (*ḥph*), חפז (*ḥpz*), חפץ (*ḥpṣ*) I and II, חפר (*ḥpr*) I and II	19; 0; 0%	17; 0; 0%	0%
תּ	חתה (*ḥth*) II, חתך (*ḥtk*), חתל (*ḥtl*), חתם (*ḥtm*), חתף (*ḥtp*), חתר (*ḥtr*), חתת (*ḥtt*)	14; 0; 0%	5; 0; 0%	0%

In terms of a general sonority scale, the findings presented in the table above conform to our hypothesis. Between *ḥ* and the unvoiced plosives *k*, *p*, and *t* and the voiced plosives *b*, *d*, and *g*, contact anaptyxis never occurs. [ḇ] and [ḡ] should be considered voiced fricatives. Voiced fricatives are generally not amongst the most sonorous sounds, but they are at least more sonorous than their voiced plosive counterparts.

So, the interesting matters concerning the *begadkefat* consonants are connected to why only *b* and *g* occur spirantised and why they do so in just some cases. We will discuss the instances of *b* and *g* below, but at the moment we do not have any concluding answers.

As far as *b* is concerned, the manifestation is [b] in 24 cases and [ḇ] in 14. These numbers can be misleading, however, since for the forms of *ḥbʾ*, *ḥbh*, *ḥbṭ*, *ḥbl II*, and *ḥbr I* – 14, one, three, one, and one instance, respectively, and 20 instances all together – the realisation is always [b]. The roots left, then, are *ḥbq*, *ḥbl I*, and *ḥbš*. As for *ḥbq* there is only one form to consider, and so the case is difficult to evaluate. As for *ḥbl I* and

II the picture is interesting. For *ḥbl* (*ḥbl I* and *II* in our terms), DeCaen (2003: 42) suggests a variation by book. He observes that the manifestations of *b* are [b] in Job but [ḇ] in Deuteronomy. This is correct, but the occurrences in those two books are few: three in Job (22:6, 24:9, and 34:31) and two in Deuteronomy (24:6 and 24:17). There is a sixth and last instance of *ḥbl* – in Ex 22:25 – in which the realisation is [b]. It is hardly possible to generalise from six examples. This is probably the reason why DeCaen suggests prosodic effects as a second explanation: the two examples in Deuteronomy are preceded by the particle *lō(ʾ)*. "Prosodic effects" do, of course, not automatically amount to epenthesis. But if this were the explanation, should we then not expect **kī-taḥăḇōl* instead of כִּי־תַחְבֹּל *kī-taḥbōl* in Job 22:6? And **lō(ʾ) ʾeḥĕḇōl* instead of לֹא אֶחְבֹּל *lō(ʾ) ʾeḥbōl* in Job 34:31? Prosody cannot be excluded as an explanation for the anaptyctic *ḥăṭāp̄* vowels in *ḥbl I*, but at least a preceding particle does not seem to be the triggering factor. As we will see in section 4.1.3.3.4 on prosodic factors, it is rather (suffixed) enclitic particles that seem to have this effect (cf. Bergsträsser 1918–1929, vol. 2: 113).

As far as the root *ḥbš* is concerned, DeCaen does not doubt that prosody is what distinguishes the variants. Having in mind whether the *b* is followed by a full vowel or a *šwā mobile* he states the following:

> "Those with a full vowel exhibit anaptyxis; while those with a *shewa mobile* [...] do not: we find minimal contrasts such as [...] *yaḥăbōš* [rather *yaḥăḇōš*] vs. *yaḥbəšēnû*." (DeCaen 2003: 42)

Above we have already stated that when the second radical is followed by a *šwā mobile*, *ḥ* never takes an anaptyctic half vowel. It either takes a *šwā quiescens* or, in a few exceptional cases, a full vowel. Thus, a form such as *yaḥbəšē-nū* where *b* and *ḥ* take *šwā mobile* and *šwā quiescens*, respectively, is unmarked (opaque). The manifestation [b] rather than [ḇ] here is in line with Vennemann's syllable contact law (Vennemann 1988: 40), which we repeat here for the sake of clarity:

> "A syllable contact A$B is the more preferred, the less the Consonantal Strength of the offset A and the greater the Consonantal Strength of the onset B; more precisely – the greater the characteristic difference CS(B)–CS(A) between the Consonantal Strength of B and that of A."

The difference in consonantal strength between *ḥ* and [b] is greater than that between *ḥ* and [ḇ]. All three forms of *ḥbš* of this kind conform to the two rules above, i.e. when *b* takes *šwā mobile*, the manifestation is [b] and *ḥ* takes *šwā quiescens*. What is puzzling about the root *ḥbš*, then, is that when *b* takes a full vowel, the instantiation is [ḇ] in 11 of 12 cases, the one exception being וְיֶחְבָּשׁ *wə-yeḥbāš* in Job 5:18. The corresponding numbers for the other roots are three out of 23. As mentioned above, DeCaen (2003: 42) ascribes the data for *ḥbš* to prosody. But, if prosody is a relevant parameter at all, why does it block anaptyxis in five roots – *ḥbʾ*, *ḥbh*, *ḥbṭ*, *ḥbl II*, and *ḥbr I* – and trigger it in one? If we look at other consonants in the corpus that have two manifestations, e.g., *k* and *p*, this question is even more justified. *k* occurs as [k] in all eight relevant cases, i.e. cases in which *k* is followed by a full vowel. As for *p*, the manifestation is [p] in all 36 cases where it takes a full vowel. The number of roots for *k* is only one, but four (or six if *ḥpṣ* and *ḥpr* are split in I and II) for *p*.

The case of *ḥbš* is truly puzzling. If we are right in suggesting that the explanation is not prosody, the issue needs further investigation.

When it comes to *g*, there are 10 instances of one root in our corpus, and an anaptyctic *ḥăṭāp̄* vowel obtains in only one. As far as *d*, *k*, *p*, and *t* are concerned, no anaptyctic *ḥăṭāp̄* vowel occurs in the respectively 21, 9, 36, and 19 examples in the corpus.

Summing up, then, for the *begadkefat* consonants an anaptyctic *ḥăṭāp̄* vowel of course never obtains in the case of *b*, *g*, *d*, *k*, *p*, and *t*, surfacing as [b], [g], [d], [k], [p], and [t], respectively. This conforms to our hypothesis, as voiced and unvoiced plosives are placed at the bottom of the sonority scales presented in 3.1. For some reason, only *b* and *g* occur spirantised, and a *ḥăṭāp̄* vowel of course always occurs in these cases. Voiced fricatives are not, as mentioned, placed at the top of the sonority scale presented in section 3.1, but at least they are more sonorous than their plosive counterparts.

So, the anaptyxis hierarchy for the Tiberian Hebrew *begadkefat* consonants is as follows: *b* > *g* > *d*, *k*, *p*, *t*.

The next consonants we will consider are the [so called] *emphatics* – *ṭ*, *ṣ*, and *q* (cf. again Rendsburg 1997: 73 and Khan 1997: 87). As the exact

Tiberian Hebrew nature of these consonants are not yet determined, they are classified somewhat differently in the literature. As for *ṭ*, some labels are "voiceless emphatic dental plosive" (Rendsburg 1997: 70), "dental affricate" (Lipiński 2001: 132) and "emphatic unvoiced alveolar plosive" (Khan 1997: 87). As to *ṣ*, Rendsburg's and Khan's characteristic is "voiceless (alveolar) emphatic sibilant". According to the former, opinions differ as to whether *ṣ* is a (lateral) fricative or an affricate (Rendsburg 1997: 71). Khan suggests that *ṣ* had a voiced allophone (1997: 99). As far as *q* is concerned, this consonant was an "unvoiced uvular plosive" (Khan 1997: 89) and a "voiceless emphatic velar plosive" (Rendsburg 1997: 71). We follow the latter, and, among others, also DeCaen (2003: 38f.) in considering *q* an emphatic consonant. So, let us consider the table below.

(57) Statistical overview: צ (*ṣ*), ט (*ṭ*), ק (*q*)

C_2	**Roots**	***a*-prefixed forms**	***e*-prefixed forms**	***a*-and *e*-prefixed forms together**
ט	חטב (*ḥṭb*), חטם (*ḥṭm*), חטף (*ḥṭp*): Including חטא (*ḥṭʾ*):	3; 1; 33% 20; 18; 90%	1; 1; 100% 42; 42; 100%	50% 97%
צ	חצב (*ḥṣb*) Including חצה (*ḥṣh*):	5; 0; 0% 5; 0; 0%	0 5; 5; 100%	0% 50%
ק	חקר (*ḥqr*)	6; 1; 17%	3; 0; 0%	11%

As far as *ṭ* is concerned, the percentage value varies significantly depending on whether one includes the root *ḥṭʾ* or not. *ḥṭʾ* is the root in 58 of the 62 cases in which *ṭ* is the second radical. As we have shown in section 4.1.3.3.3 above, roots *tertiae infirmae* and in which the second radical is a voiceless sibilant or a voiceless emphatic consonant tend to display contact anaptyxis significantly more often than other roots. Therefore, the percentage value for *ṭ* when *ḥṭʾ* is included, 97%, is most probably too high. But when the root *ḥṭʾ* is left aside, there are only four forms left to consider. Contact anaptyxis obtains in two of them. The percentage value then becomes 50%, which may also be too high, since it is, of course, problematic to operate in terms of percent when the number of examples is low. But a percentage value for *ṭ* of significantly more than 0 is explainable assuming that *ṭ* once had an emphatic (velarised) quality.

The case of *ṭ* has also been registered by DeCaen (2003: 46). However, he does not take the problematic issue of *ḥṭʾ* into consideration, and so places *ṭ* at the same level as *z* on his "T[iberian]H[ebrew]-T[iberian] A[ramaic] sonority scale" (ibid.). We think this is misleading in two respects. First, as far as a general sonority scale is concerned, there are no unvoiced phonemes above voiced fricatives. As far as we are aware, Tiberian Hebrew *ṭ* did not have a voiced allophone (cf., e.g., Rendsburg 1997: 70 and Khan 1997: 87; but cf. Goerwitz 1996: 490), and so *z* should be more sonorous than *ṭ*. Second, as we will see below, *z* is involved in epenthesis in 99% of the cases whether the third-weak root *ḥzh* is included or not. Therefore, *z* should rank higher than *ṭ* on the anaptyxis hierarchy for Tiberian Hebrew as well.

The case of *ṣ* is not straightforward either. *ṣ* is the second radical in ten instances in the corpus, five of which belong to the root *ḥṣb* and five to the root *ḥṣh*. A *ḥăṭāp̄* vowel does not obtain in any of the five first examples, but in all of the five examples of *ḥṣh*. In *ḥṣh* the third radical is weak and so some of the effect should be ascribed to this. But it is probably a mistake to place *ṣ* at the very bottom of the Hebrew sonority scale alongside *t*, since the two manifestations of the root *ḥth* do not exhibit anaptyxis, despite the final weak radical. It is impossible to arrive at an exact percentage value for *ṣ* when there are so few examples available. We can, however, get closer by comparing the case of *ṣ* with the one of *ṭ* when the final weak roots are left out. Then, for *ṭ* two of four forms exhibit anaptyxis, whereas for *ṣ* none of five does. Considering at the same time the fact that none of the two manifestations of *ḥth* exhibit anaptyxis, we can place *ṣ* on the Hebrew anaptyxis hierarchy somewhere between *ṭ* and *t*: *ṭ* > *ṣ* > *t*. However, if *ṣ* had a voiced allophone, as Khan (1997: 99) suggests, *ṣ* should rank higher than *ṭ* in a general sonority scale, and thus, according the general tendency we have discovered, the anaptyxis hierarchy. In DeCaen's sonority scale *ṣ* is placed alongside *ṭ* and *z* (DeCaen 2003: 43 and 46). We have already explained how DeCaen has arrived at the ranking of *ṭ* alongside *z*. But it is not clear why *ṣ* is placed at this same level, as the percentage for *ṣ* is just 50% even when the third-weak root is included.

If we assume that Khan is wrong and that *ṣ* did not have a voiced allophone, the ranking *ṭ* > *ṣ* conforms to Angoujard's sonority scale for Arabic/Semitic emphatics (1997: 139–154). And if Angoujard's ranking is correct, our findings conform perfectly to our hypothesis.

The last consonant in the table above is the now unvoiced plosive *q*. According to Rendsburg, *q* in ancient Hebrew was a voiceless emphatic velar or glottalised plosive (1997: 71 and 73). Khan (1997: 89) considers *q* in Tiberian Hebrew an unvoiced uvular plosive. Of the nine examples in the corpus *q* is involved in anaptyxis only once. It might be that the historical quality of the consonant is reflected here. But it might also be that Bergsträsser is right in claiming that the *ḥăṭāp̄* vowel in יַחֲקָר־ *yaḥăqor-* (Ps 44:22) is due to accent. According to Bergsträsser, verb forms may be modified through stress or a shift of accent forward (1918–1929: 113), and *yaḥăqor-* is one of his examples. He claims that in some cases where a *šwā quiescens* is the unmarked variant, i.e. when the C_2 usually does not trigger anaptyxis, a shift of accent may lead to the insertion of a *ḥăṭāp̄* vowel. The form in Ps 44:22 is יַחֲקָר־זֹאת *yaḥăqor-zō(ʾ)ṯ*, and so the *ḥăṭāp̄* vowel may be ascribed to a shift of stress to the enclitic demonstrative pronoun.

Our data does not allow for the ranking of the emphatics *ṣ* and *q* in relation to each other. As mentioned above, for *ṣ* when the final-weak root is left aside, none of five forms exhibit anaptyxis. For *q* an epenthetic vowel obtains in one of nine cases, none of which belong to a final-weak root. But if we accept Bergsträsser's explanation and ascribe the *ḥăṭāp̄* vowel for *q* to prosodic factors, *ṣ* was probably more sonorous than *q* in Tiberian Hebrew. As our hypothesis has been strengthened by other findings, *ṣ* should rank higher than *q* in the anaptyxis hierarchy as well. Thus, preliminarily we have the following anaptyxis hierarchy for the Tiberian Hebrew emphatics: *ṭ* > *ṣ* > *q*.

The next consonants to be considered are the sibilants – *z*, *s*, *ṣ*, *ś*, and *š*. *ṣ* is included in this account too, because of its likely sibilant quality in Ancient and Tiberian Hebrew. As for *ś*, the Ancient Hebrew quality was lateral (Rendsburg 1997: 71), but in Tiberian Hebrew the pronunciation was the same as of *s* (Khan 1997: 89), and so it is included in the table below.

(58) Statistical overview: ז (*z*), ס (*s*), צ (*ṣ*), שׂ (*ś*), שׁ (*š*)

C_2	Roots	*a*-prefixed forms	*e*-prefixed forms	*a*-and *e*-prefixed forms together
ז	חזק (*ḥzq*): Including חזה (*ḥzh*):	56; 55; 98% 59; 58; 98%	69; 69; 100% 90; 90; 100%	99% 99%
ס	חסם (*ḥsm*), חסר (*ḥsr*): Including חסה (*ḥsh*):	3; 0; 0% 6; 2; 33%	10; 0; 0% 18; 6; 33%	0% 33%
צ	חצב (*ḥṣb*): Including חצה (*ḥṣh*):	5; 0; 0% 5; 0; 0%	0 5; 5; 100%	0% 50%
שׂ	חשׂך (*ḥśk*), חשׂף (*ḥśp*):	8; 0; 0%	3; 2; 67%	18%
שׁ	חשׁב (*ḥšb*), חשׁך (*ḥšk*), חשׁל (*ḥšl*): Including חשׁה (*ḥšh*):	20; 4; 20% 26; 5; 19%	18; 1; 6% 27; 10; 37%	13% 28%

A first observation is that *z* triggers contact anaptyxis significantly more often than expected from Vennemann's general sonority hierarchy, where voiced fricatives are placed below liquids and nasals. In the hierarchy for Hebrew *z* finds itself right below the central liquid *r* and on the same level as the lateral liquid *l*, and far above the nasal *m*. True, there are only two roots in which the second radical is *z* and at that, one of the roots has a final weak radical. But the percentage value is 99% even when the final-weak root is left aside, and the number of examples is high – 122.

Another observation is the difference in percentage value between *s* and *ś*: when the final-weak root *ḥsh* is excluded, *s* is never involved in contact anaptyxis, whereas the percentage value for *ś* is 18%. So, *ś* ranks higher than *s* in the Tiberian Hebrew anaptyxis hierarchy. If this is a reflection of the suggested lateral quality of *ś* in Ancient Hebrew, our hypothesis is strengthened, as laterals are generally more sonorous than fricatives.

The divergence between *s* and *ś* has been registered by DeCaen as well (2003: 41). If Khan is correct in claiming that in Tiberian Hebrew the pronunciation of *ś* was the same as that of *s*, it is somewhat surprising, as DeCaen remarks (ibid.), that the historical contrast – /ś/ having a lateral quality – is preserved in Tiberian Hebrew.

As far as *š* is concerned, when the third-weak root *ḥšh* is excluded, the percentage value is 13%. This leaves us with the following ranking of the sibilants in the contact anaptyxis hierarchy so far: *z* > *ś* > *š* > *s*.

Ranking *ṣ* in the sibilant hierarchy is not unproblematic, but as a start *ṣ* should be placed above *s* and below *z*: first, when the final-weak roots for *s* and *ṣ* are excluded, the percentage value for both is 0%. But whereas the result for *ḥsh* is 73%, it is 100% for *ḥṣh*. Second, the percentage value for *z* is 99% even when *ḥzh* is excluded, whereas for *ṣ* epenthetic *ḥăṭāp̄* vowels only obtain in the root *ḥṣh*. The challenge is how to rank *ṣ* in relation to *ś* and *š*. As far as *ś* is concerned, epenthetic *ḥăṭāp̄* vowels occur even though no third-weak roots exist. Of 11 examples an anaptyctic *ḥăṭāp̄* vowel obtains in two, which renders a percentage value of 18%. The sums do not lend themselves to any conclusion, but if *ś* indeed derives from a lateral, *ś* would possibly trigger contact anaptyxis more often than would *ṣ*. As for *š* the percentage values are 13% when *ḥšh* is excluded and 67% for *ḥšh*. The corresponding values for *ṣ* are 0% and 100%. Here too it is impossible to conclude on the basis of quantity. But if Bergsträsser is correct in suggesting that some of the anaptyctic *ḥăṭāp̄* vowels involved with *š* are triggered by prosodic factors (Bergsträsser 1918–1929, vol. 2: 113), it is possible that *ṣ* would be involved in contact anaptyxis more often than would *š*. We would like to stress that the percentage values do not lend themselves to any conclusion. Therefore, we only suggest the following contact anaptyxis hierarchy for the Tiberian Hebrew sibilants: *z* > *ś* > *ṣ* > *š* > *s*.

Our ranking of the sibilants in Tiberian Hebrew in terms of sonority and the involvement in contact anaptyxis does not conform to De Caen's sibilant sonority hierarchy, which is the following: *ś* > *z* > *s* > *š* (op. cit.: 41, 43, and 46). It is not clear why *z* does not have the highest ranking, since 1) Tiberian Hebrew *ś*, according to Khan (1997: 89), was most probably pronounced in the same way as *s*, 2) voiced fricatives are more sonorous than voiceless ones, and 3) anaptyxis for *z* obtains in 99% of the cases. DeCaen has ranked *ś* higher than *s*, as we have, but it is not clear why *š* is considered the least sonorous of the four sibilants. His ranking of *s* as more sonorous than *š* is explainable if the final-weak roots are included in the sums. Then, the percentage values are 33% versus 28%. On the other hand, those values are higher than the value for *ś*, which is only 18%. What is more, a crucial factor when it comes to sonority in terms of phonetics is the size of the space of resonance, i.e. the oral cavity, when the sound is produced: the greater the space the lesser the sonority.[39] The oral cavity is greater when *s* is produced than when *š* is. When these factors are taken into consideration, the hierarchy of the Tiberian Hebrew sibilants except *ṣ*, as far as sonority is concerned, should be the following: *z* > *š* > *ś*, *s*. But the hierarchy of the same consonants as far as the involvement in contact anaptyxis is concerned, should be as follows: *z* > *ś* > *š* > *s*.

Let us continue to dwell on the Tiberian Hebrew sibilants. One reason for which we posed the question whether the prefix vowel had any influence on the insertion of epenthetic *ḥăṭāp̄* vowels was the constraint "SEGHOL-SIBILANT" suggested by DeCaen (2003: 43):

> "There is ... a phonetically conditioned alternation in those final-weak roots with medial sibilants. When the vowel of the prefix is [a], a firmly closed syllable obtains; however, when the vowel is the front [ɛ], anaptyxis is the result. Thus we find such constrasts as *maḥšê* vs. *teḥĕšê*."

In our corpus there are four final-weak roots with a medial sibilant: *ḥzh*, *ḥsh*, *ḥṣh*, and *ḥšh*. As far as *ḥzh* is concerned, there are 21 *e*-prefixed forms, all of which exhibit anaptyxis. But there is also one *a*-prefixed form, *la-ḥăzōṯ* (Ps 27:4), and an epenthetic *ḥăṭāp̄* vowel obtains in this as well. It is hard to see how these results can support DeCaen's proposal. As for *ḥsh*, six of eight *e*-prefixed forms exhibit anaptyxis, and two of three *a*-prefixed forms do. So, *ḥsh* does not support DeCaen's hypothesis either. As regards *ḥṣh*, there are five relevant forms, all of which exhibit

39 Thanks to Inger Moen for bringing this to our notice (personal communication in August 2008).

anaptyxis, and all of which are *e*-prefixed. Thus, DeCaen must have based his constraint only on the results for *ḥšh*. As we will see, however, the constraint is plausible only to a limited extent. Correctly, all nine *e*-prefixed forms exhibit anaptyxis, whereas only one of six *a*-prefixed does. But a closer look at the *a*-prefixed forms shows that in four of the five cases in which an *a*-prefixed form does not exhibit anaptyxis, the form in question is מַחְשִׁים *maḥšīm* (Neh 8:11, Judg 18:9, 1 K 22:3, and 2 K 7:9). Correctly, we also find the form מַחְשֶׁה *maḥšē* (Is 57:11), but also לַחֲשׁוֹת *la-ḥăšōṯ* (Qoh 3:7). So, in one way we can say that for *ḥšh* all nine *e*-prefixed forms exhibit anaptyxis and one of three *a*-prefixed forms do. These results hardly legitimise a constraint SEGHOL-SIBILANT. This will be even more evident in section 4.1.3.2.2 below, when nominal forms are included in the account.

The findings for the nasals *m* and *n* are interesting as well. Consider the table below:

(59) Statistical overview: *m, n*

C_2	**Roots**	***a*-prefixed forms**	***e*-prefixed forms**	***a*-and *e*-prefixed forms together**
מ	חמד (*ḥmd*), חמל (*ḥml*), חמס (*ḥms*), חמץ (*ḥmṣ*):	30; 0; 0%	13; 1; 8%	2%
נ	חנט (*ḥnṭ*), חנן (*ḥnn*), חנף (*ḥnp*): Including חנה (*ḥnh*):	6; 6; 100% 106; 106; 100%	5; 5; 100% 5; 5; 100%	100% 100%

On a general sonority scale nasals are placed in the middle, i.e. below the laterals *r* and *l* and above voiced and unvoiced fricatives. In the Tiberian Hebrew contact anaptyxis hierarchy, however, *m* and *n* find themselves on opposite ends – almost at the bottom, and at the top, respectively. *m* is involved in anaptyxis in just one of more than 40 cases, whereas for *n*, when even the third weak root is excluded, anaptyxis obtains in 11 of 11 cases. This does not seem to support our hypothesis. Above, however, we mentioned that sonority is related to the size of the oral cavity when the sound is produced: the greater the size, the lesser the sonority. The space of resonance is greater when *m* is produced than when *n* is. Thus, phonetically, *n* is probably generally more sonorous than *m*. So, the findings for the Tiberian Hebrew nasals support our hypothesis as well.

The contrast between *m* and *n* in Tiberian Hebrew has also been noted by DeCaen (2003: 38). According to him, this contrast is not controversial in cross-linguistic terms, as there is corresponding evidence in, for instance, Russian, Spanish, and Old French as well. DeCaen does not, however, state the exact nature of this evidence.

The next consonants to be considered are the liquids – the lateral liquid *l* and the central liquid *r*.

(60) Statistical overview: *l*, *r*

C_2	**Roots**	***a*-prefixed forms**	***e*-prefixed forms**	***a*-and *e*-prefixed forms together**
ל	חלם (*ḥlm*), חלף (*ḥlp*) I, חלץ (*ḥlṣ*), חלק (*ḥlq*) I and II, חלש (*ḥlš*): Including חלא (*ḥlʾ*) and חלה (*ḥlh*) I:	38; 38; 100% 40; 38; 95%	6; 6; 100% 13; 11; 85%	100% 92%
ר	חרב (*ḥrb*) I, חרד (*ḥrd*), חרך (*ḥrk*), חרם (*ḥrm*), חרף (*ḥrp*) I and II, חרץ (*ḥrṣ*) I and II, חרק (*ḥrq*), חרש (*ḥrš*) I and II: Including חרה (*ḥrh*):	84; 82; 98% 87; 85; 98%	63; 63; 100% 69; 69; 100%	99% 99%

These statistics too support our hypothesis, since the laterals are ranked *r* > *l* on a general sonority scale as well. However, as mentioned in section 4.1.3.3.3 above, the percentage value for *ḥlʾ* and *ḥlh I* is peculiar, because this is one of just two occasions (the other being *b*) in which the inclusion of final-weak roots renders the percentage value for the C_2 lower than the exclusion.

The last consonants to be considered are *w* and *y*.

(61) Statistical overview: *w*, *y*

C_2	**Roots**	***a*-prefixed forms**	***e*-prefixed forms**	***a*-and *e*-prefixed forms together**
ו	חור (*ḥwr*):	0	1; 1; 100%	100%
י	חיה (*ḥyh*):	15; 15; 100%	16; 8; 50%	74%

As regards *w*, there is only one instance in the corpus – the form יֶחֱוָרוּ *yeḥĕwā́rū* in Is 29:22 – and this has to be borne in mind when the percentage value is considered.

As for *y* the percentage values need some comments. First, *y* is a glide and so should be placed alongside or right below high vowels on a general sonority scale. Thus it is contrary to expectation that we do not find *y* at the absolute top of the Hebrew scale, i.e. that the percentage value is not 100%. A closer look at the forms in the corpus, however, tells that the value of 74% is misleading. There is only one relevant root in the corpus – *ḥyh* – of which there are 31 instances. 8 of these belong to the binyan paʿal, of which none exhibit anaptyxis. The rest of the examples – 23 – belong to hifʿīl, and anaptyxis obtains in all of them. Thus we find אֶחְיֶה *ʾeḥyē*, exemplified in 2 K 1:2, but הֶחֱיֵיתִי *heḥĕyēṯī*, as in Num 22:33. What the value of 74% tells, then, is that in 74% of the relevant cases in the corpus the form belongs to the root hifʿīl, and in 26% to paʿal.

The case of *ḥyh* and anaptyxis is puzzling. For some reason, in paʿal the prefix vowel *e* is not copied to a *ḥăṭap̄ sẹḡōl* and the prefix vowel *i* is not lowered, as in יִחְיֶה *yiḥyē* in, e.g., Gen 31:32, whereas in hifʿīl *sẹḡōl* is always copied and so *i* never occurs. At the moment we have no good explanation for this phenomenon, and neither have the grammars of Biblical Hebrew. One possibility is that there is some kind of vowel harmony operating in the background, amounting to a "*ḥăṭāp̄ i*", which is present phonetically, but not graphically (cf. sections 4.1.2.10 above and 6.3.2 below).

Concluding the section about sonority and contact anaptyxis we have seen that the likelihood of the insertion of an anaptyctic *ḥăṭāp̄* vowel after *ḥ* increases the more sonorous C_2 is. Thus, our hypothesis is corroborated.

4.1.3.3.5 Factoring in prosodic effects: the relation between prosodic factors and anaptyctic *ḥăṭāp̄* vowels in the poetic parts vs. the rest of the books of the Hebrew Bible

The background for this section is a statement made by Speiser in 1926 and a suggestion made by DeCaen in 2003. First, Speiser (1926: 153) stated the following as to the "phonetic basis for a secondary vowel with a single consonant":

> "[…] such conditions might arise […] during especially solemn recitations or else on occasions in which the emotions of the speaker have been particularly stirred. […] such developments presuppose a greater stress on the given syllable than the latter is ordinarily entitled to, […]. […] conditions favoring the development of such vowels obtained notably in the pronunciation of the synagogue, especially that of the poetical portions of the Scriptures. […]. They have never attained to the dignity of full vowels and are therefore marked with the Ḫateph-signs […]."

Thus, Speiser claimed that there is a connection between prosody and poetry, and anaptyctic *ḥăṭāp̄* vowels. In his 2003 paper DeCaen suggested the same – that prosody (2003: 42), and thus rhythm, and poetry (op. cit.: 46) are triggers of contact anaptyxis. Hence we decided to look into this matter as well, letting the Book of Psalms represent "the poetic parts of the Bible".[40] Our findings can be summed up as follows: prosody and rhythm most likely do trigger epenthetic vowels in certain environments. But the extent to which they do is one and the same across the whole Hebrew Bible. Anaptyctic *ḥăṭāp̄* vowels are not triggered by prosodic factors more often in the poetic parts than in the rest of the Bible.

The issue of prosody in the Hebrew Bible is an intriguing but very complicated one. We will not go into the details of the accentuation system of the Masoretes here, but the reader is referred to Yeivin 1980.

---

40 As poetic parts of the Bible one can count Job, Psalms, Proverbs, Ecclesiastes, and Song of Songs (Song of Solomon). In Speiser "the poetic parts" is referred to as "the poetical parts of the Scriptures" (1926: 153), cf. the quotation above, and in DeCaen as "the book of Psalms" (2003: 46).

A crucial reference when it comes to prosody and contact anaptyxis is Bergsträsser (1918–1929, vol. 2: 113). He states that certain forms, such as the forms relevant to our analysis, are sometimes modified by accent, in that a *ḥăṭāp̄* vowel obtains instead of a *šwā* due to a shift of accent forward. This phenomenon is visible in cases where the C_2 does not normally trigger contact anaptyxis. Bergsträsser gives examples such as the fact that we find נֶחְמָד *neḥmāḏ* (Gen 2:9) but נֶחֱמָדִים *neḥĕmāḏīm* (Ps 19:11), יַחְקֹר *yaḥqōr* (Job 13:9) but יַחֲקָר־ *yaḥăqor-* (Ps 44:22), and יַחְשֹׁב *yaḥšōḇ* (Is 10:7) but יַחֲשָׁב־ *yaḥăšoḇ-* (2 Sam 19:20).[41] This observation has also been made by DeCaen. He places forms that take anaptyxis contrary to expectation – against the background of modern pronunciation – in one of three groups, one of which is what he calls *prosodic conditioning* (2003: 42). What is more, he ascribes the form נֶחֱמָדִים *neḥĕmāḏīm* to an addition of a prosodic foot. Because of this extra prosodic foot, he argues, a secondary stress is applied to the prefix, and so an epenthetic *ḥăṭāp̄* vowel is inserted. Consequently, a question is whether such forms occur more often in the poetic books of the Bible than in the other books.

We arrived at the conclusion above – that *prosody most likely is a relevant parameter as far as anaptyctic vowels are concerned, but it is so irrespective of book* – by counting the *ḥăṭāp̄* forms while distinguishing between the book of Psalms and the other books. Our results, which are based on the data presented in Appendix 1, are the following:

1) In the book of Psalms there are 69 forms to be considered, 41 of which exhibit anaptyxis, and 28 of which do not. Approximately, we can say that the relationship between the total number of forms, forms involving anaptyxis, and forms which do not, is the following: 70 – 40 – 30. Operating with the exact numbers we arrive at a percentage value for the forms in the Psalms exhibiting anaptyxis, of 59%. This is lower than for the Hebrew Bible all together – about 70%. Since the number of forms is low – there are, as mentioned, about 850 relevant forms in the whole Hebrew Bible – a closer look at the roots involved is in order.

41 Bergsträsser's observations seem to be substantial. As far as C_2 = *š* is concerned, his claim is supported by הַחֲשַׁכְתִּי *haḥăšaḵtī* (Amos 8:9) – accent here on the last syllable – and נֶחֱשָׁלִים *neḥĕšālīm* (Dt 25:18). As for C_2 = *m* and *q*, Bergsträsser's examples are the only relevant ones.

2) Based on Lisowsky (1993) there are 73 relevant roots in our corpus, 48 of which are not represented in the book of Psalms: *ḥbʾ, ḥbh, ḥbṭ, ḥbl I* and *II, ḥbq, ḥbr I, ḥbš, ḥdl, ḥwr, ḥṭb I, ḥṭm, ḥkm, ḥlʾ, ḥlh I, ḥlm, ḥlṣ, ḥlq II, ḥlš, ḥml, ḥms, ḥmṣ, ḥnṭ, ḥnn I, ḥsm, ḥpṣ II, ḥpr I, ḥṣb, ḥrd, ḥrh, ḥrk, ḥrm I, ḥrp I* and *II, ḥrṣ I* and *II, ḥrš I, ḥśk, ḥśp, ḥšl, ḥth II, ḥtk, ḥtl, ḥtm, ḥtp, ḥtr*, and *ḥtt*.

3) For the following eight roots, when there are only forms with epenthetic vowels in the book of Psalms, there are only such forms in the other books as well: *ḥzh, ḥṭʾ, ḥlp I, ḥlq I, ḥnh, ḥnp, ḥṣh*, and *ḥrš II*.

4) For the following four roots, when there are only forms without epenthetic vowels in the other books, there are only such forms in the book of Psalms as well: *ḥsr, ḥpz, ḥpṣ I*, and *ḥpr II*.

5) For the last 13 roots some comments are in order:

There are some instances in the corpus that support the suggestion that contact anaptyxis is triggered more often in the book of Psalms than in the other books of the Hebrew Bible. The first concerns the root *ḥmd*, of which there are 10 instances in the corpus. Anaptyxis obtains in just one case, *neḥĕmāḏīm*, which occurs in Ps 19:11. This is the only occurrence of this root in the book of Psalms.

The other supporting example regards the root *ḥqr*, of which there are nine instances in the corpus. Just one form exhibits anaptyxis: we find יַֽחֲקָר־ *yaḥăqor-* in Ps 44:22, and this is the only example of this root in the Psalms.

The third example concerns *ḥšb*. Of this root there are 28 verbal forms in the corpus. Only three of these exhibit anaptyxis, of which two occur in the Psalms: יַֽחֲשֹׁבוּן *yaḥăšōḇūn* in Ps 35:20 and יַֽחֲשָׁב לִי *yaḥăšoḇ lī* in Ps 40:18. For the book of Psalms the relation between anaptyctic forms and non-anaptyctic forms is 2:7, whereas the relation is 1:21 for the rest of the books. The third instance in which anaptyxis occurs is אַל־יַֽחֲשָׁב־לִי *ʾal-yaḥăšoḇ-lī* in 2 Sam 19:20.

As for the root *ḥšh*, there are 15 relevant forms in the corpus. Anaptyxis obtains in ten cases. The root occurs three times in the Psalms, in all of which anaptyxis is displayed: we find פֶּן־תֶּחֱשֶׁה *pen-teḥĕšē* in Ps 28:1, וַיֶּחֱשׁוּ *way-yeḥĕšū* in Ps 107:29, and הֶחֱשֵׁיתִי *heḥĕšēṯī* in Ps 39:3.

Thus, the relation between anaptyctic forms and non-anaptyctic forms in the Book of Psalms and the other books is 3:0 and 7:5, respectively. Against this root being support for the suggestion one could argue that the number of examples is low, and that the percentage value for the rest of the Hebrew Bible is high as well.

The fifth and last example concerns the root *ḥśp*. In Ps 29:9 we find the form וַיֶּחֱשֹׂף *yeḥĕśōp̄*, whereas the two forms in the other two represented books do not exhibit anaptyxis.

There are some examples that do not support the suggestion that prosodic factors trigger anaptyxis more often in the Psalms than in the other books. The first concerns the root *ḥṭp*, of which the only two forms in the corpus occur in the Psalms. In one form anaptyxis obtains, and in the other it does not. Thus, we find לַחֲטוֹף *la-ḥăṭōp̄* – but יַחְטֹף *yaḥṭōp̄*, and at that, both forms occur in Ps 10:9.

The second example regards *ḥsh*, occurring 11 times in the corpus. Three of these forms do not exhibit anaptyxis, of which two can be found in the Psalms: אֶחְסֶה *ʾeḥsē* in Ps 57:2 and תֶּחְסֶה *teḥsē* in Ps 91:4. The relation between the forms exhibiting and not exhibiting anaptyxis is 5:2 for the Psalms and 3:1 for the rest of the books. The number of examples is low, but the percentage value of anaptyxis is 71% for the Psalms and 75% for the rest of the books. The third non-anaptyctic form is לַחְסוֹת *la-ḥsōṯ* in Is 30:2.

As for the root *ḥgr* there are 11 forms in our corpus, of which only one exhibits anaptyxis. The two forms in the Psalms, תַּחְגֹּרְנָה *taḥgōrnā(h)* in Ps 65:13 and תַּחְגֹּר *taḥgōr* in Ps 76:11, do not. The only anaptyctic form, לַחֲגֹר *la-ḥăḡōr*, is found in Is 22:12. The infinitive here forms a prosodic unit with the following complement *śāq*, לַחֲגֹר שָׂק *la-ḥăḡōr śāq* 'to put on [the] sack'. As the accent (*sillūq*) here moves rightward onto *śāq*, the insertion of the epenthetic *ḥăṭāp̄* vowel is plausible in this case.

As far as *ḥšk* is concerned, there are nine forms in the corpus, and anaptyxis obtains in just one. The three forms in the Psalms, תֶּחְשַׁכְנָה *teḥšaḵnā(h)* in Ps 69:24, וַיַּחְשִׁךְ *way-yaḥšiḵ* in Ps 105:28, and לֹא־יַחְשִׁיךְ *lō(ʾ)-yaḥšīḵ* in Ps 139:12, do not. The form that exhibits anaptyxis is וְהַחֲשַׁכְתִּי *wə-haḥăšaḵtī* in Amos 8:9. Note that this form carries stress on the ultima.

The only manifestation of *ḥph* in the corpus is found in the Book of Psalms. In Ps 68:14 we find נֶחְפָּה *neḥpā*.

As we have seen above for *ḥsh*, *ḥgr*, and *ḥšk*, exceptional anaptyctic forms occur in non-poetic books as well. An example for roots not occurring in the Book of Psalms is לַחֲשׁוֹת *la-ḥăšōṯ* of *ḥšh* in Qoh 3:7. As this form carries pausal accent, no "prosodic" explanation is possible. This is the only instance, of six, in which an anaptyctic vowel occurs in an *a*-prefixed form of *ḥšh*.

If we have interpreted him correctly, DeCaen (2003: 43) suggests that factors related to prosody may *block* anaptyxis as well:

> "[…] our hypothesis […] still leaves out two forms. […] The other case is marked as a *hapax* in the margin by the Tiberians: *ʾeḥsê* (Ps. 57:2) […] vs. the expected *ʾeḥĕsê* (*passim* 3x; 4x with other prefixes). (It might very well be the prosodic effect of minor pause on *ʾatnaḥ*.)"

The tenth and eleventh of the 13 roots worthy of a closer look may shed some light on this issue. First, as for the root *ḥzq* there are 125 forms in the corpus, only one of which does not exhibit anaptyxis. The only form in the Psalms does exhibit anaptyxis – we find הַחֲזֵק *haḥăzēq* in Ps 35:2, prosodically plausible, since the last syllable carries a conjunctive accent (*mūnaḥ*). The form in which anaptyxis does not obtain is וְאַחְזֵק *wə-ʾaḥzēq* in Is 42:6 (admittedly also carrying a *mūnaḥ*). As regards the second root, *ḥrb I*, there are 28 forms in the corpus, of which only two exhibit anaptyxis. There is one example of this root in the Book of Psalms, and in it anaptyxis obtains: we find וַיֶּחֱרָב *way-yeḥĕrāḇ* in Ps 106:9. The exceptional forms are found in 2 K 19:24 and Is 37:25. The form is וְאַחְרִב *wə-ʾaḥrīḇ* in both cases.[42]

The last two roots are *ḥyh* and *ḥrq*. As to the former, the forms in the Book of Psalms exhibit anaptyxis in exactly the same cases as the other books, i.e. never in paʿal but always in hifʿīl. As to *ḥrq* the only form in the corpus is יַחֲרֹק *yaḥărōq* in Ps 112:10. But there is nothing peculiar about this form, since the form וַיַּחַרְקוּ־ *way-yaḥarqū-* in Lam 2:16 exhibits anaptyxis as well, though in this case the epenthetic vowel is the unreduced *a*-vowel (marked by *pattāḥ*).

42 According to the apparatus a *way-yiqṭol* form וָאַחְרִב *wā-ʾaḥriḇ*.

Summing up, in this section we have investigated whether prosodic factors trigger or block contact anaptyxis more often in the poetic parts of the Bible, represented by the Book of Psalms, than in the prosaic parts. There are about 850 relevant forms in our corpus, approximately 70 of which are found in the Book of Psalms. In the corpus all together, based on Lisowsky (1993), 73 roots are represented. 25 of these occur in the Psalms. In brief, as far as the hypothesis is concerned that links contact anaptyxis and (prosodical features in) poetry, these are our results:

1) For 18 roots the forms in the Psalms follow more or less the same pattern as do the forms in the other books.
2) For two roots the only anaptyctic forms occur in the Psalms.
3) For two roots none of the anaptyctic forms occur in the Psalms.
4) For one root the other books exhibit anaptyxis more often than do the Psalms.
5) For two roots the Psalms exhibit anaptyxis more often than do the other books.

To our method in this analysis, one could object that it is unfair to oppose the forms in *one* book, the Psalms, to the forms in *a group* of books. One could argue that for the score to be 0 – 1 in a match between the arguments for and against the relevance of prosody in the poetic parts of the Bible in particular, if there are only non-anaptyctic forms of a certain root in the Psalms, there should be at least one anaptyctic form in *each* of the other books represented. On the other hand, we have given evidence that exceptional anaptyctic and non-anaptyctic forms occur in the prosaic books as well. Therefore, our assertion is that if prosodic factors trigger or block contact anaptyxis, they do so across the *whole* Hebrew Bible, not just in the poetic parts.

4.1.3.3.6 Summary

As for the פ״ח forms in the Hebrew Bible, our hypothesis is that *the higher the second radical is on the sonority scale, the greater the likelihood of an anaptyctic half vowel between* ḥ *and the second radical*. So far in this chapter we have thoroughly investigated all relevant verbal forms in the Hebrew Bible, as presented in Lisowsky (1993: 441-559), where *ḥ* is the first radical. We have arrived at the following conclusions:

1a) When the second radical is a voiceless sibilant, represented by *s* and *š*, or a voiceless emphatic consonant, represented by *ṭ* and *ṣ*, and the third radical is weak, represented by *ʾ* and *h*, the likelihood of contact anaptyxis between *ḥ* and the second radical increases significantly.

1b) The likelihood of contact anaptyxis is slightly greater when the weak radical is *h* than when it is *ʾ*.

1c) Two C_2-s – *b* and *l* – represented by three roots – *ḥbʾ*, *ḥbh*, and *ḥlh* – need further investigation in this respect. These are the only cases where the percentage value for final-weak forms alone is lower than the value for the regular forms. As for *b*, the percentage value for contact anaptyxis is 61% when the final-weak forms are excluded and 0% for the weak forms alone. As for *l*, the percentage value is 100% when the final-weak forms are excluded and 43% for *ḥlh* alone.

2) As the percentage values in the strictly quantitative presentation in item (55) above have been modified through the exclusion of final-weak roots, matters of prosody and discussions of the phonetic quality of the Tiberian Hebrew sibilants and emphatics, it is difficult to rank the C_2-s in terms of percent. Therefore, we confine ourselves to presenting linear hierarchies of the Tiberian Hebrew consonants in terms of how often they are involved in contact anaptyxis:

– the voiced and unvoiced plosives: *b* > *g* > *d, k, p, t*;
– the emphatics: *ṭ* > *ṣ* > *q*;
– the sibilants: *z* > *ś* > *ṣ* > *š* > *s*;
– the nasals: *n* > *m*;
– the laterals: *r* > *l*.

Against the background of our analysis we suggest the following overall hierarchy, as far as our investigation is concerned:

(62) Overall hierarchy (chances of *ḥăṭāp̄* epenthesis)[43]
w, y > *l, n* > *z, r* > *b* (*ḇ*) > *ṭ* > *ś* > *ṣ* > *g, š* > *s* > *d, k, m, p, q, t*

43 Thus, we do not entirely agree with DeCaen's "sonority hierarchy" for Tiberian Hebrew and Tiberian Aramaic (2003: 46), which he has arrived at through looking into verb forms *primae gutturalis* in general:
y, w, n, l, r, ś > *z, ṣ, ṭ* > *ḥ* > *b* > *s* > *m* > *š* > *ʿ* > *h, q* > *ʾ*.

A general sonority hierarchy can be presented as follows (cf., e.g., Vennemann 1988: 9):

(63) General sonority hierarchy
glides > central liquids > lateral liquids > nasals > voiced fricatives > voiceless fricatives > voiced plosives > voiceless plosives

Thus, we can see that our hypothesis is strengthened: the more sonorous the C_2, the greater the likelihood of contact anaptyxis between *ḥ* and this consonant.

3) In our analysis we also considered the suggestion that prosody or prosody related factors trigger or block contact anaptyxis in the poetic parts of the Bible in particular. We compared data from the book of Psalms and the rest of the Hebrew Bible and arrived at the following conclusion: if prosody and prosody related factors such as rhythm trigger or block contact anaptyxis, they do so most probably across the whole Bible, not only in the poetic parts. The possible influence of prosody on contact anaptyxis needs further investigation.

4.1.3.4 The Tiberian Hebrew nominal forms

4.1.3.4.1 Introductory remarks

The basis of our hypothesis on the Hebrew פ״ח forms, that there is a connection between the sonority of C_2 and the likelihood of contact anaptyxis between *ḥ* and this consonant, was discoveries we made after investigating Modern Hebrew verbal forms in Bolozky's (1996/2008) *501 Hebrew Verbs*, hence the "לַחְשׁוֹב *la-ḥšōḇ*, but לַחֲזוֹר *la-ḥăzōr*?" in the title of this monograph. Having looked deeper into such verbal forms our hypothesis seemed to be strengthened. The hypothesis also seemed plausible, against the background of DeCaen's 2003 article "Hebrew sonority and Tiberian contact anaptyxis: the case of verbs *primae gutturalis*". As DeCaen does in his article we first concentrated upon verbal forms. However, there was no reason the hypothesis should not be of relevance to nominal forms as well, and so we decided to investigate these forms, too.

4.1.3.4.2 Principles underlying the analysis

In order to test our hypothesis against nominal forms we looked into all relevant *m*- and *t*-prefixed nominal forms – no relevant *h*-prefixed forms are attested – of the פ״ח type as listed in Lisowsky (1993), Gesenius (1995), and Koehler and Baumgartner's (1994) Hebrew and Aramaic dictionaries of the Old Testament. Unless otherwise mentioned the sums and statistics are based on Lisowsky (1993). For rare instances of (proper) nouns with a *y*-prefix, most of which are lexicalised verb forms, cf. section 2.6 above.

In Lisowsky (1993), 37 *m*-prefixed and six *t*-prefixed nominal forms are listed. First, a couple remarks on the selection of the forms are in order, since some forms are excluded from our account: lexical entries where the voweling is arrived at through induction are not included in the analysis, even in cases where, according to our findings for the verbal forms, the voweling is most probably correct.

The first two excluded forms are instances where the nominal form does not occur in the form of the lexical entry or another relevant form: **maḥălap̄* and **maḥlap̄ōṯ*.[44] The former is only attested as מַחֲלָפִים *maḥălāp̄īm* (Ezra 1:9) and the latter only in the construct state, i.e. as מַחְלְפוֹת *maḥləp̄ōṯ* (Judg 16:13, 19). Considering our findings for the $C_2 = l$ verbal forms – contact anaptyxis obtains in more than 90% of the cases – the voweling of **maḥălap̄* is probably correct, whereas **maḥlāp̄ōṯ* is most likely incorrect. The expected form of the latter would be **maḥălap̄ōṯ*.

The next eliminated form is the lexical entry **maḥămāʾā* of which the only occurrence is the construct form מַחְמָאֹת פִּיו *maḥmāʾōṯ pī-w* (Ps 55:22). It is difficult to say whether or not **maḥămaʾā* would be the correct voweling. On the one hand, for the $C_2 = m$ verbal forms, contact anaptyxis obtains in only one case – נֶחֱמָדִים *neḥĕmāḏīm* – which should be ascribed to accentuation, cf. section 4.1.3.3.5 above on prosodic effects. On the other hand final-weak forms tend to exhibit anaptyxis more often than regular ones (cf. section 4.1.3.3.3 above on the special status of final-weak forms).

44 Henceforth, unattested forms will be marked with an asterisk.

The lexical entry **maḥămōḏ* is not considered either. This noun only occurs in מַחֲמֻדֶּיהָ *maḥămūḏē-hā* (Lam 1:7), which, according to Bergsträsser (1918–1929, vol. 2: 113), could not have been voweled otherwise: מַחֲמֻדֶּיהָ *maḥămūḏē-hā* exhibits contact anaptyxis due to a shift of accent forward, not the sonority of $C_2 = m$,[45] since, for $C_2 = m$, contact anaptyxis otherwise does not occur. The case of $C_2 = m$ and the verbal forms is the following: out of 43 forms contact anaptyxis obtains in only one: נֶחֱמָדִים *neḥĕmāḏīm* in Ps 19:11. This is the only occasion of $C_2 = m$ where, in De Caen's (2003: 42) terms, "an extra prosodic foot is added". Therefore, to vowel a noun **maḥămōḏ* is most probably a mistake. We do consider the entry מַחְמָד *maḥmāḏ* (e.g. Ez 24:21), however, since this noun occurs in exactly this form. Forms such as מַחֲמַדִּים *maḥămāḏīm* occur (e.g., Ct 5:16), but again, according to Bergsträsser, these forms could not have been voweled otherwise in the first place.

The form **meḥqār* is not accounted for either, since this form only occurs in the construct state – מֶחְקְרֵי־אָרֶץ *meḥqərē-ʾāreṣ* (Ps 95:4), a situation in which C_2 takes a *šwā mobile* and thus an epenthetic *ḥăṭāp* after *ḥ* cannot obtain anyway (Blau 1993: 39). The voweling of **meḥqār* is most probably correct, though, in the light of our findings for the $C_2 = q$ verbal forms.

As far as the *t*-prefixed forms are concerned, the lexical entries **taḥănūn* and **taḥănōṯ* need some comments. As there are no occurrences that fit into this pattern, i.e. have the accent on the third syllable, these two forms cannot be verified. In the attested forms the accent is on the last syllable (ultima), as in, e.g., תַּחֲנוּנִים *taḥănūnīm* (Jer 31:9) and תַּחֲנוֹתִי *taḥănōṯ-ī* (2 K 6:8). For both lexical entries, though, the voweling is most likely correct. We have decided to account for them, despite the non-occurrence, for two reasons. Most importantly, we have included the entries מַחֲלָצוֹת *maḥălāṣōṯ*, מַחֲרָאוֹת *maḥărāʾōṯ*, and תַּחֲלֻאִים *taḥălūʾīm*, which are of the same type. Correctly, these entries do occur in this form in the Bible, and so are justified. But since Bergsträsser's comments concern roots in which the second radical otherwise is not involved in contact anaptyxis, such as *m* and *q*, the *ḥăṭāp* vowels in תַּחֲנוּנִים *taḥănūnīm*

45 We already treated this phenomenon in the section on prosodic effects on verbal forms (4.1.3.3.5 above).

and תַּחֲנוֹתִי *taḥănōṯ-ī* should most likely be ascribed to the high sonority of *n*. On these grounds we have included **taḥănūn* and **taḥănōṯ* in the second table below, and thus in our analysis, even though the lexical entries should have been תַּחֲנוּנִים *taḥănūnīm* and תַּחֲנוֹתִי *taḥănōṯ-ī*, respectively.

This leaves us with 32 *m*-prefixed and six *t*-prefixed nominal forms to consider, all of which will be presented in two tables below. As our findings for the nominal forms to a great extent conform to our results for the verbal forms, we will only go into a few details as far as numbers are concerned.

4.1.3.4.3 Tables and findings

In the tables below we will present the lexical entries alphabetically according to C_2. For each lexical entry there are two cells. In the first cell there are two numbers, which represent the number of relevant occurrences and the number of these forms involved in contact anaptyxis, respectively. The gloss can be found in the second cell. The share of anaptyctic forms will not be given in percent, as the numbers in most cases are too low to be statistically significant.

(64) Tiberian Hebrew *m*-prefixed nominal forms[46]

Lexical entry	Relevant occurrences; contact anaptyxis	Gloss
מַחֲבֵא	1; 1	'hiding-place'
מַחֲבֹאִים	1; 1	'hiding-places'
מַחְבֶּרֶת	8; 0	'place of joining, juncture'
מַחֲבַת	5; 5	'baking-, frying-pan'
מַחֲגֹרֶת	1; 1	'girding'
מַחֲזֶה	4; 4	'vision'
מֶחֱזָה	4; 4	'window'
מִחְיָה	8; 0	'preservation of life, sustenance'

46 מֶחֱזָה occurs twice in two different sentences (1 K 7:4 and 7:5).

Lexical entry	Relevant occurrences; contact anaptyxis	Gloss
מַחֲלֶה	2; 2	‘sickness’
מַחֲלָה	4; 4	‘sickness’
מַחֲלֻיִים	1; 1	‘diseases’
מַחֲלָצוֹת	2; 2	‘robes’
מַחֲלֹקֶת	7; 7	‘share, division, group’
מַחֲלַת	2; 2	a musical term
מַחְמָד	0; 5	‘desire, loveliness, treasure’
מַחְמָל	0; 1	‘desire’?
מַחְמֶצֶת	0; 2	‘soured, leavened’
מַחֲנֶה	216; 216	‘camp, host, army’
מַחֲנָק	1; 1	‘suffocation’
מַחְסֶה / מַחֲסֶה	20; 5	‘refuge’
מַחְסוֹם	1; 0	‘muzzle’
מַחְסוֹר	13; 0	‘need’
מַחְצֵב	3; 0	‘wound’
מֶחֱצָה	2; 2	‘half’
מַחֲצִית	16; 16	‘half’
מַחֲרָאוֹת	1; 1	‘privies’
מַחֲרֵשָׁה	3; 3	‘ploughshare’
מַחְשֹׂף	1; 0	‘laying bare’
מַחֲשָׁבָה	21; 21	‘thought, device, invention’
מַחְשָׁךְ	3; 0	‘dark place’
מַחְתָּה	21; 0	‘fire-pan’
מַחְתֶּרֶת	2; 0	‘breaking in’

Let us comment on these results before moving on to the *t*-prefixed forms. The first observation concerns the forms with a final weak radical. The roots in question are *ḥbʾ*, *ḥzh*, *ḥyh*, (*ḥlʾ*,) *ḥlh*, *ḥnh*, *ḥsh*, *ḥṣh*, *ḥrʾ*, and *ḥth*. In addition, there is possibly an underlying weak radical in מַחֲבַת *maḥăḇaṯ* 'baking-, frying-pan' and certainly in מַחֲלַת *maḥălaṯ* (a liturgical/musical term).[47]

While some modern dictionaries (notably Even-Shoshan) point to a (fictituous) root *ḥbt*, there is no fitting root in other related Semitic languages. A suggestion proposed originally by Gesenius to connect מַחֲבַת *maḥăḇaṯ* with the root *ḫ-b-z*, as in Arabic *ḫubz* 'bread' ("s.th. baken") is generally rejected today. In Gəˁəz one finds both a root *ḫ-b-y* and a root *ḫ-b-b*, both revolving around "to be a vessel for food". *Faute de mieux*, it is legitimate to associate these roots with מַחֲבַת *maḥăḇaṯ* (a connection with Hebrew *ḥ-b-y* 'to hide' is less likely). In terms of morpho-phonology, this correspondence would constitute an analogous case to מַחֲלַת *maḥălaṯ* (a musical term), which the Hebrew dictionaries associate with Gəˁəz *ḫ-l-y* 'to sing' (cf. also Hebrew *ḥ-l-l*).

This means that at least 14 of the 32 *m*-prefixed nominal forms are of the type III-weak. If we are right concerning *maḥăḇaṯ* and *maḥălaṯ*, 50% of the relevant nominal forms have a final weak radical.

There is more to be said about the final-weak forms. As far as the roots *ḥbʾ*, *ḥzh*, (*ḥlʾ*,) *ḥlh*, *ḥnh*, *ḥṣh*, and *ḥrʾ* are concerned, all relevant manifestations exhibit anaptyxis. As for *ḥyh*, of which all relevant forms have the prefix vowel *i*, anaptyxis never obtains, which is the case for *ḥth* as well. As for *ḥsh*, an epenthetic *ḥăṭāp̄* vowel is present in one fourth of the cases. These findings conform perfectly to our results for the verbal forms of the same roots except three: *ḥbʾ*, *ḥlh*, and *ḥsh*. Whereas both (or all three, if מַחֲבַת *maḥăḇaṯ* is included) *ḥbʾ* nominal forms exhibit anaptyxis, none of the 14 verbal forms do. As for *ḥlh*, an epenthetic *ḥăṭāp̄* vowel is present in all three nominal forms, but in just three of the seven verbal forms. The numbers for both *ḥbʾ* and *ḥlh* are too low, however, to conclude as to whether or not an epenthetic *ḥăṭāp̄* vowel occurs more often in

47 Due to the high sonority of *l* contact anaptyxis would probably have obtained in a form with $C_2 = l$ anyway (independently of the quality of C_3), but a final weak radical would explain the *ḥăṭāp̄* vowel in מַחֲבַת *maḥăḇaṯ*. An unmarked form of *ḥbt* would be **maḥbaṯ*. On the other hand, the share of contact anaptyxis for the $C_2 = b$ verbal forms, when the final-weak forms are excluded, interestingly, is 61%.

the nominal forms of these roots than in the verbal ones. As for *ḥsh*, 73% (eight of 11) verbal forms exhibit anaptyxis, whereas just 25% of the nominal forms do.

The numbers for מַחְשָׁךְ *maḥšāḵ* deserve a comment, too. No relevant occurrences exhibit anaptyxis. One does find the forms מַחֲשַׁכִּים *maḥăšakkīm* (e.g., Ps 88:7) and מַחֲשַׁכֵּי־ *maḥăšakkē-* (Ps 74:20), but here contact anaptyxis *has to* obtain: both forms are due to accentuation (cf. again Bergsträsser 1918–1929, vol. 2: 113) and to the gemination of *k* (before a geminated consonant *šwā* cannot occur).

The last comment to the *m*-prefixed forms is a peculiar observation connected to the lexical entry מַחֲלֹקֶת *maḥălōqeṯ*. In 1 Chr 23:6 we find the form מַחְלְקוֹת *maḥləqōṯ*, which in this situation is a construct only in morphological terms. Syntactically, however, it is not.[48]

Now, let us move on to the *t*-prefixed forms.

(65) Tiberian Hebrew *t*-prefixed nominal forms

Lexical entry	Relevant occurrences; contact anaptyxis	Gloss
תַּחְבֻּלוֹת	6; 0	'devices'
תַּחֲלֻאִים	5; 5	'diseases'
תַּחְמָס	2; 0	a species of owl
תַּחֲנוּן	18; 18	'supplication'
תַּחֲנוֹת	1; 1	'place of encampment'?

Among the five *t*-prefixed forms three are of the type final-weak. The instances of *ḥlh* and *ḥnh* exhibit anaptyxis. The two former observations conform to the results for the corresponding verbal forms and the *m*-prefixed forms.

48 Cf. Gesenius 1910: 321 = § 130: "The construct state, which, according to § 89a, primarily represents only the immediate government by one substantive of the following word (or combination of words), is frequently [!] employed in rapid narrative as a connecting form, even apart from the genitive relation; ..."

4.1.3.4.4 The nominal ע״ח forms

The connection between sonority and the insertion of epenthetic *ḥăṭāp̄* vowels is to some extent evident in Biblical Hebrew ע״ח forms as well. The interesting forms are the nominal forms, since the verbal forms all exhibit contact anaptyxis irrespective of the quality of the third radical. The analysis below is based on all relevant ע״ח nominal forms in the Hebrew Bible, presented in Appendix 2.

Altogether there are 52 forms. As regards the roots, some comments are in order. First, אַחְלָמָה *ʾaḥlāmā* ‘amethyst’ probably derives from the Old Egyptian root *ḥnmt*, but synchronically the form is of the type ע״ח. Besides, it is unlikely that the noun belongs to the root *ḥlm* ‘to dream’ even if the form appears to be an Aramaic variant of the hifʿīl verbal noun *haC₁C₂āC₃ā*. It is difficult to operate with the concept “root” in אַחֲרַח *ʾaḥăraḥ* (n. pr.) and יַחְזֵרָה *yaḥzērā* (n. pr.), too, but in synchronic terms they belong to the ע״ח type. The form נַחֲמָנִי *naḥămānī* (n. pr.) derives from *nḥm*. As for תַּחְמָס *taḥmās* (name of a bird) it is unlikely that the root is *ḥms* ‘be violent’, and so arguably this form also is of the ע״ח type. The form תַּחְפַּנְחֵס *taḥpanḥes*, an Egyptian place name, is included in our account since the second radical is *ḥ* and the third radical takes a full vowel. Finally, the form תַּחְרָא *taḥrā(ʾ)* ‘armour plate’ most likely derives from the root *tḥr* and the final *ʾālep̄* is probably an Aramaic ending. (This holds for זַחֲלָא *zaḥălā(ʾ)* ‘creeping locust’, too.) Besides, it is implausible that the form תַּחְרָא *taḥrā(ʾ)* derives from the root *ḥrʾ*, as the meaning of *ḥrʾ* is connected to ‘sewer’. The roots and consonantal skeletons in question, then, are the following 39: *ʾḥz, ʾḥw, ʾḥl, ʾḥlm, ʾḥr, ʾḥrḥ, zḥl, ṭḥn, yḥd, yḥzr, yḥm, lḥy, lḥm, lḥṣ, mḥw, mḥzʾ* (the root here may also be *ḥzʾ*, i.e. of the פ״ח type), *mḥl, mḥr, nḥl, nḥm, nḥn* (byform of אֲנַחְנוּ *ʾanaḥnū*), *nḥr, nḥš, sḥr, pḥd, pḥz, ṣḥn, ṣḥ(ṣḥ), rḥb, rḥm, rḥṣ, šḥṭ, šḥṣ, šḥr, šḥt, tḥms, tḥpnḥs, tḥr*, and *tḥt*. For each occurring C_3 the table below shows the total number of forms and the number of forms where an epenthetic *ḥăṭāp̄* vowel is inserted.

(66) Nominal ע״ח forms with and without *ḥăṭāp̄* epenthesis

C_3	**Total number of forms**	**Number of forms with an epenthetic *ḥăṭāp̄* vowel**
ב	1	1
ד	2	0
ו	2	2
ז	4	2
ט	1	1
י	1	0
ל	10	5
מ	9	4
נ	3	2
פ	1	0
צ	4	2
ר	9	7
שׁ	1	0
ת	4	0

The table shows that 26, i.e. half of the 52 nominal forms of the ע״ח type in the Old Testament exhibit contact anaptyxis. In the cases where an epenthetic *ḥăṭāp̄* vowel obtains, the C_3 is *b, w, z, ṭ, l, m, n, ṣ*, and *r*. If we rank these consonants in terms of how often they are involved in contact anaptyxis – bearing in mind, though, the low number of examples – we arrive at the following hierarchy: *b, w, ṭ > r > n > z, l, ṣ > m*. As we can see, when an epenthetic *ḥăṭāp̄* vowel is inserted, the third radical is a glide such as *w*, a lateral such as *l* and *r*, a voiced sibilant such as *z*, or an emphatic consonant such as *ṭ* and *ṣ*. When C_3 is *d, y, š*, and *t*, contact anaptyxis does not obtain.[49] This conforms perfectly to our findings for the verbal and nominal forms of the type פ״ח, with two minor divergences:

49 As a glide, *y* is highly sonorous, but the root in question is *ḥyh*, which is an exceptional case in several respects (contact anaptyxis obtains only in hifʕīl).

when the consonant after *ḥ* is *l* or *m* the ע"ח forms are involved in contact anaptyxis less often and more often, respectively, than are the פ"ח forms. Despite the case of *l* and *m*, our hypothesis is corroborated by the ע"ח forms as well: the higher the sonority of the consonant following *ḥ*, the greater the likelihood of the insertion of an epenthetic *ḥăṭāp* vowel between *ḥ* and this following consonant.

4.1.3.4.5 Summary

Summing up, the findings for the Tiberian Hebrew nominal forms conform to a great extent to the ones for the respective verbal forms. As far as the III-weak forms are concerned, contact anaptyxis obtains when C_2 is *b, z, l, n,* and *ṣ*, but not *t* and *y*, to a limited extent when it is *s*, and when it is *r*. As to the strong roots, epenthetic *ḥăṭāp* vowels occur when C_2 is *l, n,* and *r*, but not in the case of *b, m, s, ś,* and *t*. *š* should be placed somewhere in between. Thus, our hypothesis is strengthened: the more sonorous the C_2, the greater the likelihood of contact anaptyxis.

Two more comments are in order. First, we have seen in this section that Bergsträsser's observation concerning the voweling of certain verbal forms also holds for the corresponding nominal forms. Second, we have seen that the share of final-weak forms of the total amount of relevant nominal forms is unduly large. But whether or not the latter is a coincidence, i.e. just the case for פ"ח forms, needs further investigation.

4.1.4 The (Tiberian) Aramaic forms

The few Tiberian Aramaic פ"ח forms (cf. item **(42)** above) confirm the observations made on the corresponding Tiberian Hebrew forms (cf. also DeCaen 2003: 45). Epenthesis in the finite hafᶜel forms of the verb *ḥwh*, e.g., יְהַחֲוֵה *yəhaḥăwē* 'he will announce' (Dan 5:12), is expected due to the high sonority of /w/ and the ל"ה factor. The same holds for the infinite pəᶜal form *meḥĕzē* 'to see' (Ezra 4:14). The only unexpected form found is הֶחֱסִנוּ *heḥĕsīnū* 'they took in possession' (Dan 7:22). The remaining finite form יַחְלְפוּן *yaḥləpūn* 'they will pass' (Dan 4:13 etc.), as well as the two participles מְהַחְצְפָה *məhaḥṣəpā* and מַחְצְפָה *maḥṣəpā* 'severe' (Dan 2:15 and 3:22) do not permit any conclusions in this context.

4.2 The Modern Hebrew forms

4.2.1 Introduction

This monograph grew out of observations we made as to the פ"ח verbal forms listed in Bolozky's (1996/2008) *501 Hebrew Verbs*. There seemed to be a certain connection between the presence of epenthetic *ḥăṭāp̄* vowels after *ḥ* and the sonority of C_2: the more sonorous the C_2, the greater the likelihood of contact anaptyxis.[50] In this part of the chapter we will first account for our first findings – the findings that made us extend our analysis to Modern Hebrew written nominal forms, verbal and nominal forms in Latin transcription on the internet, oral verbal and nominal forms, and Tiberian Hebrew forms. Thus, in this section we will

1) present our starting point in terms of a hierarchy;
2) account for our findings for the פ"ח verbal and nominal forms in modern dictionaries;
3) present these findings in tables;
4) discuss the relation between the modern tendencies and the results for Tiberian Hebrew;
5) account for discrepancies between voweling and transcription in certain modern dictionaries; and
6) present some observations made as to the Latin transcription of relevant verbal and nominal forms on the Internet.

We will give a summary of our analysis at the end of the section.

In this part of the chapter we will try to focus on the differences between what seems to be the modern tendencies and the results for Tiberian Hebrew. Since there are significant similarities, this account will not be as thorough as the one provided for in the previous section.

4.2.2 The modern dictionaries: statistical analysis

4.2.2.1 Introduction

This analysis is based on the data presented in the tables in Appendices 3–6. In these appendices are listed the פ"ח verbal and nominal forms

50 We continue to use this term, based on the "Masoretic" voweling in the modern reference works, even though the term is strictly speaking anachronistic in Modern Hebrew.

occurring in Bolozky 1996/2008, Lavi (Langenscheidt Achiasaf) 2004, Even-Shoshan 2003, and Bantam-Megiddo 1975.

4.2.2.2 The verbal forms

4.2.2.2.1 A preliminary account

As mentioned previously, the starting point of this monograph was a statistical analysis of the פ"ח roots in Bolozky's (1996/2008) *501 Hebrew Verbs* as to the connection between the second radical and epenthetic *ḥăṭāp̄* vowels. Before we present the hierarchy we arrived at, some remarks are in order. First, in all but one case (the case of *l*) the number of relevant roots is too low – often just one, two or three – to render a statistical account meaningful. Second, it has to be stressed that this hierarchy is strictly introductory, in the sense that it is based on a significantly less thorough analysis than our subsequent ones. Thus, the ranking as to the involvement of the C_2-s represented in Bolozky 1996/2008 in contact anaptyxis is as follows:

(67) Chances of *ḥăṭāp̄* epenthesis based on Bolozky 1996/2008

z, k, m, n, r > *l, b* > *y* > *s* > *g, d, q, š, ś, t*

As we can see, nasals, liquids, and the voiced sibilant *z* are involved in anaptyxis, whereas voiced and unvoiced plosives are not. In view of our findings for the Tiberian Hebrew forms, however, some consonants are ranked in a perhaps somewhat unexpected manner, and so some comments as to *k, m, b, y, s, š* and *ś* are in order.

First, as far as *k* is concerned, the occurring root is *ḥkh* and the form לַחֲכוֹת *la-ḥăḵōṯ* (*la-xakhot*) 'to hope, expect (lit.)'.[51] The final weak radical may be the trigger of contact anaptyxis here. When it comes to *m*, the only relevant form exhibits anaptyxis – נֶחֱמַם *neḥĕmām* (*nexemam*) 'to get hotter; become desirous'. As for *b*, three roots are represented: *ḥbb, ḥbq*, and *ḥbr*. For *ḥbb* we find לַחֲבוֹב *la-ḥăḇōḇ* (*la-xavov*) 'to like, be fond of,

51 Here and in the following, we render both the normative Masora-based vowelling in Bolozky 1996/2008 and a modern transcription of the forms in question. Only the crucial *ḥăṭāp̄* vowels (or their absence) are marked in the Hebrew script. Post-vocalic spirantisation of /g, d, t/ would be a gross anachronism, though.

love' but יַחְבּוֹב *yaḥbōḇ* (*yaxbov*); for *ḥbq* לַחֲבוֹק *la-ḥăḇōq* (*la-xavok*) 'to hug, embrace; encircle, surround' and יַחֲבוֹק *yaḥăḇōq* (*yaxavok*), and for *ḥbr* we have לַחֲבוֹר *la-ḥăḇōr* (*la-xavor*) 'to join together, unite' and יַחֲבוֹר *yaḥăḇōr* (*yaxavor*), but נֶחְבַּר *neḥbār* (*nexbar*) as well as לְהַחְבִּיר *lə-haḥbīr* (*le-haxbir*) and הֶחְבִּיר *heḥbīr* (*hexbir*). The case of $C_2 = y$ is hard to judge, as the only relevant root is *ḥyh* 'to live, be alive etc.', which is a special case in several respects. When *y* is C_2, it is involved in anaptyxis in hifᶜīl,[52] but not in paᶜal, just as in Tiberian Hebrew.

When it comes to the sibilants, the roots represented for *s* are *ḥsk* and *ḥsr*. For *ḥsk* we find לַחֲסוֹךְ *la-ḥăsōḵ* (*la-xasokh*) 'to save (money); withhold, spare, hold back', but יַחְסוֹךְ *yaḥsōḵ* (*yaxsokh*) and נֶחְסַךְ *neḥsāḵ* (*nexsakh*). Forms of *ḥsr* are לַחְסוֹר *la-ḥsōr* (*la-xsor*) 'to diminish; be absent/ missing; lack, be without' and יֶחְסַר *yeḥsār* (*yexsar*), נֶחְסַר *neḥsār* (*nexsar*), לְהַחְסִיר *lə-haḥsīr* (*le-haxsir*), מַחְסִיר *maḥsīr* (*maxsir*), and מוּחְסָר *muḥsār* (*muxsar*). As for *š* there are two roots represented: *ḥšb* and *ḥšd*. The former occurs as לַחְשׁוֹב *la-ḥšōḇ* (*la-xshov*) 'to think' and יַחְשׁוֹב *yaḥšōḇ* (*yaxshov*), נֶחְשַׁב *neḥšāḇ* (*nexshav*), לְהַחְשִׁיב *lə-haḥšīḇ* (*le-haxshiv*), and מַחְשִׁיב *maḥšīḇ* (*maxshiv*). The forms of *ḥšd* are לַחְשׁוֹד *la-ḥšōd* (*la-xsod*) 'to suspect' and יַחְשׁוֹד *yaḥšōd* (*yaxshod*), נֶחְשַׁד *neḥšād* (*nexshad*), לְהַחְשִׁיד *lə-haḥšīd* (*le-haxshid*), מַחְשִׁיד *maḥšīd* (*maxshid*), and מוּחְשָׁד *muḥšād* (*muxshad*). The only root in which $C_2 = ś$ is *ḥśp*: we find לַחְשׂוֹף *la-ḥśōp̄* (*la-xsof*) 'to expose, bare, uncover' and יַחְשׂוֹף *yaḥśōp̄* (*yaxsof*), נֶחְשַׂף *neḥśāp̄* (*nexsaf*), לְהַחְשִׂיף *lə-haḥśīp̄* (*le-haxsif*), and מַחְשִׂיף *maḥśīp̄* (*maxsif*).

Interestingly, if a *ḥăṭāp̄* vowel is inserted in some form of a root at all, it is always in the infinitive and in some cases the future of paᶜal, the only exception being the hifᶜīl form of *ḥmm*. Thus, it seems that the paᶜal infinitive to a great extent is a lexicalised form.

It should be mentioned that some of these forms in Bolozky 1996/ 2008 are listed as "infrequent verbs sharing the same root". According to our informant Rikki Bliboim (personal communication), some forms would not even be accepted by native speakers of Modern Hebrew.

52 Bolozky (2008: 189) gives hufᶜal forms without *ḥăṭāp̄* vowels, i.e. הוּחְיָה *huḥyā* (*huxya*) 'he was revived', יוּחְיֶה *yuḥyē* (*yuxye*) 'he will be revived', and מוּחְיֶה *muḥyē* (*muxye*) 'being revived' (m.sg.).

4.2.2.2.2 Principles underlying the analysis

The observations presented above made us want to investigate the phenomenon thoroughly. Thus, we extrapolated 374 פ״ח verbal forms spread across 94 different roots from Bolozky 1996/2008, Lavi 2004, Even-Shoshan 2003, and Bantam-Megiddo 1975. The only dictionary in which all 374 forms are listed is Even-Shoshan 2003, where a *ḥăṭāp̄* vowel is inserted only in alternative forms of the root *ḥwh*. The share of *ḥăṭāp̄* forms of the total number of forms is 70% in Bantam-Megiddo 1975, 57% in Lavi 2004, and 54% in Bolozky 1996/2008. It should be borne in mind here that several roots – not always the same ones – are not represented in all dictionaries, and the number of dictionaries is low. Based on Lisowsky for Tiberian Hebrew and Lavi and Bolozky for Modern Hebrew, though, the share of forms that exhibit contact anaptyxis has decreased by 15 percentage points – from 70 to 55%. Considering the findings for Even-Shoshan as well, it seems that the insertion of epenthetic *ḥăṭāp̄* vowels in פ״ח forms is on its way out (even) in written Hebrew (when voweled at all).

Possibly, the voweling in Bantam-Megiddo is based directly on the voweling in dictionaries of Biblical (Tiberian) Hebrew.

In the first table below we have compared percentage values for all relevant פ״ח forms listed in Lisowsky 1993 for Tiberian Hebrew and the four dictionaries mentioned above for Modern Hebrew, as to how often a given C_2 is involved in contact anaptyxis. When considering the table, though, it should be borne in mind that whereas the special status of the third-weak forms is accounted for in the Tiberian Hebrew data, it is not in the data for Modern Hebrew. This means that in the sums for Tiberian Hebrew the results for final-weak forms are excluded, whereas such forms are included in the sums for Modern Hebrew. Thus, the differences in voweling of פ״ח forms between Tiberian Hebrew and Modern Hebrew is probably somewhat greater than expressed in item **(68)** below.

The values for Tiberian and Modern Hebrew in item **(68)** are based on the presentation in item **(41)** and Appendices 3–6 and are arrived at in the following way: non-attested and unmarked forms are not included in the sums. In the "– (+)" cases, i.e. when a *ḥăṭāp̄* form is only *also accepted*, the form is ascribed a share of 25%. For each C_2 and each dictionary we have summed up the total number of verbal forms and the number of forms that exhibit anaptyxis and arrived at a value in percent. Then, we have summed up the average of the values for each dictionary. For each C_2 this final percentage value is presented in the second column in the first table below.

As far as the values for Tiberian Hebrew are concerned, a few comments are in order, since some consonants are hard to ascribe an exact value in percent. The consonants in question are *m*, *s*, *ṣ*, *q*, and *š*.

As to *m* and *q*, the epenthetic *ḥăṭāp̄* vowels in the one and only form for each C_2 are due to the addition of a syllabic foot, i.e. a shift of accent forward, cf. Bergsträsser 1918–1929, vol. 2: 113, and so the correct value should be 0% in both cases. The case of the sibilants is challenging because this is where the results for final-weak forms make the most impact on the statistics. Against the background of the discussions in section 4.1.3.3.4 above, though, we have attributed *s*, *ṣ*, and *š* a sum of 5, 25, and 15%, respectively. Finally, it is worth mentioning that for $C_2 = w$ only one instance is attested.

As far as both Tiberian and Modern Hebrew are concerned, it is also noteworthy why *y* is not placed in the table. The reason is that the only root listed for both Tiberian and Modern Hebrew is *ḥyh*, which is consistently voweled *with* epenthetic *ḥăṭāp̄* vowels in hifᶜīl, and *without* epenthetic *ḥăṭāp̄* vowels in paᶜal.

4.2.2.2.3 Tables and findings

Now, let us consider the table, in which contact anaptyxis in Tiberian Hebrew is statistically compared with anaptyxis in Modern Hebrew:[53]

(68) Contact anaptyxis (ḥ(v)C_2) in written Hebrew:
Tiberian Hebrew vs. modern dictionaries

%	**C_2 in Tiberian Hebrew**	**C_2 in Modern Hebrew**
96-100%	ז, ו, ל, נ, ר	
71-75%		ו, ז

53 As in item **(52)** above, irrelevant 5% intervals are omitted in the chart.

%	C_2 in Tiberian Hebrew	C_2 in Modern Hebrew
61-65%	ב	ר
56-60%		ל, נ
46-50%	ט	
36-40%		ב, ט
21-25%	צ	מ
16-20%	שׂ	צ, שׂ
11-15%	שׁ	ס
6-10%	ג	
1-5%	ס	כ
0%	כ, מ, פ, ק, ת	ג, ד, פ, ק, שׁ, ת

A first observation is that the ranking of the consonants is approximately the same: contact anaptyxis obtains the most when the voiced fricative *z* and *w*, the laterals *r* and *l*, and the nasal *n* are involved, and never when the voiced (now) plosive *g* and *d*, and the unvoiced (now) plosive *q* and *t* are involved. In both hierarchies *b* and *ṭ* are placed in the middle. The essential difference between the results for Tiberian Hebrew and the ones for Modern Hebrew concerns the frequency of contact anaptyxis: as for *z* and *w*, there is a decrease of 25 percentage points, for *r* 35, and for *l* and *n* 40. For *b* and *t* the decrease is 25 and 15, respectively; for *ṣ* it is 10, and for *ś* and *g* it is 20 and 10, respectively. The higher a C_2 is in the hierarchy for Tiberian Hebrew, the steeper the fall in the hierarchy for Modern Hebrew. The horizontal ranking of the consonants is approximately one and the same in Tiberian and Modern Hebrew. But in a vertical ranking the sums in percentage fall proportionately from Tiberian to Modern Hebrew.

In the table above there are some peculiarities, however, that deserve some comments. They concern *k*, *m*, *s*, and *š*, the only cases in which we can observe a rise in percentage points from Tiberian to Modern Hebrew. The rise in percentage points is approximately 2.5, 25, 5, and 5, respectively. As for *k*, there are three roots in question: *ḥkk*, *ḥkm*, and *ḥkr*. None of these roots are listed in Bolozky, and so there are three dictionaries to consider. The total number of occurrences, i.e. forms multiplied with dictionaries, is 42, only one of which – לַחֲכוֹךְ *la-ḥăḵōḵ* (*la-xakhokh*) 'to scratch' in Lavi – exhibits contact anaptyxis. In the same dictionary, however, we find the form יַחְכוֹךְ *yaḥkōḵ* (*yaxkokh*).

As far as *m* is concerned, there are seven roots to consider: *ḥmʾ*, *ḥmd*, *ḥmm*, *ḥms*, *ḥmṣ*, *ḥmq*, and *ḥmr*. The only root for which the relevant dictionaries agree is *ḥmr*. (The relevant dictionaries in this case are Lavi and Even-Shoshan, since in Bolozky the root is not listed, and in Bantam-Megiddo the forms are unmarked.) For *ḥmʾ* there is consistency in both relevant dictionaries: Even-Shoshan does not insert epenthetic *ḥăṭāp̄* vowels, whereas Lavi does. As for *ḥmd* there are eight occurrences, only one of which exhibits contact anaptyxis: we find נֶחֱמָד *neḥĕmād* (*nexemad*) in Lavi. In the same dictionary, however, an epenthetic vowel is not inserted in the participle. When it comes to *ḥmm* we find נֶחֱמַם *neḥĕmām* (*nexemam*) in Bolozky, but נֶחְמַם *neḥmām* (*nexmam*) in Even-Shoshan. As for *ḥms* the two forms are listed *with* an epenthetic *ḥăṭāp̄* vowel in Bantam-Megiddo, but *without* in Lavi and Even-Shoshan. The next root is *ḥmṣ*, for which all three anaptyctic forms occur in Lavi. All three are hifʿīl forms, and, surprisingly perhaps, the infinitive is not amongst them. Finally, for *ḥmq* one of four occurrences exhibits anaptyxis: we find לַחֲמוֹק *la-ḥămōq* (*la-xamok*) (but יֶחְמַק *yeḥmāq* (*yexmak*)) in Lavi. As for $C_2 = m$, then, the share of occurrences with anaptyxis of the total number of occurrences is 23%. It is peculiar that epenthetic *ḥăṭāp̄* vowels are inserted between *ḥ* and *m* more often in modern dictionaries than in Tiberian Hebrew. We do not have any explanation for this phenomenon.

The next C_2 to consider is *s*. There are six roots in question: *ḥsh*, *ḥsk*, *ḥsl*, *ḥsm*, *ḥsn*, and *ḥsr*. For the three last roots none of the relevant dictionaries insert an epenthetic *ḥăṭāp̄* vowel. For the three first, there is disagreement, and so first we find לַחֲסוֹת *la-ḥăsōt* (*la-xasot*) and יֶחֱסֶה *yeḥĕsē* (*yexese*) in Lavi, but לַחְסוֹת *la-ḥsōt* and יֶחְסֶה *yeḥsē* (*yexse*) in Even-Shoshan. For *ḥsk* the only anaptyctic form, לַחֲסוֹךְ *la-ḥăsōḵ* (*la-xasokh*) is found in Bolozky, where we also, however, find יַחְסוֹךְ *yaḥsōḵ* (*yaxsokh*). When it comes to *ḥsl*, there are two anaptyctic forms, which both occur in Bolozky: לַחֲסוֹל *la-ḥăsōl* (*la-xasol*) and יַחֲסוֹל *yaḥăsōl* (*yaxasol*). Thus, for $C_2 = s$ in the modern dictionaries contact anaptyxis obtains five times, of which two occurrences are of the final-weak root *ḥsh*. But whereas $C_2 = s$ is *not* involved in contact anaptyxis when the final-weak *ḥsh* is excluded in Tiberian Hebrew, it is involved in contact anaptyyxis three times in Bolozky's (1996/2008) survey of Modern Hebrew verbs.

The last C_2 that deserves some remarks is *š*, for which there are seven roots to consider: *ḥšb*, *ḥšd*, *ḥšh*, *ḥšk*, *ḥšl*, *ḥšq*, and *ḥšš*. As for *ḥšb*, *ḥšk*, and *ḥšq*, all relevant dictionaries agree: no anaptyctic forms. As for *ḥšd*, all four hifʿīl forms exhibit anaptyxis in Bolozky, but not in Lavi and Even-Shoshan. For *ḥšl* epenthesis obtains in Lavi, but not in Even-Shoshan. There are two forms of *ḥšš*, both of which are listed in all four dictionaries. The forms exhibit anaptyxis only in Bantam-Megiddo. So far we have seven occurrences of epenthesis, spread across three roots. The last 12 occurrences of epenthesis belong to the final-weak root *ḥšh*: anaptyxis obtains in all six forms in Lavi and Bantam-Megiddo, but not in Even-Shoshan. If we ignore the occurrences of *ḥšh*, the share of anaptyctic occurrences of the total number of occurrences is approximately 10%, which is lower than the 13% for Tiberian Hebrew, and thus more in accordance with the overall finding: that the C_2-s are involved in contact anaptyxis to a lesser extent in Modern than in Tiberian Hebrew.

We have already touched upon the final-weak forms in our modern dictionaries, but some more paragraphs are in order. There are 15 final-weak roots in our corpus: *ḥbʾ*, *ḥwh*, *ḥzh*, *ḥṭʾ*, *ḥyh*, *ḥlh*, *ḥmʾ*, *ḥnh*, *ḥsh*, *ḥph*, *ḥṣh*, *ḥrʾ*, *ḥrh*, *ḥšh*, and *ḥth*. First, none of the dictionaries suggest epenthesis for *ḥbʾ*, as well as the paʿal of *ḥyh*, *ḥph*, and *ḥth*, which conforms to our findings for Tiberian Hebrew. For *ḥzh*, *ḥṭʾ*, *ḥlh*, *ḥmʾ*, *ḥsh*, *ḥṣh*, *ḥrʾ*, *ḥrh*, and *ḥšh* Even-Shoshan never suggests epenthesis, whereas the other dictionaries agree: an epenthetic vowel occurs in all forms. *ḥwh* is the only root in which Even-Shoshan ever accepts anaptyctic forms, and even then only in parenthesis. Thus, we find לחוות *la-ḥăwōt* (*la-xavot*), להחוות *lə-haḥăwōt* (*le-haxavot*), and החווה *heḥĕwē* (*hexeve*). In the other represented dictionaries an epenthetic *ḥăṭāp* vowel is inserted in all forms. For *ḥnh* we find only non-anaptyctic forms in Bolozky and Even-Shoshan, but only anaptyctic ones in Lavi and Bantam-Megiddo. As for the hifʿīl forms of *ḥyh*, epenthetic *ḥăṭāp* vowels are inserted in all forms in all dictionaries except Even-Shoshan. We see, then, that as far as the final-weak forms are concerned, the findings for Bolozky, Lavi, and Bantam-Megiddo conform to the results for Tiberian Hebrew. In percent the share of anaptyctic forms of the total number of final-weak forms is approximately 75% for Bolozky, 85% for Lavi, and 80% for Bantam-Megiddo. The corresponding sums when all forms are considered together are about 55, 55, and 70%, respectively. Admittedly, certain forms may have a disproportionate impact on the sums, but we should be able to conclude that final-weak forms exhibit contact anaptyxis more often than strong forms do.

4.2.2.2.4 Summary

In this section we have investigated פ"ח verbal forms in four different dictionaries of Modern Hebrew – Bantam-Megiddo 1975, Even-Shoshan 2003, Lavi 2004, and Bolozky 1996/2008. In Even-Shoshan all forms were listed, but an epenthetic *ḥăṭāp̄* vowel was only suggested in parenthesis for three forms of the root *ḥwh*.

The first overall finding is that the hierarchy of C_2-s as to how often they are involved in contact anaptyxis to a great extent conforms to our results for Tiberian Hebrew. But – and this is the second main finding – in Modern Hebrew the share of anaptyctic forms for all relevant C_2-s, i.e. cases where the share for Tiberian Hebrew is more than 0%, is significantly lower than in Tiberian Hebrew. There is one striking exception to this second finding: in the case of $C_2 = m$ contact anaptyxis does not obtain in Tiberian Hebrew (the only exception is due to prosody), whereas in the dictionaries of Modern Hebrew *m* is involved in contact anaptyxis in almost 25% of its occurrences. This issue needs further investigation.

4.2.2.3 The nominal forms

4.2.2.3.1 Principles underlying the analysis

In this section we will present an analysis of all *h*-, *m*-, and *t*-prefixed nominal forms of the type פ"ח listed in Bantam-Megiddo 1975, Lavi (Langenscheidt Achiasaf) 2004, and Even-Shoshan 2003.[54] All forms are pre-

54 Only verbal forms are listed in Bolozky 1996/2008.

sented in Appendices 4–6. Before we present our results some remarks are in order. First, before we analysed the forms we asked one of our informants to read the forms aloud so that we could exclude the forms that are not accepted.[55]

This left us with 29 *h*-prefixed, 82 *m*-prefixed, and 24 *t*-prefixed forms to consider. For each prefix we will point out whether or not there are cases in which the dictionaries agree as to the insertion of an epenthetic *ḥăṭāp̄* vowel. In doing this we will, unless otherwise mentioned, cite the symbol "– (+)" in support of contact anaptyxis, i.e. the cases included are "+ + +" and "+ + – (+)".

An interesting overall observation is that Even-Shoshan accepts epenthetic *ḥăṭāp̄* vowels in more than half of the nominal forms (70 out of 135), as against only three of the 374 verbal forms.

4.2.2.3.2 Analysis and findings

As far as the 29 *h*-prefixed forms are concerned the dictionaries agree in inserting an epenthetic *ḥăṭāp̄* vowel in just one instance – החיאה *haḥăyāʾā* (*haxaya'a*) 'revitalisation', belonging to the root *ḥyh*. In Bantam-Megiddo this is one of only two forms listed. The second root is *ḥdr*, in which contact anaptyxis does not obtain. In Lavi all forms are listed, and anaptyxis

55 The non-accepted *h*-prefixed forms are הֶחבֵר 'association', הַחזָיָה 'making visible' and הַחנָיָה 'parking'. The non-accepted *m*-prefixed forms are מַחבֵא 'hiding place', מַחבֵטָה 'threshing-machine', מַחבֵצָה 'butter-machine', מַחבָר 'joint (carpentry)', מַחבֵר 'joint (machinery), מַחגֵר 'inhibition', מַחדֵד 'pencil sharpener', מֶחזָה 'look', מַחזירור 'reflector', מַחזֵק 'handle', מַחזֵר 'back-switch', מַחזורֶת 'period', מַחטֵטָה 'slotting-machine', מַחטופֶת 'razzia', מַחלוב 'milking level', מַחלָפָה 'plait (of hair)', מַחלָצָה 'festive costume', מַחלֵק 'smoothing machine', מַחמֵאָה 'butter box', מַחמָץ 'mixed pickles (sour)', מַחמֶצֶת 'sour dough', מַחמָק 'refuge', מַחמושֶת 'note system (5 lines)', מַחפָה 'protected position', מַחפֶה 'protective shoe', מַחפֵר 'dredging-machine', מַחצֵב 'hewing of stones', מֶחרָב '*miḥrāb* (in a mosque)', מֶחרָד 'reflex', מַחרוץ 'cheese knife', מַחרוסֶת 'dessert cup', מֶחרָץ 'cut', מַחרֵצָה 'bung plane ("Hobel")', מַחרָקָה 'insectarium', מַחשבי 'thought-related', מַחשבָן 'computer specialist', מַחשָך 'darkness', מַחשֵף 'trigger', מַחתָה 'coal shovel', מֶחתָך 'horizontal cut', מַחתֵך 'cutting machine' and מַחתֵכָה 'bread-cutter'. There are four non-accepted *t*-prefixed forms: תַחבלָן 'tactician', תַחזורֶת 'reconstructed model', תַחנאי 'station attendant' and תַחצָה 'cross-walk'. The list illustrates our principle, to test forms with our informants, without indicating the pointing (*šwā* or *ḥăṭāp̄*) of /ḥ/.

is exhibited only in the form of *ḥyh* mentioned above. All forms are listed in Even-Shoshan as well, but in this dictionary 23 of them are marked with "– (+)". The roots in these cases are the following: *ḥyh* (as mentioned), *ḥwr, ḥzq, ḥzr, ḥṭʾ, ḥlṭ, ḥlm, ḥlp, ḥlq, ḥmṣ, ḥmr, ḥnp, ḥnq, ḥsn, ḥsr, ḥṣn, ḥrb, ḥrm, ḥrp, ḥrš, ḥšb,* and *ḥšd*. The findings for C_2 = *l* (four cases), *n* (two cases), *z* (two cases), *r* (four cases), and *w* (one case) are in line with our hypothesis, as all these radicals have little consonantal strength (high sonority). The result for *ḥṭʾ* is probably due to the final weak radical. The epenthetic vowels in the instances of C_2 = *m, s, š,* and *ṣ* conform to our hypothesis to a lesser extent.

Against the background of our findings for the verbal forms it is surprising that an epenthetic *ḥăṭāp̄* vowel is inserted only once in Lavi and in 23 cases in Even-Shoshan. One should have expected the opposite result. Considering only the findings in Even-Shoshan, then, one could argue that nominal forms are more likely to exhibit contact anaptyxis than verbal forms are. But this observation, which was certainly supported by the Tiberian Hebrew data, needs, of course, further investigation.

Our informant did not pronounce any of the *h*-prefixed nominal forms with an epenthetic vowel.

The dictionaries agree in *not* inserting an epenthetic *ḥăṭāp̄* vowel in six forms, which belong to the roots *ḥbʾ, ḥdr, ḥzr, ḥkr, ḥlṭ,* and *ḥtm*. The findings for *ḥbʾ, ḥdr, ḥkr,* and *ḥtm* conform to our results for Biblical Hebrew, Modern Hebrew verbal forms, and our hypothesis: the lesser the sonority of C_2, the lower the likelihood of contact anaptyxis.

As far as the *m*-prefixed forms are concerned, there are 33 cases in which all the dictionaries agree when it comes to the insertion of an anaptyctic *ḥăṭāp̄* vowel. The forms belong to the following roots: *ḥbʾ, ḥwh, ḥzh, ḥzr, ḥzmr, ḥlh, ḥlʾ, ḥlm, ḥlp, ḥlq, ḥmʾ, ḥnh, ḥnq, ḥṣh, ḥrʾ, ḥrb, ḥrz, ḥrṭ, ḥrd, ḥrš, ḥrm,* and *ḥšb*. As we can see, the second radical is *r* in seven cases, *l* in five, *z* in three, *n* in two and *w* in one case. This conforms perfectly to our hypothesis. In three cases – when C_2 is *b, m,* and *ṣ* – the epenthetic vowel should be ascribed to the final weak radical.

Our informant pronounced 13 *m*-prefixed forms with an epenthetic *ḥăṭāp̄* vowel: מחזאי *maḥăzāʾī* (*maxaza'i*) 'playwright', מחזה *maḥăzē* (*maxaze*) 'play, drama', מחזמר *maḥăzémer* (*maxazémer*) 'musical', מחלה *maḥălā* (*maxala*) 'disease', מחנה *maḥănē* (*maxane*) 'camp', מחניק *maḥănīq* (*maxanik*) 'suffocating' (in this case an anaptyctic vowel is not inserted in Even-Shoshan), מחסה *maḥăsē* (*maxase*) 'shelter' (in this case an anaptyctic vowel is not inserted in Lavi), מחצית *maḥăṣīt* (*maxatsit*) 'half', מוחרב *moḥŏrāḇ* (*moxorav*) 'destructed', מחרוזת *maḥărōzet* (*maxarózet*) 'row; neck-chain', מחריב *maḥărīḇ* (*maxariv*) 'destructive', מחריד *maḥărīd* (*maxarid*) 'causing fear', and מחריש *maḥărīš* (*maxarish*) 'deafening'. These results, too, conform to our hypothesis, since the second radical is *r* in five cases, *z* in three, *n* in two and *l* in one case. The cases of epenthesis when $C_2 = s$ and *ṣ* (*maḥăsē* (*maxase*) and *maḥăṣīt* (*maxatsit*)) should be ascribed to the final weak radical.

Continuing the account of the *m*-prefixed forms we observe that the dictionaries agree in *not* inserting an epenthetic *ḥăṭāp* vowel when it comes to the following roots: *ḥbṭ, ḥbr, ḥdl, ḥzr, ḥzq, ḥyh, ḥkm, ḥkr, ḥlb, ḥld, ḥlṭ, ḥlp, ḥlṣ, ḥlq, ḥlš, ḥmd, ḥmʾ, ḥmr, ḥml, ḥmṣ, ḥsm, ḥsn, ḥpr, ḥṣb, ḥṣl, ḥṣn, ḥṣṣ, ḥqr, ḥśp, ḥšk, ḥšš*, and *ḥtr*. The findings for $C_2 = b, d, k, m, s, p,$ *ṣ*, *q*, *š*, *ś*, and *t*, i.e. for approximately two thirds of the roots, conform to our hypothesis, as they have great consonantal strength. Considering our findings for Biblical Hebrew and for Modern Hebrew so far, however, a somewhat surprising observation is the existence of many non-anaptyctic forms in which the second radical is *l*. On the other hand, two of those roots build forms that do exhibit contact anaptyxis as well. Thus, of 11 $C_2 = l$ roots in the dictionaries we find anaptyctic and non-anaptyctic forms of two of them, only anaptyctic forms of four and only non-anaptyctic forms in five, which still leaves us with a large share of anaptyctic forms for *l*.

As for the *t*-prefixed forms, there are 11 instances where the dictionaries agree in inserting an epenthetic *ḥăṭāp* vowel. The following roots are in question: *ḥzq, ḥzh, ḥlʾ, ḥlp, ḥlb, ḥnh, ḥnn, ḥrh,* and *ḥšb*. The second radicals except *š* are highly sonorous, which supports our hypothesis. Our informant inserts an epenthetic *ḥăṭāp* vowel in three cases: תחזית *taḥăzīt* (*taxazit*) 'forecast', תחנה *taḥănā* (*taxana*) 'station', and תחרות *taḥărūt* 'competition'. The second radical is highly sonorous in all cases. Moreover, all the roots are of the type ל"ה.

The dictionaries agree in *not* inserting an epenthetic vowel in the rest of the cases (13), in which the roots are *ḥbl, ḥbr, ḥbb, ḥbš, ḥdš, ḥmḥ, ḥmš, ḥpš, ḥqr, ḥrt,* and *ḥrm*. The second radical is consonantally strong in all cases except the instances of *r*.

Finally, some remarks concerning the forms *tertiae infirmae* are in order. There are 25 forms to consider, of which three are *h*-prefixed and belong to the roots *ḥbʾ, ḥṭʾ,* and *ḥyh*. There are 17 final-weak *m*-prefixed forms belonging to the roots *ḥbʾ, ḥwh, ḥzh, ḥyh, ḥlh, ḥlʾ, ḥmʾ, ḥnh, ḥsh, ḥṣh,* and *ḥʾ*. As for the *t*-prefixed forms there are five cases and four roots: *ḥzh, ḥlh, ḥnh,* and *ḥrʾ*. *Considering only the occurrences of "+ + +"*, the dictionaries agree in inserting an epenthetic *ḥăṭāp̄* vowel in 10 of the 25 cases. If we *include the cases of "+ + – (+)"*, the number is 20. The number of forms for which an epenthetic *ḥăṭāp̄* vowel is *suggested in one or more dictionaries* (i.e. here one occurrence of "–(+)" is sufficient) is 22, which renders a share of approximately 90%. The corresponding share for strong roots is approximately 50%. This is in accordance with our findings for Biblical Hebrew verbal and nominal forms and for verbal forms in dictionaries of Modern Hebrew: final-weak roots are involved in contact anaptyxis to a greater extent than strong roots are.

As for the final-weak forms in which the dictionaries agree in *not* inserting an epenthetic *ḥăṭāp̄* vowel, the roots are *ḥbʾ, ḥyh,* and *ḥmʾ*, and the forms החבאה *haḥbāʾā* (*haxba'a*) 'hiding', מחיה *miḥyā* (*mixya*) 'subsistence' and מחמיא *maḥmī(ʾ)* (*maxmi*) 'flattering', respectively. But these roots are represented amongst the forms that are involved in contact anaptyxis as well. We find מחבוא *maḥăḇō(ʾ)* (*maxavo*) 'hiding' – and מחבא *maḥăḇē(ʾ)* (*maxave*) 'hiding place', but this noun was not accepted by our informant – of *ḥbʾ*, and of *ḥyh* we find החיאה *haḥăyāʾā* (*haxaya'a*) 'revitalisation'. Of *ḥmʾ* we have מחמאה *maḥămāʾā* (*maxama'a*) 'compliment'. The epenthetic *ḥăṭāp̄* vowels in החיאה *haḥăyāʾā* (*haxaya'a*) and מחמאה *maḥămāʾā* (*maxama'a*) possibly have a prosodic explanation. As compared to מחיה *miḥyā* (*mixya*) and מחמיא *maḥmī(ʾ)* (*maxmi*), the forms החיאה *haḥăyāʾā* (*haxaya'a*) and מחמאה *maḥămāʾā* (*maxama'a*) have an additional syllabic foot, in terms of Bergsträsser (1918–1929, vol. 2: 113) and DeCaen (2003: 42), and so there is a parallel to the phenomenon that in Biblical (Tiberian) Hebrew we have נֶחְמָד *neḥmāḏ* (Gen 2:9), but נֶחֱמָדִים

neḥĕmāḏīm (Ps 19:11). On the other hand, this does not explain why we have מחבוא *maḥăḇō(ʾ)* (*maxavo*) (and מחבא *maḥăḇē(ʾ)* (*maxave*)), unless one takes recourse to the III-weak factor again.

4.2.2.3.3 Summary

Let us sum up our findings for פ"ח *h-*, *m-*, and *t*-prefixed nominal forms in dictionaries of Modern Hebrew in a unified table. The second radical is presented in the first column. In the second column the number of forms in which the consonant in the left cell is the second radical can be found. The sum in the third column is the number of forms for each C_2 where an epenthetic *ḥăṭāp̄* vowel is suggested in one or more of our dictionaries. "Suggested" means that one instance of the symbol "– (+)", which occurs only in Even-Shoshan, is included, i.e. "– – –(+)" is sufficient.

(69) Modern *h-*, *m-*, and *t*-prefixed nominal forms in a unified table

C_2	Number of forms	Number of forms where an epenthetic *ḥăṭāp̄* is suggested in one or more dictionaries
ב	11	3
ד	3	0
ו	4	4
ז	12	10
ט	1	1
י	2	1
כ	4	0
ל	27	14
מ	11	3
נ	8	8
ס	6	4
פ	3	0
צ	8	4
ק	2	0

C_2	**Number of forms**	**Number of forms where an epenthetic *ḥăṭāp̄* is suggested in one or more dictionaries**
ר	17	15
שׁ	12	6
שׂ	1	0
ת	2	0

There are few examples, but we can see that epenthetic *ḥăṭāp̄* vowels are inserted exceptionally often when the second radical is *z*, *n*, and *r*, and to a certain extent *l*, considering the high number of occurrences. These consonants are, together with *y* and *w*, generally the most sonorous of the Hebrew consonants. Thus, our hypothesis is supported again.

4.2.2.3.4 The nominal ע"ח forms

In order to investigate the extent to which contact anaptyxis obtains after *ḥ* in nominal forms of the type ע"ח, we extrapolated 215 relevant forms from three dictionaries of Modern Hebrew – Bantam Megiddo (1975), Milon Even-Shoshan (2003) and Langenscheidt Achiasaf (2004). All forms are listed together with the ע"ח verbal forms in Appendix 7. Not all 215 forms are listed in all three dictionaries. Therefore, we will treat the dictionaries separately.[56]

As for Bantam Megiddo, only 40 forms are considered, since 130 forms are not attested and in 45 forms the vowels are not marked. Of the 40 forms listed, an epenthetic vowel is inserted in all but one, in which the third radical is the non-spirantised allophone of *p*. As for the instances where contact anaptyxis obtains, the consonants represented as the third radical are *w*, *r*, *l*, *z*, *n*, *m*, *s*, the spirantised allophone of *p*, *ṣ*, and *q*. The six first of these 10 consonants are highly sonorous in general phonological terms.

In Milon Even-Shoshan, all but one form are attested. In about 50 forms, or between 20 and 25% of the cases, an epenthetic *ḥăṭāp̄* vowel is inserted. The third radical in these cases are *r*, *l*, *z*, *n*, *m*, the spirantised

56 We have not considered the ע"ח verbal forms, since *ḥ* in such forms always takes an epenthetic vowel, irrespective of the quality of the following radical.

allophone of *b*, *s*, *š*, the spirantised allophone of *p*, *ṭ*, *ṣ*, and *q*. In addition, in about 35 cases a form with *ḥăṭāp̄* is *also acceptable*. Then, ʾ and *t* (the latter reflecting a feminine form) are represented in the third radical position as well. Thus, as far as Milon Even-Shoshan is concerned, a form with epenthesis is the only acceptable form, or *also* an acceptable form, in about 40% of the cases.

In Langenscheidt Achiasaf, 80 forms are not attested, which leaves us with 135 forms to investigate. Of these 135 cases, an epenthetic *ḥăṭāp̄* vowel is inserted in about 60, or more than 40%. In about 20 of the 60 cases, however, the epenthetic vowel is not inserted in the transcription (cf. section 4.2.2.4 below). The consonants represented as the third radical when an epenthetic *ḥăṭāp̄* vowel is inserted are *w*, *r*, *l*, *z*, *n*, *m*, *s*, *š*, the spirantised allophone of *p* and *k*, *ṭ*, *ṣ*, *q*, and ʾ.

Concluding this section, it seems that the sonority of the following radical is of lesser significance in the ע״ח forms than in the פ״ח forms. In the ע״ח forms *ḥ* is quite often involved in contact anaptyxis also when the following radical has great consonantal strength. Whether or not epenthesis obtains more often in ע״ח forms than in פ״ח forms, however, needs further investigation. It is also questionable whether sonority is a relevant parameter at all as far as ע״ח forms are concerned.

4.2.2.4 The modern dictionaries: discrepancies between data in Masoretic representation and in Latin transcription

The dictionary of Even-Shoshan often gives alternatives with *ḥăṭāp̄* vowels in parentheses, in case C_2 is of high sonority, e.g., מַחְוָן or מַחֲוָן, *maxvan* or *maxavan* 'indicator'. This holds also in cases where C_2 is of lower sonority, e.g., /š/, but where the modern word is not formed spontaneously, but borrowed from Biblical Hebrew, and the *ḥăṭāp̄* insertion is due to factors such as relatively remote accent, as in מַחֲשָׁבָה *maxašava* (Masoretic *maḥăšāḇā*) 'thought'. But synchronically, preference is given to the forms without *ḥăṭāp̄*, which are *also* spelled out in the Masoretic system, in principle a non-trivial (because non-normative) decision. An interesting development can be observed, when the 1975 version and the 2004 version of Lavi's Hebrew-German dictionary are compared. Both editions give nominal forms in a Masoretic representation as well as in Latin transcription. While the older 1975 edition mirrors all *ḥăṭāp̄* vowels in the Masoretic transcription by full vowels in the Latin transcription, the 2004 edition discontinues this practice in all cases, where the actual pronunciation is no longer in tune with the Masoretic precepts. As can be inferred from the following list, the crucial factor is again the sonority of C_2, the point being that even in case of high sonority, forms without *ḥăṭāp̄* may be more natural due to the modern quality of /ḥ/. Still, Lavi 2004 is not entirely systematic in this respect. While one finds מַחֲרָטָה *maxrata* (Masoretic *maḥărāṭā*) 'turnery' ("turning (lathe) factory"), the nearly homonymous form מַחֲרֵטָה 'turning lathe', i.e. the instrument as opposed to the factory, is transcribed *maxaréta* (Masoretic *maḥărēṭā*). What is more, the two forms מָחֳרָב *moxrav* (Masoretic *moḥŏrāḇ*) 'destructed' and מָחֳרָם *moxram* (Masoretic *moḥŏrām*) 'boycotted' are intriguing. While the *ḥăṭāp̄* vowel is no longer transcribed, the *o*-quality of the first vowel still reflects the "old" form with the epenthetic vowel (as opposed, for instance, to מֻחְכָּר *muxkar* (Masoretic *muḥkār*) 'under lease'). Here is an overview of the relevant forms with a *h*-, *m*-, *n*-, or *t*-prefix in Lavi 2004 (in all other cases, the *ḥăṭāp̄* vowel is still reflected in the Latin transcription):

(70) Nominal פ"ח forms in Masoretic representation and Latin transcription (Lavi 2004)

Masoretic	**Transcription**	**Gloss**
הַחֲיָאָה	*haxyaʾa*	'revitalisation'
הַחֲנָיָה	*haxnaya*	'parking'
מַחֲבַת	*maxvat*	'frying-pan'
מַחֲוֶה	*maxve*	'pointer' (for reading the *Tora*)
מֶחֱוָה	*mexva*	'gesture'
מַחֲוָן	*maxvan*	'indicator'
מַחֲזוֹרֶת	*maxzoret*	'period'
מַחֲלִיא	*maxli*	'disgusting'
מַחֲלִים	*maxlim*	'convalescent'
מַחֲלִיף	*maxlif*	'substitute' (person)

Masoretic	Transcription	Gloss
מַחֲלִיקַיים	*maxlikayim*	'skates'
מַחֲלָצָה	*maxlatsa*	'festive costume'
מַחֲלוֹקֶת	*maxloket*	'difference of opinion'
מַחֲמָאָה	*maxmaʾa*	'compliment'
מַחֲנִיק	*maxnik*	'suffocating'
מַחֲנָק	*maxnak*	'lack of air'
מַחֲרָאָה	*maxra'a*	'latrine'
מָחֳרָב	*moxrav*	'destructed'
מַחֲרוֹץ	*maxrots*	'cheese knife'
מַחֲרוֹזֶת	*maxrozet*	'row; neck-chain'
מַחֲרָטָה	*maxrata*	'turnery'
מַחֲרִיב	*maxriv*	'destructive'
מַחֲרִיד	*maxrid*	'causing fear'
מַחֲרִישׁ	*maxriš*	'deafening'
מָחֳרָם	*moxram*	'boycotted'
מחֲרוֹסֶת	*maxroset*	'dessert cup'
מַחֲרֵצָה	*maxretsa*	'bung plane' ("Hobel")
מַחֲרָקָה	*maxrata*	'insectarium'
מַחֲרֵשָׁה	*maxreša*	'plow'
מַחֲשָׁבָה	*maxšava*	'thought'
מַחֲשֶׁבֶת	*maxševet*	'applied art'
מַחֲשַׁבְתִּי	*maxšavti*	'thought-related; related to applied art'
נֶחֱרָץ	*nexrats*	'finally decided'
נֶחֱשָׁל	*nexshal*	'retarded'
תַּחֲזוּקָה	*taxzuqa*	'maintenance'
תַּחֲלוּאָה	*taxlu'a*	'spreading of a disease'
תַּחֲלוּפָה	*taxlufa*	'exchange'
תַּחֲלִיב	*taxliv*	'emulsion'
תַּחֲלִיף	*taxlif*	'surrogate'

Masoretic	Transcription	Gloss
תַּחֲנוּנִים	*taxnunim*	'supplication'
תַּחֲצָה	*taxtsa*	'cross-walk'
תַּחֲשִׁיב	*taxšiv*	'calculation'

Comparable cases can be found for ע"ח roots. Here are a few examples extracted from our corpora.

(71) Nominal ע"ח forms in Masoretic representation and Latin transcription (Lavi 2004)

Masoretic	Transcription	Gloss
אַחֲרָאִי	*'axra'i*	'responsible'
דַּחֲפָן	*daxfan*	'impulsive person'
דַּחֲקוּת	*daxkut*	'pressure'
לַחֲשׁוּשׁ	*laxshush*	'whisper' (n.)
נַחֲשָׁן	*naxshan*	'soothsayer'
צַחֲקָנוּת	*tsaxkanut*	'laughter'
רַחֲמָן	*raxman*	'forgiving person'
רַחֲפָנִי	*raxfani*	'suspended'
שַׁחֲפָן	*shaxpan*	'smitten with tuberculosis'
שַׁחֲצִית	*shaxtsit*	'boasting' (n.)
שַׂחֲקָן	*saxkan*	'actor'
שַׁחֲרוּר	*shaxrur*	'blackbird'

4.2.3 Internet forms in Latin transcription

4.2.3.1 Introduction

Having investigated and analysed the פ"ח verbal forms in Bolozky 1996/2008 we became curious as to the extent to which Modern Hebrew as used by native speakers would conform to our findings. First we asked one informant to transcribe 100 פ"ח verbal forms extrapolated from Bolozky 1996/2008. Not in any of the forms was an epenthetic *ḥăṭāp̄* vowel inserted. We wanted to look deeper into this matter and so we decided to search for hits on the Internet with the help of Google.

The searches on the Internet were performed in March, April, and October 2008. The forms searched for are identical to some of the forms that our informants read aloud so that we could conduct acoustical analyses. All the forms are presented in Appendices 3–8.

We investigated the transcription of a form by searching for it in different spellings. For example, when investigating a form such as the third person singular masculine of nifᶜal of *ḥlṣ*, we would perform four searches – "nechlats", "nechelats", "nechlac", and "nechelac". As far as, say, *maḥlīpā* (*maxlifa*) is concerned, we would search for "machlifa" and "machalifa", but also "machelifa". Thus, we wanted to look into the issue as thoroughly as possible, but at the same time we had to confine ourselves. Thus, as far as the exact context is concerned, in which a certain form occurred, we looked into at most the first fifty hits.

As for the transcription of *ḥ*, we are aware that the correct (scholarly) transcription is *x*. For some reason, however, the most frequent (popular) transcription on the Internet is *ch*. For example, on one occasion we got 400 hits on "maxshev", but 4900 on "machshev", and likewise six on "yaxzor", but almost 1000 on "yachzor".

Finally, it must be pointed out that analysing פ"ח forms in Latin transcription on the Internet was a very difficult task. We wanted to find out how פ"ח forms are transcribed by native speakers, but on the Internet of course you cannot be sure who the author is. Another fact is that the vast majority of our forms occur in English texts, and so are extrapolated from other sources. Therefore, no conclusions will be drawn in this section. We will rather confine ourselves to presenting some general observations and representative examples and come up with a hypothesis at the end.

4.2.3.2 Analysis

By way of introduction we can say that פ"ח forms in Latin transcription on the Internet occur in texts that can be split into four different groups. The majority of the forms occur in representations of old religious texts, typically on web sites where the exact meaning of specific phrases is discussed. In this group we can also include forums where Jews living outside Israel, typically in the United States, share their views and experiences. The second group of forms occur in Hebrew songs, and the third group consists of forums for foreign students of Hebrew, including online dictionaries. The fourth and final group of texts is found in online forums for native speakers of Modern Hebrew. This is the group of primary interest to us, but unfortunately it is also the smallest one, as these texts are the hardest ones to find.

A search for "machashiv" vs. "machshiv" and "machashava" vs. "machshava" gives two good examples from the first group. They both illustrate how Hebrew words occur in Latin transcription in the middle of English texts. In the first context a person has submitted a question to a discussion forum of *dafyomi*, a web site related to the study of the Talmud.[57]

(72) "Moshe asked:
Does the concept that we find by Hotza'ah, "if you are Matznia (**Machshiv**) something [sic] then you are Chayav even on a Kol Shehu", apply to other Malachos as well. [sic] For example, if I am Machshiv a little piece of food and want to cook it, will I be Chayiv for Bishul because of my **Machshava**?
Moshe"[58]

The other example is from a forum called *haskafah* and a discussion initiated about what it means to be "yeshivish":

(73) "I don't think you are yeshivish. I think people who are not familiar with the yeshivish community use 'frum' and 'yeshivish' interchangeably. I would think that you and your husband are **machshiv** torah and live a very frum lifestyle but are not necessarily yeshivish."[59]

The search for "machshiv" gave 250 hits, whereas the search for "machashiv" gave none. We got 190 hits on "machashava" and 8600 on "machshava".

57 In the examples below the bold script is ours.

58 http://www.mail-archive.com/daf-discuss@shemayisrael.co.il/msg00426.html.

59 http://www.hashkafah.com/Yeshivisht45640.html&st=20&p=975627#entry 975627.

An example from the second group of texts, Hebrew songs, was found through a search for "lachkor" vs. "lachakor". In the example below, "lachkor" occurs in the refrain of a song called *Al nevakesh*. On the same website we find an English translation of the song:

(74) "(...)
Yesh dvarim nistarim
Lo navin lo neda
Na'ase gam dvarim
Shenirim bli siba
Lo tzarich kol davar **lachkor** velishol
Lifamim gam mutar lo lada'at hakol
(...)"
"(...)
There are hidden things
we will never know nor understand
We will do things
without a reason
we don't have to question every thing [sic]
some times [sic] we are allowed not to know
(...)"[60]

The form "lachkor" occurred 100 times, and to our surprise we got as many as seven hits on "lachakor" as well.[61] The example below represents the first group of texts in which our forms occur. The example is extrapolated from the Torah network *Shema Yisrael*'s web site and the headline is "Sedrah selections Mishpotim-Shkolim 5761 BS"D".

(75) "Ch. 21, v. 1: "V'ei'leh hamishpotim" - The Baal Haturim says that each letter of this verse can be the first letter of a list of basic rules for judges. V'chayov Odom **Lachakor** Hadin (Pirkei Ovos 1:1)"[62]

60 http://www.hebrewsongs.com/?songID=161.

61 Doubtful hits are excluded, such as one occurring in a discussion about what would be the Hebrew root for 'hacker' (http://osdir.com/ml/linux.region.israel/2003-01/msg00707.html). Another doubtful example is a transcription of the book לחקור שמות וכינויים בתלמוד (מוסד) Lachakor Shmvs VchynvayYem Betalmud (Mosad) (http://www.discountseforim.com/Hebrew-Seforim-ISS9125.html).

62 http://www.shemayisrael.com/parsha/fleisher/archives/mishpatim61.htm.

"Lachakor" occurs in another reference to Pirkei Ovos (= Avot) as well, this time to 1:9:

(76) "(...) The author begins, "be extensive in questioning the witnesses," that is, be as thorough as possible gathering the information available. "In questioning" comes from the Hebrew phrase *lachakor*, which also has the sense of "for exploring.""[63]

"Lachakor" also occurs in a scientific article. It deals with Torah work on a more abstract level.

(77) "(...) there is a type of Torah work reminiscent of this approach. A typical discussion of this genre would open, for example, with the words, *"Yesh lachakor"* ("There is room to inquire...")."[64]

The fourth example of "lachakor" occurs in the second group of texts, i.e. Hebrew songs. The example below is from a song called *Kol hachaim rak chipus echad* in a Russian songbook. (The transcription is inconsistent).

(78) "Kol ha-chaim hem rak hipus ehad
shel hashalem vehameuchad
Kulam yodim zot aval shochachim
Lachakor ma hu hataam bachai
(...)"[65]

Our final example of "lachakor" is found in the bibliography of two works by Fred Rosner. The first work is the book *Biomedical Ethics and Jewish Law*, and the second the article "Pig Organs for Transplantation into Humans. A Jewish View":

63 http://scottsrandombits.blogspot.com/2007_12_01_archive.html.

64 http://www.haretzion.org/alei/12-03garmiek.doc (p. 30).

65 http://www.kabbalah.info/ruskab/spingseminar2004/seminar_book_2004.pdf.

(79) "Metzger, Z: *Nisuyim Refuyim BeBa'ale Chayim* (Medical experiments on living animals). In *Harefuah Le'Ohr Hahalachah*. Jerusalem. *Machon* ***Lachakor*** *Harefuah Behalacha* (Institute for the Investigation of Medical Matters in Jewish Law. 1983, pp. 1-50."[66]

Searching for "nechshav" vs. "necheshav" we found an example from group three, i.e. texts for non-native speakers and/or students of Modern Hebrew. Whereas we got 360 hits by searching for "nechshav", we found only one example of "necheshav", occurring on a Finnish site for discussions on the Hebrew language. Below is an excerpt from a section on the consonant ח, submitted by a participant.

(80) "ח puoli CHE (chataf segol) נֶחֱשַׁב **NECHESHAV** näyttää jltkn; tulla otetuksi lukuun; olla jnkn arvoinen"[67]

The last examples we will provide for are from our search for "lachgog" vs. "lachagog". "lachgog" gave us 50 hits, of which one is presented below. The example is extrapolated from a discourse in a *Yahoo* forum, in which someone needs help to translate a speech into Hebrew.

(81) "It is an amazing thing that we all were able to fly in and celebrate Sarah's new step into adulthood."
"Ze davar niflaa she kulanu tasnu lepo **lachgog** et ha tzaad shel sara lebagrut."[68]

We got two hits for "lachagog" as well. One was from a text belonging to our first group, i.e. on the interpretation of old Jewish documents. The other, however, was the interesting one. In this case we are as sure as we can be that the author is a native speaker of Hebrew. If we are right, the example below belongs to our fourth group, i.e. the group of primary interest to us as far as transcription of Modern Hebrew is concerned. The

66 The web sites are http://books.google.no/books?id=T7w2oAmohpEC&pg=PA345&lpg=PA345&dq=lachakor&source=web&ots=gSgD6W8owQ&sig=IPbTBPcqsXujyBLGd2XfV7SLiXk&hl=nn&sa=X&oi=book_result&resnum=10&ct=result and http://www.mssm.edu/msjournal/66/PAGE314_319.PDF, respectively.

67 http://p3.foorumi.info/shalom/viewtopic.php?t=87.

68 http://answers.yahoo.com/question/index?qid=20070511175715AAeXkMR.

example is from an Israeli web site, and the participants in the chat write in both Hebrew and Latin letters.

(82) "?who cares
(…)
!ani mitkaven lachagog"[69]

If we presuppose that the writer is a native speaker, and a young one at that, it is very interesting that an epenthetic *ḥăṭāp̄* vowel is inserted in this context.

4.2.3.3 Summary

Summing up our most important observations, the vast majority of פ"ח forms in Latin transcription occur in texts not written in Hebrew. Most often the language is English, and as far as web sites concerning religion are concerned, the texts seem to be meant for Jews living outside Israel, most frequently in the United States. Typically, the meaning of specific phrases in the Tanakh or Talmud is discussed. One can, for example, find online Bar/Bat Mitzva tutors in English, Spanish, and Russian, and on http://www.bible.ort.org one can "navigate the Bible".

A smaller group of פ"ח forms in Latin transcription occur in Hebrew songs, and a third group is found on sites devoted to Hebrew linguistics. In connection to the third group are typically found online dictionaries between Hebrew other languages, most often Slavic ones, such as Czech and Polish. The last group comprises forms found in forums where the users are native speakers of Hebrew. These are the most interesting forms, but also the most difficult ones to find.

Throughout our searching on the Internet we have found פ"ח forms in Latin transcription both with and without epenthetic vowels in all four groups. Against the background of our overall observations we suggest the following hypotheses for further research: the epenthetic vowels in representations of Jewish religious documents are due to the original transcription, which is a study in its own right, unless the source is the Hebrew Bible itself. The epenthetic vowels in songs are due to

69 http://www.news1.co.il/showTalkBack.aspxdocId=56070&subjectId=1&talkBackId=477643.

rhyme and rhythm. The epenthetic vowels occurring in online dictionaries are mainly due to a Masora-based transcription. Finally, we suggest that epenthetic *ḥăṭāp̄* vowels are inserted by native speakers only in exceptional cases, a highly sonorous second radical and/or a final weak radical being the crucial triggering factors.

5 The evidence of the living language: normative forms vs. spoken Modern Hebrew

5.1 Introduction

In chapter 4 we analysed 850 verbal forms and 40 nominal forms in Biblical Hebrew, and 375 verbal forms and 135 nominal forms in dictionaries of Modern Hebrew, of the type פ״ח. Of the 850 verbal forms in Biblical Hebrew the share of epenthetic forms is approximately 70%. In four dictionaries of Modern Hebrew the percentages are 70%, 57%, 54%, and practically 0%. The dictionaries (and verb lists) are from 1975, 2004, 2008 and 2003, respectively. In order to investigate to what extent spoken Hebrew conforms to the norm, we contacted 12 informants and established an oral corpus consisting of about 1080 פ״ח and 320 ע״ח verbal and nominal forms.

5.2 The informants

Our group of 12 informants is comprised of two middle-aged men and two women aged 30-40 living in Oslo, one middle-aged man living in the USA, one middle-aged woman living in Sweden, three women aged 30-40, one young and one middle-aged woman living in Israel, and one man aged 30-40 living in Austria, all of whom are native speakers of Modern Hebrew. They all have at least a basic academic education, and they have different levels of consciousness as far as the Masoretic base (or correlate) of the modern forms are concerned.

Thus, in terms of sex, our informants consist of four men and eight women. In terms of age, five are middle-aged, six are between 30 and 40, and the last is a teenager.

In light of our aim it could be argued that the distribution of informants in terms of sex and age should have been more equal. When it comes to the acoustical analysis, this objection is even more justified. Therefore, our results from this analysis are mere indications and so can serve as working hypotheses for further research.

5.3 Method

We presented texts to our informants, one in which 44 פ״ח and 3 ע״ח forms occurred in context, and some in which relevant forms were listed. (All texts can be found in Appendix 8.) Our informants all consented to letting us record their speaking, which we did by using iPods. We then loaded the sound-files from the iPod onto a computer, listened to them and investigated under what circumstances epenthetic (*ḥăṭāp̄*) vowels were inserted.

As our project came along, more and more forms became interesting to us. To begin with, we made a list of 100 פ״ח verbal forms as listed in Bolozky (1996/2008). Then, we wrote a text of 30 sentences – some of which are extrapolated from Bolozky (1996/2008) – in which 44 פ״ח and 3 ע״ח forms were hidden. Later on, we also made lists of 30 *h*-prefixed, 82 *m*-prefixed and 23 *t*-prefixed פ״ח nominal forms, and about 400 forms of the type ע״ח, including 260 verbal and 135 nominal forms, and some prepositions, adverbs, and interjections. Our final lists completed our first list so that all consonants occurring as second radical in a verbal form of a פ״ח root would be represented.

Since our recordings were made at different stages of our project, not all texts are read by all our informants. The number of informants consulted will be made clear in all sections of 5.4 below.

5.4 Findings

5.4.1 The context forms

The text of 30 sentences including 44 פ״ח and 3 ע״ח verbal and nominal forms was presented to nine informants. Our corpus of context forms then comprises about 400 פ״ח forms and 27 ע״ח forms. In our context forms of the פ״ח type, the second radical is *g* in two cases, *z* in eight, *y* in three, *l* in nine, *n* in two, *s* in two, *p* in two, *q* in three, *r* in four, *š* in five, *ś* in two, and *t* in two cases. The third radical is *r* in all three ע״ח forms.

An epenthetic *ḥăṭāp̄* vowel was inserted in only 19 – less than 4,5% – of the 427 cases. The only word all the informants pronounced with a *ḥăṭāp̄* vowel was אחרון *(')axaron* (*ʾaḥărōn*) 'last, latter', of the type ע״ח. Five of the informants read *soxorei* (*sōḥărē*) 'businessmen of' for סוחרי.

One informant pronounced יחנוך 'he will inaugurate' *yaxanokh* (*yaḥănōḵ*). One informant read *hexerifu* (*heḥĕrīp̄ū*), *la-xalot* (*la-ḥălōt*), and *la-xasof* (*la-ḥăśōp̄*) for החריפו 'they worsened (intr.); they made worse', לחלות 'to fall sick, be sick', and לחשוף 'to expose, bare, uncover', respectively. Finally, one informant read *la-xagog* (*la-ḥăgōg*) for לחגוג 'to celebrate, observe (holiday)'. As we can see, in 15 of the 19 cases where epenthesis obtains, the consonant following *ḥ* is *r*. This does correspond to our hypothesis about sonority. But as we are now dealing with *Modern* Hebrew, it is not certain that the explanation lies in sonority alone (or anymore), but rather in closeness of place of articulation (Shmuel Bolozky, Outi Bat-El, and Matthew Monger, personal communication on October 27, 2008). This point, however, needs further investigation.

In the last four cases where an epenthetic *ḥăṭāp̄* vowel is inserted, the consonant following *ḥ* is *l*, *n*, *g* and *ś*. *l* and *n* conform to our hypothesis.

For one of our informants, five forms are pronounced such that it is difficult to hear whether an epenthetic vowel is inserted or not. The forms in question are להחזיק 'hold, seize', יחזיק 'he will hold out', להחזיר 'return (trans.), restore; reflect (light); turn (trans.)', מוחזרים '(are) being returned / restored; (are) reflected (light) (m. pl.)', and מחליפה 'she (ex)changes; replaces'. Even though this applies only to one informant, it is interesting that C_2 is *z* in four instances and *l* in one, and thus in accordance with our hypothesis about sonority.

5.4.2 The isolated verbal forms

Our list of 100 פ"ח verbal forms was presented to eight informants. In these forms, the following consonants are represented as the second radical: *b* (six cases), *g* (three), *d* (three), *z* (seven), *y* (three), *k* (one), *l* (19), *m* (one), *n* (three), *s* (nine), *p* (seven), *q* (four), *r* (seven), *š* (11), *ś* (four), and *t* (12 cases).

Five informants did not insert an epenthetic vowel in any of the cases. The last three, all middle-aged, inserted an epenthetic vowel in 18, 20, and 32 cases, respectively. They have the following five cases in common: *la-xavok* (*la-ḥăḇōq*) and *yaxavok* (*yaḥăḇōq*) for לחבוק 'to clamp' and

יחבוק 'he will clamp', *la-xavor* (*la-ḥăḇōr*) for לחבור 'to join', and *la-xanokh* (*la-ḥănōḵ*) and *yaxanokh* (*yaḥănōḵ*) for לחנוך 'to inaugurate' and יחנוך 'he will inaugurate'. The second consonant in these cases are *ḇ* (three cases) and *n* (two cases), and the forms are paᶜal infinitive (three cases) and future (two cases).

Two of the three informants – not always the same two – have the following 16 forms in common: *yaxavor* (*yaḥăḇōr*) for יחבור 'he will join', *yeḥĕzāq* (*yexezak*) and *le-haxazik* (*lə-haḥăzīq*) for יחזק 'he will be strong' and להחזיק 'to seize', *le-haxazir* (*lə-haḥăzīr*) for להחזיר 'to return (trans.)', *le-haxayot* (*lə-haḥăyōt*) for להחיות 'to revive', *la-xalot* (*la-ḥălōt*) for לחלות 'to fall sick', *yaxalof* (*yaḥălōp̄*) for יחלוף 'he will pass by', *la-xalok* (*la-ḥălōq*) and *yaxalok* (*yaḥălōq*) for לחלוק 'to allot' and יחלוק 'he will allot', *la-xasokh* (*la-ḥăsōḵ*) and *la-xasor* (*la-ḥăsōr*) for לחסוך 'to save (money)' and לחסור 'to lack', *le-haxasir* (*lə-haḥăsīr*) for להחסיר 'to subtract', *la-xapos* (*la-ḥăpōś*) (sic!) and *yaxapos* (*yaḥăpōś*) (sic!) for לחפוש 'to investigate' and יחפוש 'he will investigate',[1] and *la-xarof* (*la-ḥărōp̄*) and *yaxarof* (*yaḥărōp̄*) for לחרוף 'to spend the winter' and יחרוף 'he will spend the winter'. The second consonant in these cases are *ḇ* (one case), *z* (three), *y* (one – hifᶜīl infinitive), *l* (four), *s* (three), *p* (two) (non-spirantised) and *r* (two cases). The forms are paᶜal infinitive (six cases), paᶜal future (six), and hifᶜīl infinitive (four cases).

One – but not always the same – informant pronounced the following 23 forms with an epenthetic vowel: לחבוב 'to love' and יחבוב 'he will love' *la-xavov* (*la-ḥăḇōḇ*) and *yaxavov* (*yaḥăḇōḇ*), לחזוק 'to be strong' *la-xazok* (*la-ḥăzōq*), יחזיק 'he will seize' *yaxăziq* (*yaḥăzīq*), לחזור 'to return' and יחזור 'he will return' *la-xazor* (*la-ḥăzōr*) and *yaxăzor* (*yaḥăzōr*), יחלה 'he will fall sick' *yexele* (*yeḥĕlē*), לחלוט 'to pour boiling water' *la-xalot* (*la-ḥălōṭ*), יחלום 'he will dream' *yaxalom* (*yaḥălōm*), לחלוף 'to pass by' and להחליף 'to exchange' *la-xalof* (*la-ḥălōp̄*) and *le-haxalif* (*lə-haḥălīp̄*), אחסר 'I will lack' *ˀaxasor* (*ˀaḥăsōr*) [should be *ˀexsar* (*ˀeḥsar*)!] , יחסר 'he will lack' *yexĕsar* (*yeḥĕsār*), לחפור 'to dig' *la-xafor* (*la-ḥăpōr*), לחקור 'to investigate' and יחקור 'he will investigate' *la-xakor* (*la-ḥăqōr*) and *yaxakor* (*yaḥăqōr*),

1 This form is now considered obsolete in paᶜal. The informant did not spirantise the *p* in these instances.

לחרוט *la-xarot* (*la-ḥărōṭ*) 'to engrave', יחרוט *yaxarot* (*yaḥărōṭ*) 'he will engrave', and להחריט *le-haxarit* (*lə-haḥărīṭ*), יחשוב 'he will think' *yaxashov* (*yaḥăšōḇ*), לחשוד 'to suspect' *la-xashod* (*la-ḥăšōd*), as well as לחשוף 'to expose' and יחשוף 'he will expose' *la-xasof* (*la-ḥăśōp̄*) and *yaxasof* (*yaḥăśōp̄*). The second consonant in these cases are *ḇ* in two cases, *z* in four, *l* in five, *s* in two, *ṕ* in one, *q* in two, *r* in three, *š* in two, and *ś* in two cases. The forms belong to paᶜal infinitive (10 cases), paᶜal future (10 cases), hifᶜīl infinitive (two cases), and hifᶜīl future (one case).

Summing up the results of our list of 100 isolated פ"ח verbal forms, our corpus consists of 800 forms, of which 70 were pronounced with an epenthetic vowel. In these 70 cases the second radical is *ḇ* in 13 cases, *n* in six, *z* in ten, *y* in two (hifᶜīl infinitive), *l* in 13, *s* in eight, *p* in four, *p̄* in one, *q* in two, *r* in seven, *š* in two, and *ś* in two cases. One has to be aware, though, that the number of forms for each second radical is not the same. Thus, the interesting matter here is which consonants are the second radical when an epenthetic vowel is inserted. The fact that *r*, *l*, *n* and *z* are involved when epenthesis obtains conforms to our findings for Biblical Hebrew and to our hypothesis about sonority. The same is true of *y* in the hifᶜīl infinitive form. The findings for *ḇ* and *p̄* correspond to the findings for Biblical Hebrew, and as to *ḇ* the result is also in line with our hypothesis about sonority. The observation that *ś* is involved in epenthesis conforms to our findings for Biblical Hebrew, but probably not to our hypothesis about sonority, as in Modern Hebrew *ś* and *s* are homophonous. The results for *s* and *š* do not conform either to our results for Biblical Hebrew, nor to our hypothesis about sonority. The same is true of *p* and *q*.[2]

As far as the binyanim involved in epenthesis are concerned, the form is paᶜal infinitive in 31 cases, paᶜal future in 28 cases, hifᶜīl infinitive in 10 cases, and hifᶜīl future in one case. One has to be aware, though, that the number of paᶜal and hifᶜīl forms is not identical, as there are far more of the former type than of the latter.

In our first list of 100 פ"ח verbal forms, the consonants *w*, *ṭ*, *k*, *m*, and *ṣ* are not represented as second radical. In the light of our findings

2 Correctly, *q* is involved in epenthesis once in the Hebrew Bible, but this is most probably due to prosodic factors rather than sonority.

for Biblical Hebrew, however, forms involving these consonants would be of interest as well. Therefore, we asked one informant to read eight, 11, 12, and 18 forms in which the second radical was *w*, *ṭ*, *k* and *ṣ*, respectively. As for *w*, an epenthetic vowel was inserted in one case only – *le-haxavot* (*lə-haḥăwōt*) was read for להחוות 'to show'. None of the forms with *ṭ*, *k*, or *ṣ* were pronounced with an epenthetic vowel. *k* was non-spirantised in all cases. We asked another informant to read 24 forms with *m* as second radical. An epenthetic vowel was pronounced in two cases: *hexemi* (*heḥĕmī(ʾ)*) and *le-haxamits* (*lə-haḥămīṣ*) were read for החמיא 'to flatter' and להחמיץ 'to become sour', respectively. As far as *w* is concerned, only one root – *ḥwr* – is represented in the Hebrew Bible, and epenthesis obtains in the only form attested – יֶחֱוָרוּ *yexevaru* (*yeḥĕwā́rū*) 'they turn pale' – in which the epenthetic vowel may also be due to prosodic factors (pausal form). At least, however, our informant's use of an epenthetic vowel in the case of *w* may be in accordance with our sonority hypothesis, as *w* is a glide. The fact that *m* is involved in epenthesis does not conform to our findings for Biblical Hebrew, where the only instance of epenthesis is most probably due to prosodic factors. In terms of phonetics, the result is not in accordance with our sonority hypothesis either.

5.4.3 The nominal forms

As far as the *m*-prefixed nominal forms are concerned, we presented our list of 125 forms to four informants. All informants are women – two middle-aged and two between 30 and 40. In these 125 *m*-prefixed nominal forms, the following consonants are represented as the second radical: *b* (10 cases), *g* (one), *d* (two), *w* (three), *z* (12), *ṭ* (four), *y* (one), *k* (three), *l* (22), *m* (11), *n* (four), *s* (five), *p* (four), *ṣ* (eight), *q* (one), *r* (16), *š* (12), *ś* (one), and *t* (five cases). There were 40 forms that one of our informants did not read since she did not accept them. The list of the *m*-prefixed nominal forms is presented in Appendix 5.

Our four informants inserted an epenthetic vowel in between eight and 16 of the 125 cases. The number of cases of epenthesis does not correspond in any way to the age of our informants.

The informants have the following five cases of epenthesis in common: *maxaza(')i* (*maḥăzāʾī*) for מחזאי 'playwright', *maxaze* (*maḥăzē*) for מחזה 'play, drama', *maxala* (*maḥălā*) for מחלה 'disease', *maxane* (*maḥănē*) for מחנה 'camp', and *maxase* (*maḥăsē*) for מחסה 'shelter'. The second radical in these cases is *z* in two cases, *l* in one, *n* in one, and *s* in one case. The epenthesis-supporting effect of *z*, *l*, and *n* conforms both to our findings for Biblical Hebrew and modern dictionaries of Israeli Hebrew, and to our hypothesis about sonority. Interestingly, the roots in all five forms are of the type *tertiae infirmae*, which, as we have seen, increases the likelihood of epenthesis between *ḥ* and the following radical.

Three informants, but not the same three in the two cases, have the forms *maxazemer* (*maḥăzémer*) for מחזמר 'musical' an *maxatsit* (*maḥăṣīt*) for מחצית 'half' in common.[3] In the former, the second radical is *z*, and the root in the latter form is of the type *tertiae infirmae*. Again, this conforms to our previous findings.

There are three forms in which an epenthetic vowel is inserted by two informants, though not the same two in all cases: *maxana(')ut* (*maḥănāʾūt*) for מַחֲנָוּת 'camping', *maxarozet* (*maḥărózet*) for מחרוזת 'row; neck-chain', and *maxata* (*maḥătā*) for מחתה 'coal shovel'. The epenthesis-supporting effect of *r* and *n* corresponds to our previous results. In the case of *n* the root is in addition of the type *tertiae infirmae*. The insertion of an epenthetic vowel in מחתה, however, does not conform to our sonority hypothesis or to our previous findings, as the root *ḥth* has not been involved in epenthesis in one single case, despite the final weak radical. So, the compensatory ל"ה factor seems to be at work here, in spite of the low sonority of /t/.

In 15 cases, only one informant inserts an epenthetic vowel. Again, the informant is not one and the same in all cases. The forms in question are *maxavo* (*maḥăbō(ʾ)*) for מחבוא 'hiding place',[4] *maxavat* (*maḥăḇat*) for מַחֲבַת 'frying pan', *maxave* (*maḥăwē*) for מַחֲוֶה 'pointer', *mexeva* (*meḥĕwā*)

3 The informant who pronounces מַחצית *maxtsit* (*maḥṣīt*) is the only informant to insert an epenthetic vowel in מֶחֱצָה 'half', and thus pronounces it *mexetsa* (*meḥĕṣā*).

4 The same informant, however, pronounces מַחבֵא 'hiding place' *maxve* (*maḥḇē(ʾ)*).

for מְחוּוָה 'gesture', *mexeza* (*meḥĕzā*) for מֶחֱזָה 'look', *maxazer* (*maḥăzer*) for מַחֲזֵר 'reset-switch', *mexelak* (*meḥĕlāq*) for מֶחֱלָק '(police) division', *maxanik* (*maḥănīq*) for מחניק 'suffocating', *maxafe* (*maḥăp̄ē*) for מחפה 'protected position', *mexetsa* (*meḥĕṣā*) for מֶחֱצָה 'half', *moxorav* (*moḥŏrāḇ*) for מוחרב 'destructed',[5] *maxarots* (*maḥărōṣ*) for מַחרוץ 'cheese knife', *maxariv* (*maḥărīḇ*) for מחריב 'destructive', *maxarid* (*maḥărīd*) for מחריד 'causing fear', and *maxarish* (*maḥărīš*) for מחריש 'deafening'. As we can see, for these 15 forms, the second radical is *ḇ* in two cases, *w* in two, *z* in two, *l* in one, *n* in one, *p̄* in one, *ṣ* in one, and *r* in the last five examples. As far as *ḇ*, *w*, *z*, *l*, *n*, and *r* are concerned, the results conform perfectly to our sonority hypothesis and our findings for Biblical Hebrew and written Modern Hebrew. As for *p̄*, the root in question – *ḥph* – is, correctly, of the type *tertiae infirmae*. However, this root is never involved in contact anaptyxis in our written corpus, neither in Biblical Hebrew nor in Modern Hebrew. When it comes to *ṣ*, the root in question is *ḥṣh*, and so the result conforms to our previous findings. Thus, of the 15 forms that only one informant pronounced with an epenthetic *ḥăṭāp̄* vowel, the second radical is amongst the most sonorous consonants in 13. This conforms perfectly to our hypothesis. In seven cases, including the two cases where the second radical is low on the sonority scale, the root in question is of the type *tertiae infirmae*. This is in line with our previous findings.

Summing up the results for the *m*-prefixed nominal forms, contact anaptyxis obtains when the second radical has relatively little consonantal strength, i.e. is highly sonorous. Furthermore, a final weak radical increases the likelihood of epenthesis.

As for the *h*-prefixed forms, a list of 30 forms was presented to one of our informants. The following consonants were represented as the second radical: *b* (one case), *d* (one), *w* (one), *z* (three), *ṭ* (one), *y* (one), *k* (one), *l* (five), *m* (two), *n* (three), *s* (two), *w* (one), *ṣ* (one), *r* (five), *š* (two), and *t* (one). Our informant did not insert an epenthetic vowel in any of the cases. The list is presented in Appendix 4.

5 Two informants pronounce the word *moxrav* (*moḥrāḇ*) and thus keep the [o] even though the epenthetic *ḥăṭāp̄* vowel has disappeared. The last informant pronounces the word *muxrav* (*muḥrāḇ*).

As far as the *t*-prefixed forms are concerned, a list of 32 forms was presented to one of our informants, who accepted 23 of them. The list is presented in Appendix 6. The consonants occurring as second radical are the following: *b* (five cases), *d* (one), *w* (one), *z* (two), *l* (four), *m* (three), *n* (two), *p* (one), *q* (one), *r* (three), and *š* (one). An epenthetic vowel was inserted in three cases: *taxazit* (*taḥăzīt*) was read for תחזית 'forecast', *taxana* (*taḥănā*) for תחנָה 'station', and *taxarut* (*taḥărūt*) for תחרות 'competition'. First, the second radical is highly sonorous in all three cases. Second, all three forms are of the type *tertiae infirmae.*

Concluding this section about isolated פ"ח nominal forms, we have considered about 180 *m*-, *h*-, and *t*-prefixed forms. Taking into account the number of informants for each list, the total number of forms investigated is approximately 550. Of these, an epenthetic *ḥăṭāp̄* vowel was inserted in 50, which renders a percentage value of 11%. The corresponding value for verbal forms in the Hebrew Bible is more than 70%, and for three out of four dictionaries of Modern Hebrew more than 50%. Thus, the share of epenthetic forms is significantly lower, but the circumstances under which contact anaptyxis occurs are the same: for the 50 epenthetic forms amongst the 550 oral nominal forms, the second radical is *z* in 14 cases, *n* in eight, *r* in eight, *l* in five, *ṣ* in four (the root is *ḥṣh* – *tertiae infirmae* – in all four cases), *s* in four (the root is *ḥsh* – *tertiae infirmae* – in all four cases), *w* in two, *ḇ* in two (in both cases the root is of the type *tertiae infirmae*), *t* in two (the root is *ḥth* – *tertiae infirmae*), and *p̄* in one case (the root is *ḥph* – *tertiae infirmae*). In all, of the 50 forms in which an epenthetic vowel is inserted, the root in question is of the type *tertiae infirmae* in 37 cases, which gives a percentage value of about 75%.

5.4.4 The ע"ח forms

5.4.4.1 An overall account

In order to test our hypothesis against oral ע"ח forms, we presented the list in Appendix 7 to one of our informants, who read the accepted forms for us and let us record. According to our informant, speakers of Modern Hebrew would most certainly pronounce the forms differently if reading them a second time. Our findings, however, were so striking that they deserve a section of their own.

The list presented to our informant is an earlier version of the one referred to in 4.2.2.3.4 above. This earlier version consists of about 400 ע"ח forms extrapolated from the dictionaries of Bantam Megiddo (1975), Milon Even Shoshan (2003) and Langenscheidt Achiasaf (2004). Of the 400 forms about 260 are verbal, of which only 20 are infinite, all pi[cc]el infinitives. About 110 forms are nouns, 25 adjectives, and the rest prepositions, adverbs, or interjections. In this section we will give an overall statistical account of all forms together. In two sections below we will treat verbal forms and nominal forms separately.

Almost 90 of the forms were not accepted by our informant. These forms are not included in the account below, except for the 10 of them that were read all the same.

Our first and perhaps most surprising finding was that an epenthetic vowel was pronounced in 160 cases. That is, of 320 ע"ח forms an epenthetic vowel was present in half. In table **(83)** below we have, for each consonant occurring as third radical, presented the total number of accepted forms, and the share of forms with epenthesis in terms of number and percent. Percentage values are only given in cases where the number of forms is higher than 10. Two forms in which the third radical was *m* and *r* were difficult to judge and are not included in the account. Occurring *begadkefat* consonants are given three values – one for the phoneme and two for each allophone.

(83) A first, strictly quantitative ranking

C_3	**Number of accepted forms**	**Number of forms with epenthesis**	**Percentage of forms with epenthesis**
א	3	2	–
ב	13	9	69%
[b]	2	0	–
[ḇ]	11	9	82%
ד	21	16	76%
ו	3	1	–

C_3	Number of accepted forms	Number of forms with epenthesis	Percentage of forms with epenthesis
ז	16	3	19%
ט	5	2	–
י	2	0	–
כ	9	5	–
[k]	4	0	–
[k̠]	5	5 (all)	–
ל	39	16	41%
מ	31	14	45%
נ	8	8 (all)	–
ס	17	11	65%
פ	15	7	47%
[p]	1	0	–
[p̄]	14	7	50%
צ	20	10	50%
ק	33	11	33%
ר	35	19	54%
שׁ	27	17	63%
ת	20	10	50%

In table **(84)** below the consonants occurring as third radical are ranked according to the percentage values in table **(83)** above. The forms for which an epenthetic vowel occurred in all or no forms are also included in the table.

(84) A ranking according to percentage

Percentage value	C_3
100%	[ḵ], נ
90%	
80%	[ḇ]
	ד
70%	
	ס, ב, שׁ
60%	
	ר
50%	צ, [p̄], ת
	מ, פ
40%	ל
	ק
30%	
20%	ז
10%	
0%	[b], י, [k], [p]

As was the case for nominal forms of the type ע״ח in dictionaries of Modern Hebrew (cf. section 4.2.2.3.4 above), it seems that the sonority of the following radical is of lesser significance in ע״ח forms than in פ״ח forms. In table **(83)** above we can see that *ḥ* is quite often involved in contact anaptyxis even when the following radical has great consonantal strength. Consider, for example, the high ranking of *d*, *ṣ*, *q*, and *t*, and the low percentage value for *z*. Consider also the fact that *s* and *š* are found higher up in the table than *r* and *l*.

Another early overall observation was that there seemed to be a connection between the vowel in the syllable preceding *ḥ* and the likelihood of epenthesis. In our corpus of accepted ע״ח forms there are about 85 forms in which the vowel in the syllable preceding *ḥ* is [i]. In more than 50 of these cases *ḥ* is followed by an epenthetic vowel. There are about 215 cases where *ḥ* is preceded by a syllable in which the vowel is [a]. *ḥ* is followed by an epenthetic vowel in slightly less than half of these instances. Thus, the distribution of epenthesis when the vowel preceding *ḥ* is [i] vs. [a] is approximately 60% vs. 50%. As we will return to below, however, the trigger of epenthesis is not necessarily the preceding vowel, but rather the lexical category of the word as well as gender for verbal forms and vowel pattern for nominal forms.

5.4.4.2 The ע״ח verbal forms

Our informant accepted 195 of our 260 verbal forms. Analysing the results we discovered that there were differences between binyanim, between different forms of the same binyan, and in some cases between different binyanim of the same root, as far as the insertion of an epenthetic vowel is concerned.

Let us begin with the differences between binyanim. As for the nifᶜal past forms our informant inserted an epenthetic vowel in all forms, both third person singular feminine and third person plural forms. Thus, our informant consistently read *nivxara* (*niḇḥărā*) and *nivxaru* (*niḇḥărū*) 'she was/they were elected' etc. instead of **nivxəra* and **nivxəru* etc.

As for piᶜᶜel the infinitive and three past forms are represented: third person singular masculine and feminine, and third person plural. There are 15 piᶜᶜel infinitives in our corpus, of which an epenthetic vowel was inserted in just one case: לְאַחֵזֵק 'maintain (in good condition)' was pronounced *le-(')axazek* (*lə-ʾaḥăzeq*), and not **le-(')axzek)*. None of the past forms of third person masculine singular were pronounced with an epenthetic vowel. So, we have, e.g., *(')ixzek* (*ʾiḥzeq*) 'he maintained (in good condition)', and not **(')ixazek*. As far as the past forms of third person singular feminine and third person plural are concerned, there are 35 forms to consider. 29 of these forms, i.e. more than 80%, exhibit anaptyxis. For example, for *ʾḥd* 'unite (oneself)' our informant read

(')ixada (*ʾiḥădā*) and *(')ixadu* (*ʾiḥădū*), whereas for *rḥq* 'remove', for example, *rixka* and *rixku* were read. None of the instances of the verbal noun piʿʿul were pronounced with an epenthetic vowel.

When it comes to hitpaʿʿel, the groups of forms represented in our corpus are the past form of the third person singular feminine and the third person plural. There are 24 such forms altogether, of which 16, i.e. two thirds, exhibit anaptyxis. Thus, we have, e.g., the surface forms *hityaxada* (*hityaḥădā*) and *hityaxadu* (*hityaḥădū*) 'she/they isolated herself/themselves' of *yḥd* 'devote' (in piʿʿel), but *hit'axda* and *hit'axdu* of *ʾḥd* 'unite (oneself)'.

As regards paʿal, there are 80 forms to consider. The forms are past forms of the third person singular feminine and the third person plural. 60 of these forms, i.e. 75%, exhibit epenthesis. For example, for *bḥr* 'choose' our informant read *baxara* (*baḥărā*) and *baxaru* (*baḥărū*), but for *dḥq* 'push' *daxka* and *daxku* were read.

For all the considered verbal forms together the share of epenthetic forms is 68%.

Now, let us continue with the variations across different forms of the same binyan. In our corpus there are eight cases where two verbal forms in different persons but in the same binyan vary when it comes to the presence or absence of an epenthetic vowel. In six of these cases contact anaptyxis obtains in the third person singular feminine but not in the third person plural. Thus, for paʿal past our informant read *naxăla* (*naḥălā*) but *naxlu* – 'she/they acquired possession' – and *naxata* (*naḥătā*) but *naxtu* – 'she/they descended/landed'. The forms of *sḥr* – 'trade' – were difficult to hear, but most probably the pronunciation was *saxara* (*saḥărā*) but *saxru*. As regards piʿʿel past, our informant read *kixaša* (*kiḥăšā*) but *kixšu* – 'she/they denied' – and *(')ixala* (*ʾiḥălā*) but *(')exlu* – 'she/they congratulated'. For hitpaʿʿel past were read *hitraxatsa* (*hitraḥăṣā*) but *hitraxtsu* – 'she/they took a shower'. Against these six examples there are two examples of the opposite pattern, i.e., where epenthesis obtains in the third person plural but not in the third person singular feminine. Thus, for paʿal past our informant read *(')axza* but *(')axazu* (*ʾaḥăzū*) – 'she/they gripped/held'. The piʿʿel past forms of the root *rḥm* were difficult to hear, but the pronunciation was most likely *rixma* but *rixămu* (*riḥămū*) – 'she/they had pity'.

Finally, let us account for the cases where there are variations across different binyanim of one and the same root. If we leave out the instances treated in the paragraph above, i.e. cases where there are variations across different forms of the same binyan, there are 19 roots to consider. The following 19 roots occur in two or more binyanim: *ʾḥd, bḥr, dḥp, dḥq, yḥd, yḥs, kḥd, kḥš, lḥm, lḥṣ, lḥš, nḥm, sḥb, pḥd, pḥt, rḥb, rḥq, rḥš*, and *šḥq*. In five of these cases there are differences across binyanim. The roots in question are *ʾḥd, dḥq, sḥb, rḥq*, and *šḥq*. As regards *dḥq, sḥb*, and *šḥq*, epenthesis obtains in nifᶜal, but not in paᶜal. Thus, our informant read *nidxaka* (*nidḥăqā*) and *nidxaku* (*nidḥăqū*), but *daxka* and *daxku*; *nisxava* (*nisḥăḇā*) and *nisxavu* (*nisḥăḇū*), but *saxva* and *saxvu*; and *nišxaka* (*nišḥăqā*) and *nišxaku* (*nišḥăqū*), but *šaxka* and *šaxku*. For *ʾḥd*, epenthesis obtains in piᶜᶜel, but not in hitpaᶜᶜel. Thus, we have *(')ixada* (*ʾiḥădā*) and *(')ixadu* (*ʾiḥădū*), but *hit'axda* and *hit'axdu*. Finally, for *rḥq*, epenthesis obtains in paᶜal, but not in piᶜᶜel and hitpaᶜᶜel. Thus, our informant read *raxaka* (*raḥăqā*) and *raxaku* (*raḥăqū*), but *rixka* and *rixku* and *hitraxka* and *hitraxku*. We see, then, that there is variation between different binyanim of one and the same root in just one fourth of the cases where one root occurs in different binyanim. For the remaining 14 roots above, epenthesis obtains in all forms of all binyanim.

Summing up our results for all accepted verbal forms, 68% of them exhibit epenthesis. As far as the third person singular feminine and third person plural past forms are concerned, 75% of the forms of paᶜal, more than 80% of piᶜᶜel, all of nifᶜal, and two thirds of the forms of hitpaᶜᶜel exhibit epenthesis. Moreover, the feminine forms seem to be slightly more likely to exhibit anaptyxis than the plural forms.

5.4.4.3 The ע"ח nominal forms

In our analysis of the nominal forms we discovered that epenthesis seems to be linked to certain morphological patterns. Our account has been concentrated on nouns of the following types, where "v" signifies an epenthetic vowel:

1) $C_1aC_2(v)C_3a$, e.g., בָּחְשָׁה *bax(a)ša;*

2) $C_1aC_2(v)C_3an$, e.g., לַחְשָׁן *lax(a)šan;*[6]

3) $C_1aC_2(v)C_3ut$, *-iyut*, and *-anut*, e.g., יַחסוּת *yax(a)sut*, יַחסיוּת *yax(a)siyut*, and יַחסָנוּת *yax(a)sanut;*

4) $C_1aC_2(v)C_3it$, and *-anit*, e.g., לַחמית *lax(a)mit* and לַחצָנית *lax(a)tsanit.*

We also looked into adjectives of the type

5) $C_1aC_2(v)C_3i$, and *-ani*, e.g., יַחסי *yax(a)si* and יַחסָני *yax(a)sani.*

As for 1) there are 12 nouns of this type in our corpus. 11 of them are pronounced with an epenthetic vowel. אַחוָוה is the only noun that is pronounced without, and thus pronounced *(')axva*. It is also worth mentioning that six of these 12 nouns have a corresponding third person feminine singular past form (paᶜal), of which five are pronounced in the same way. The exception is נָחרָה 'she snores', and נַחרָה 'snoring', which was read *naxra* and *naxara* (*naḥărā*), respectively.

As for 2) there are 19 instances to be considered. Of these 19, only two are pronounced with an epenthetic vowel. Thus, גַחכָן 'jester' and בַּחרָן 'choosy' were read *gaxakhan* (*gaḥăḵān*) and *baxaran* (*baḥărān*), respectively.

When it comes to 3) there are 16 cases to be accounted for. There are eight instances of the type *-anut*, none of which exhibit anaptyxis. The two *-iyut*-forms were pronounced with an epenthetic vowel. Finally, an epenthetic vowel was inserted in three of the six nouns of the nominal type *-ut*. Thus, for *yḥs* our informant read *yaxasut* (*yaḥăsūt*) 'relativity' and *yaxasiyut* (*yaḥăsiyūt*) 'relativism', but *yaxsanut* 'arrogance'.

There are eight nouns of the type in 4), i.e. of the *-it*- or *-anit*-type. Three of the six *-it*-nouns exhibit anaptyxis, whereas none of the nouns of the *-anit*-type do.[7]

6 In one case the vowel between C_1 and C_2 was not [a], but [i]. Thus, יחפָן was pronounced *yixfan*, not *yaxfan*.

7 The fact that none of the $C_1aC_2(V)C_3anut$ and $C_1aC_2(V)C_3anit$ nouns exhibit anaptyxis may somehow be related to the rules concerning the (maximal) number of open syllables.

As for 5) there are 10 adjectives to be looked into. First, there are seven instances of the *-ani*-type, and none of them are pronounced with an epenthetic vowel. Only one of the three *-i*-adjectives exhibits anaptyxis – *yaxasi* (*yaḥăsī*) was read for יַחסי 'relative'.

In the list below we have summed up our findings for the oral ע"ח nominal forms. The numbers express the amount of epenthetic forms of the total number of forms.

(85) The oral ע"ח nominal forms

1) $C_1aC_2(v)C_3a$, e.g.,	בָּחשָׁה	*bax(a)ša*:	11 of 12;
2) $C_1aC_2(v)C_3an$, e.g.,	לַחשָׁן	*lax(a)šan*:	2 of 19;
3) $C_1aC_2(v)C_3ut$, e.g.,	יַחסוּת	*yax(a)sut*:	3 of 6;
$C_1aC_2(v)C_3ut$, *-iyut*, e.g.,	יַחסיוּת	*yax(a)siyut*:	2 of 2;
$C_1aC_2(v)C_3anut$, e.g.,	יַחסָנוּת	*yax(a)sanut*:	0 of 8;
4) $C_1aC_2(v)C_3it$, e.g.,	לַחמית	*lax(a)mit*:	3 of 6;
$C_1aC_2(v)C_3anit$, e.g.,	לַחצָנִית	*lax(a)tsanit*:	0 of 2;
5) $C_1aC_2(v)C_3i$, e.g.,	יַחסי	*yax(a)si*:	1 of 3;
$C_1aC_2(v)C_3ani$, e.g.,	יַחסָני	*yax(a)sani*:	0 of 7.

As we can see, the likelihood of epenthesis is significantly higher in nominal forms of the type $C_1aC_2(v)C_3a$, e.g., בָּחשָׁה, than in the other types we have considered. The share of epenthetic forms of the total number of nominal forms is approximately one third, but since there are clear differences between the groups, this value may be misleading.

5.4.4.4 Conclusion

A preliminary conclusion is that if sonority is a relevant parameter at all when epenthesis in ע"ח forms is concerned, it is so to a lesser extent than in פ"ח forms. In ע"ח forms one trigger of epenthesis is word class: epenthesis obtains more often in verbal forms than in nominal forms. In our corpus epenthesis obtains in two thirds of the verbal forms and one third of the nominal forms. Another trigger in verbal forms is gender:

past forms of the third person singular feminine are slightly more often involved in epenthesis than the third person plural forms are. As for nominal forms, nouns of the type $C_1aC_2(v)C_3a$ exhibit contact anaptyxis significantly more often than other types do. Interestingly, past forms of the third person singular feminine follow, or end in the same way as, the $C_1aC_2(v)C_3a$ pattern.

In order to pinpoint the exact triggers of contact anaptyxis in the ע"ח forms, further investigation is needed. But the obvious importance of the factors mentioned above can explain the fact that the consonants involved in contact anaptyxis in the ע"ח forms are spread across the whole sonority scale. Thus, it may be the case that epenthesis is triggered by different factors depending on whether the form is of the type פ"ח or ע"ח.

5.5 Acoustical analysis

5.5.1 Introduction

Having recorded our informants on iPod – with their consent – we loaded the sound-files onto a computer. At the outset our intention was to subject the forms to a quantitative analysis in terms of the morphological circumstances under which epenthetic vowels were inserted. As our project came along, however, we became curious as to how the speech could be analysed qualitatively by means of, say, spectrograms. This is how we were introduced to the PRAAT program. We started to isolate our recorded forms creating one new sound-file for each form. In the end we had more than 1400 sound-files to consider.

5.5.2 The PRAAT program

The PRAAT program is a scholarly software program developed for acoustic analysis – phonetic analysis of speech. The program is downloadable from the Internet. When sound-files are loaded onto a computer (e.g., from iPod), this tool allows for spectrograms in which one can investigate factors such as duration, frequency, spectral power, pitch, intensity, formants and pulses. We arrived at our hypothesis in this acoustical analysis against the background of forms such as the two in **(86)** and **(87)** below. Both forms are read by one and the same informant. Below the spectrograms are marked the intervals that represent *ḥ*, the following consonant, and the interval in between.

(86) נחקר *nexkar* (*neḥqār*)

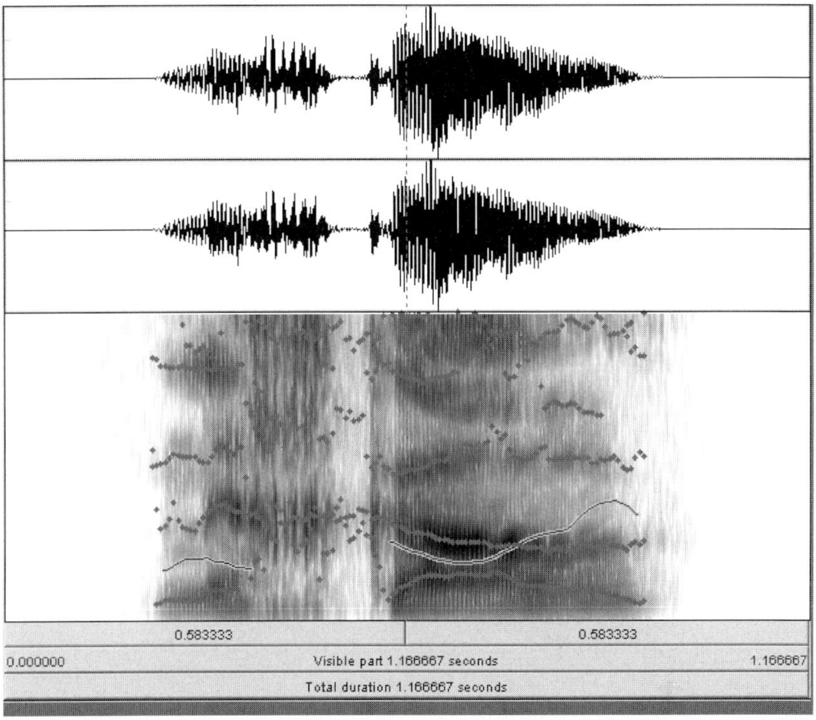

ḥ		*q*

Practically nothing can be heard or seen between *ḥ* and *q* in **(86)**, as opposed to between *ḥ* and *r* in **(87)** *ˀaḥărōn* below:

(87) אחרון *(')axaron* (*ʾaḥărōn*)

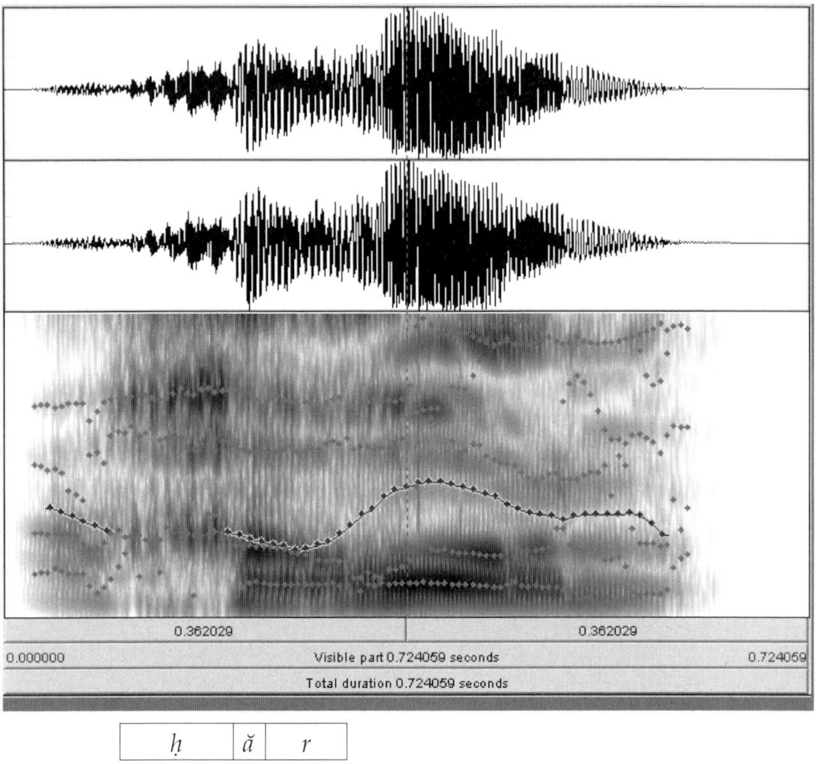

0.362029 0.362029
0.000000 Visible part 0.724059 seconds 0.724059
Total duration 0.724059 seconds

ḥ	*ă*	*r*

Whereas there is no epenthetic vowel present in *nexkar* (*neḥqār*) in **(86)**, there *is* one in *(')axaron* (*ʾaḥărōn*) in **(87)**. It is easy to see the difference. Against this background we arrived at our hypothesis.

5.5.3 Hypothesis

The higher the sonority of the consonant following *ḥ*, the longer the duration of any vowel interval between *ḥ* and this following radical.

5.5.4 Challenges

Analysing the forms and measuring the duration of the interval between *ḥ* and the following radical turned out to be a lot more complicated than expected. First, an advanced and comprehensive tool, the PRAAT program is made for phoneticians. Phonetics, however, is not our main linguistic field, and so we had to consult phoneticians and use the program with care. Second, on some occasions there was no interval between *ḥ* and the following radical at all. In, e.g., **(88)** below, *ḥ* and *r* have practically merged into one phoneme.

(88) החרפת *haxrafat* (*haḥrap̄at*)

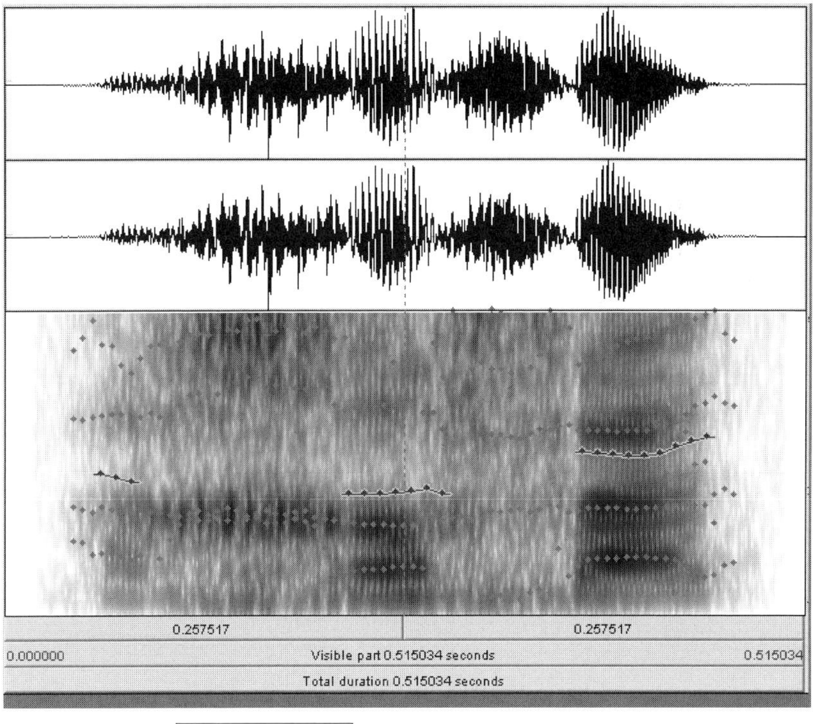

A third challenge is connected to the duration of the intervals in time. In the majority of the cases the duration of a form is not more than half a second. The duration of any interval between *ḥ* and the following consonant is only a share of this. In cases such as **(88)** above one can ask if there is any interval to measure at all.

Another challenge is connected to the fact that the PRAAT program is a phonetic tool. In David Crystal's *A Dictionary of Linguistics and Phonetics*, "sonority" is described in the following terms (p. 282):

> "Sonority (sonorous):
>
> A term in AUDITORY PHONETICS for the overall LOUDNESS of a sound relative to others of the same PITCH, STRESS and DURATION. Sounds are said to have an 'inherent sonority', which accounts for the impression of a sound's 'carrying further', e.g. [s] carries further than [ʃ], [a] further than [i]. The notion has also been used in attempts to define the SYLLABIC STRUCTURE of UTTERANCES. It is, however, very difficult to define sonority objectively, and analyses involving this notion are usually somewhat controversial."

According to this definition the sonority of a sound is the effect of several factors, and thus cannot be read straightforwardly from the spectrograms. Moreover, recent research suggests that the sonority scale is not categorical, but gradient and language-specific. For example, referring to Parker 2002, Pons Moll (2008) writes that sound sonority differences can be detected between males and females, within one sex depending on the physiology of the speakers, between different word forms pronounced by the same speaker, and differences depending on the immediately preceding and following syllable. This latter point makes it a probability that the sonority scale is language-specific. Considering this, including the fact that we are operating with very fine values, in order to arrive at meaningful statistics, far more than 12 informants and 1400 forms are needed. For example, working on *schwa* elision in French, Bürki, Fougeron, and Gendrot (2007) created a corpus of 18553 French words uttered by many different persons. In addition they used a corpus of 24h of radio broadcasted news produced by 574 different speakers.

For these reasons we will in the following confine ourselves to presenting some of our spectrograms and thus show how some of the consonants of Modern Hebrew may be expressed visually. Below the spectrograms will be marked as accurately as possible the interval of *ḥ* and the interval of the following radical. The interval between *ḥ* and the following radical will be marked if there is one. All consonants will be classified in phonological terms and presented successively from the least to the most sonorous. We will also show that there may be something to the idea of a phonetically present "*ḥăṭāp i*". Finally we will present the minimal pair להחזיק *le-haxzik* (*lə-haḥzīq*) and להכזיב *le-hakhziv* (*lə-hak̲zīb̲*) so that *ḥ* [x] and *k̲* [kh] can be compared.

Unless otherwise stated the forms are not produced by the same informant.

5.5.5 Selected examples

5.5.5.1 The complex plosive ṣ

(89) החציף *hextsif* (*heḥṣīp̄*)

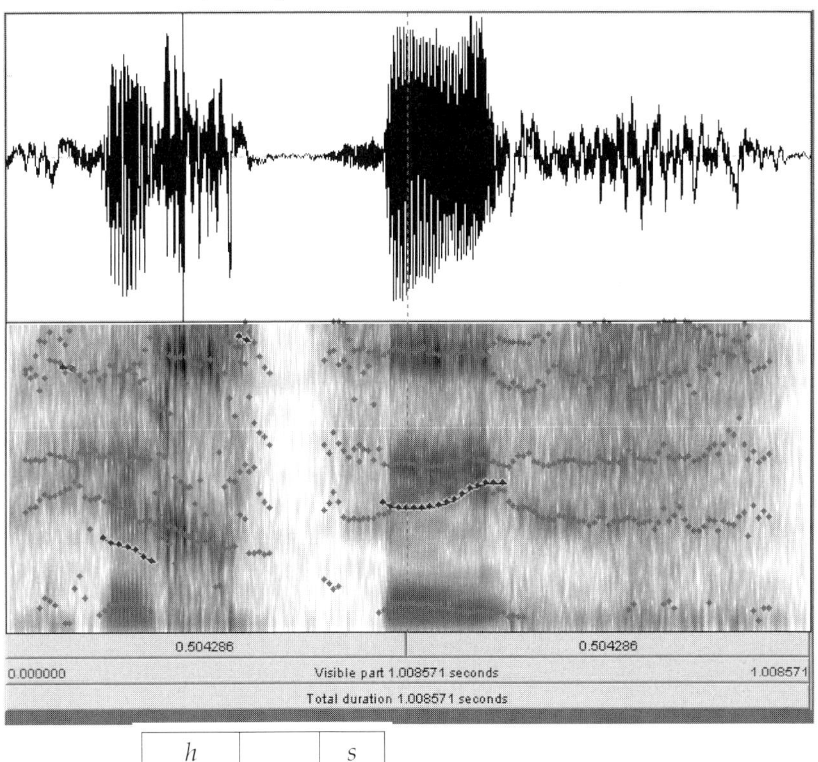

5.5.5.2 The unvoiced plosives *ṭ* and *t*

(90) לחטור *la-xtor* (*la-ḥṭōr*)

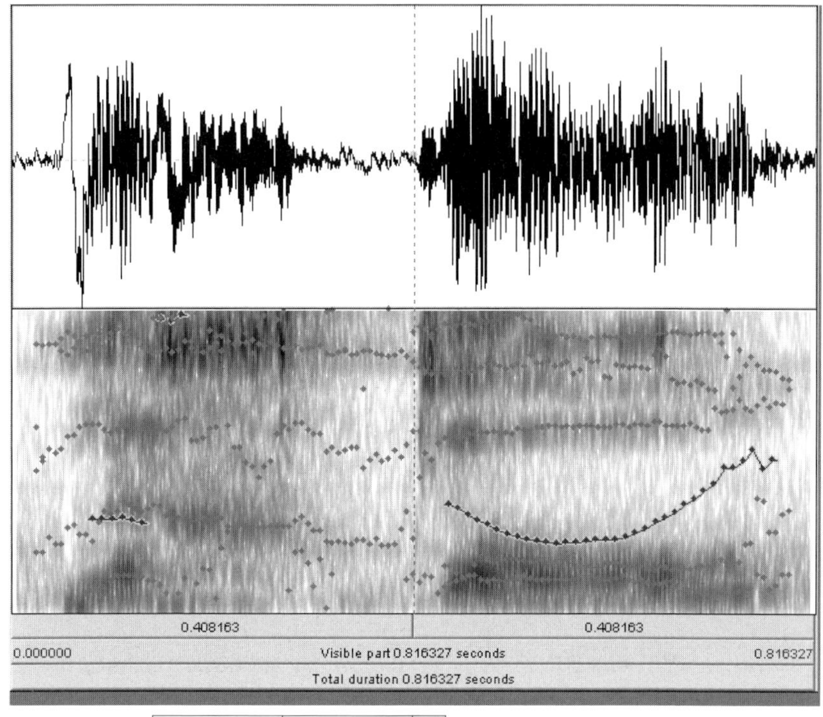

ḥ		*ṭ*

(91) לחתום *la-xtom* (*la-ḥtōm*)

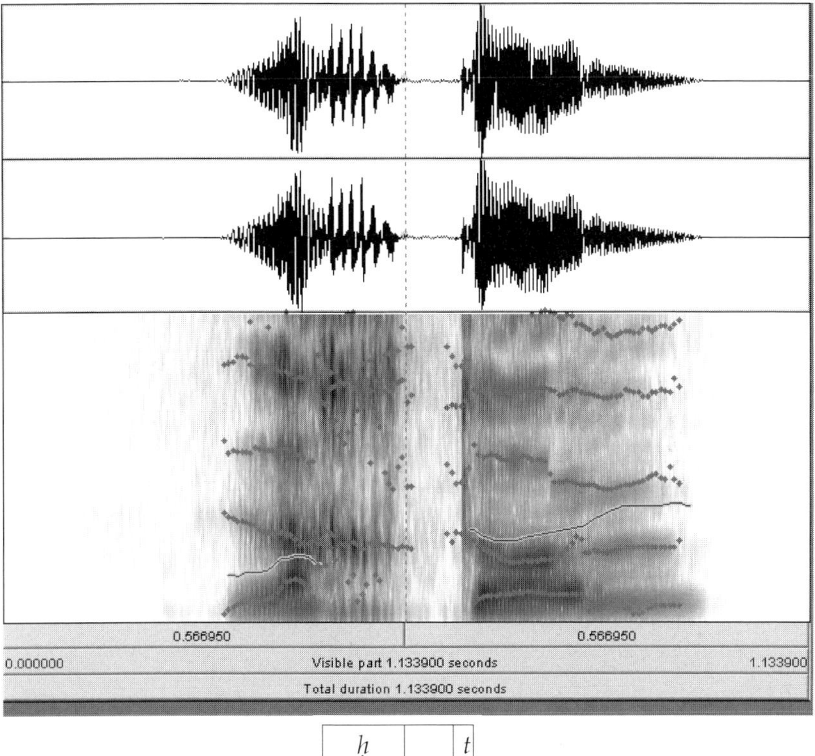

5.5.5.3 The voiced plosives *g* and *d*

An interval between *ḥ* and a voiced plosive is usually not "empty" as the interval between *ḥ* and the unvoiced plosive *q* in *nexkar* (*neḥqār*) in **(86)** and *t* in *la-xtom* (*la-ḥtōm*) in **(91)** above. When *ḥ* is followed by a voiced plosive, the interval is most often both audible and visible, and pinpointing the exact starting point and duration of the plosive is not straightforward. Consider **(92)** and **(93)** below.

(92) אחגוג *(ʾ)exgog* (*ʾeḥgōg*)

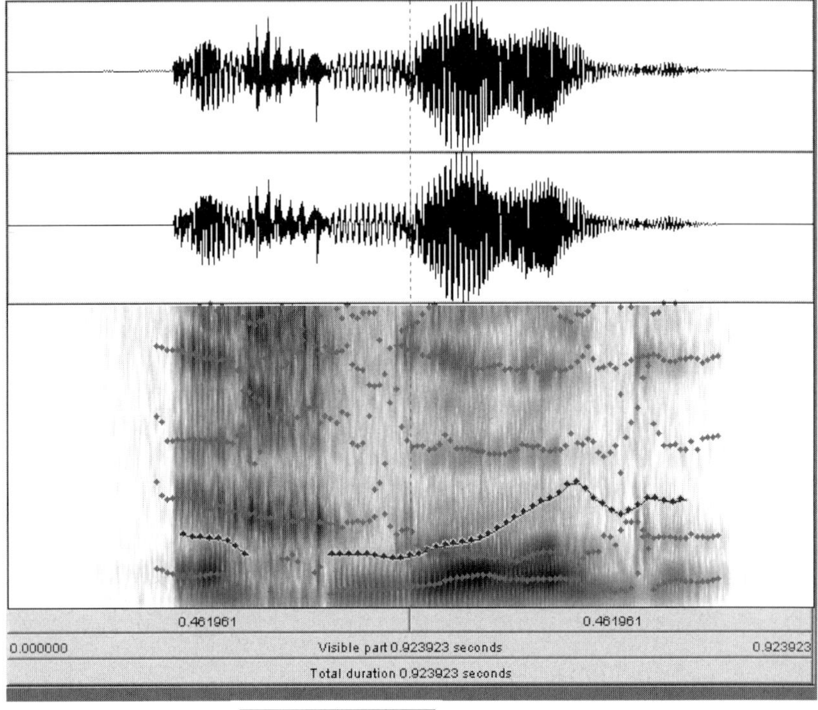

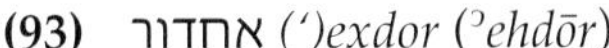

(93) אחדור *(')exdor* (*ʾeḥdōr*)

0.545952 0.545952
0.000000 Visible part 1.091905 seconds 1.091905
Total duration 1.091905 seconds

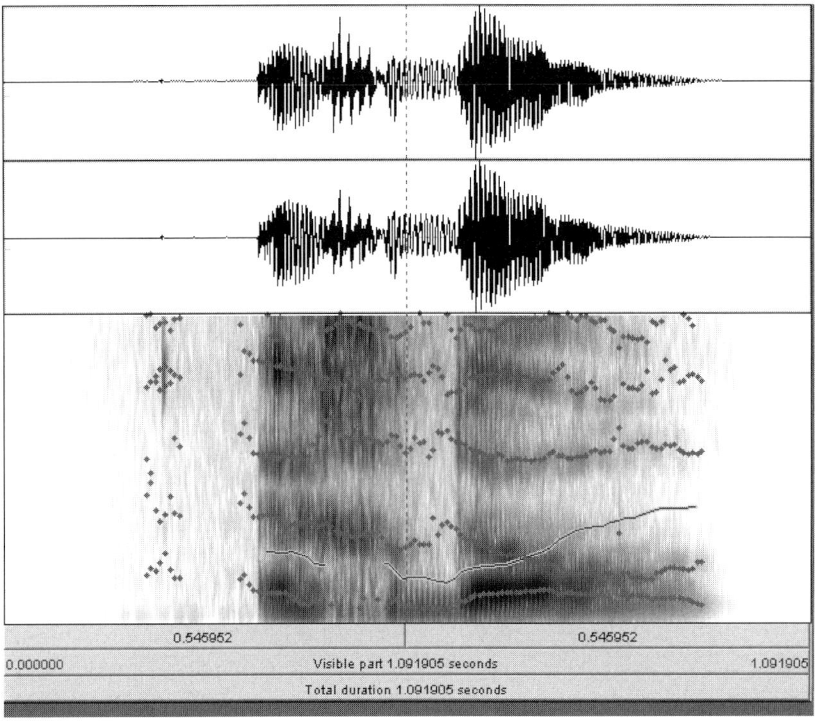

ḥ		*d*

5.5.5.4 The unvoiced fricatives *s*, *ś*, and *p̄*

(94) לחסוך *la-xsokh* (*la-ḥsōḵ*)

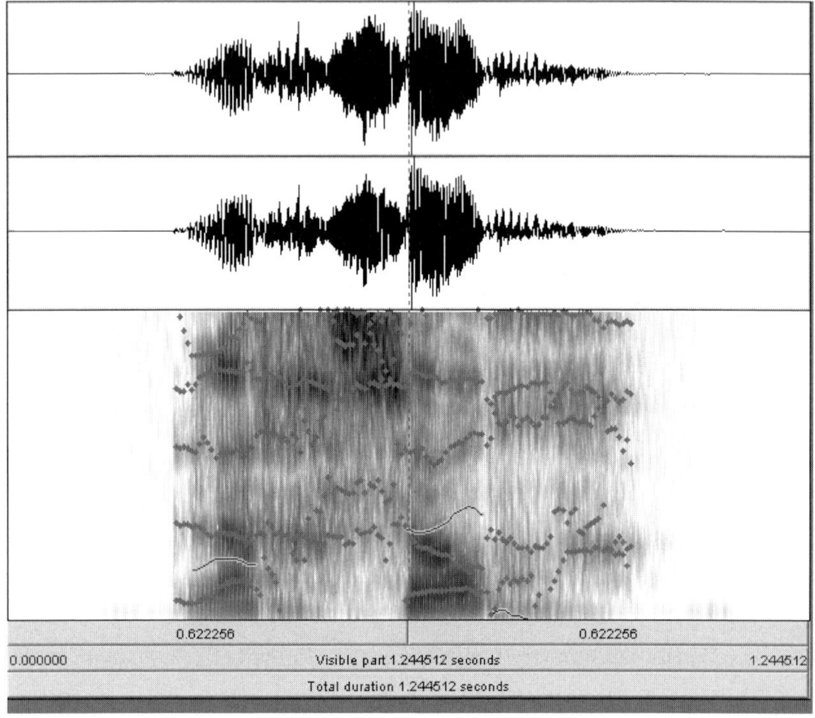

ḥ	*s*

(95) לחשׁוף *la-xsof* (*la-ḥśōp̄*)

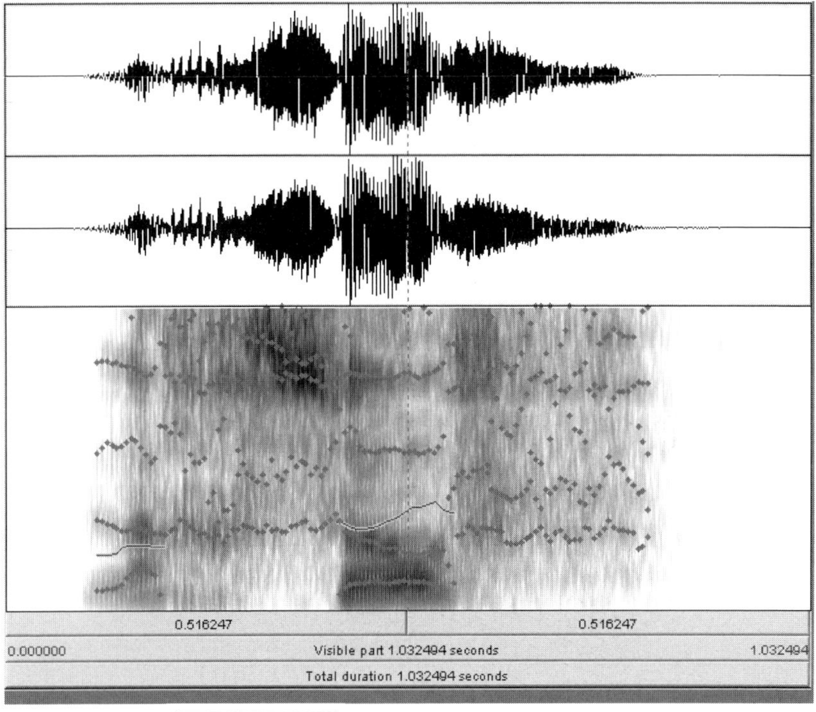

ḥ	*ś*

(96) לחפור *la-xfor* (*la-ḥp̄ōr*)

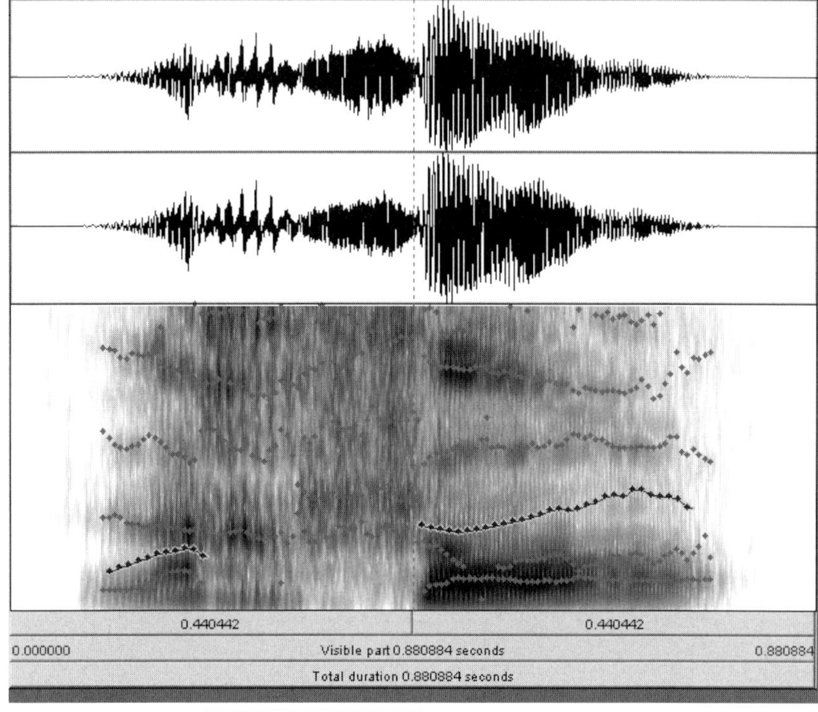

ḥ	*p̄*

5.5.5.5 The voiced fricatives *w* and *z*

(97) יחויר *yaxvir* (*yaḥwīr*)

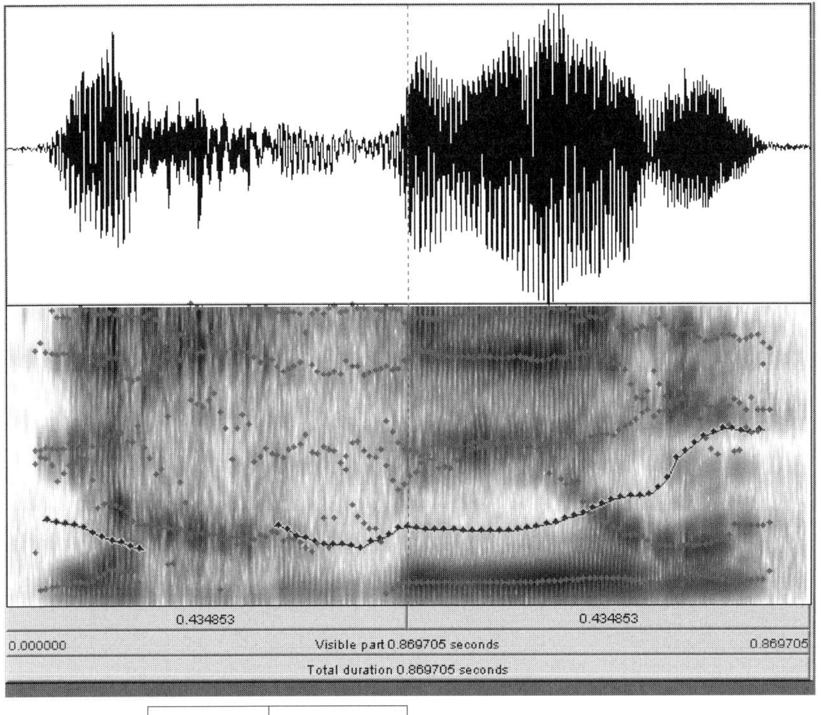

ḥ	*w*

(98) לחזוק *la-xzok* (*la-ḥzōq*)

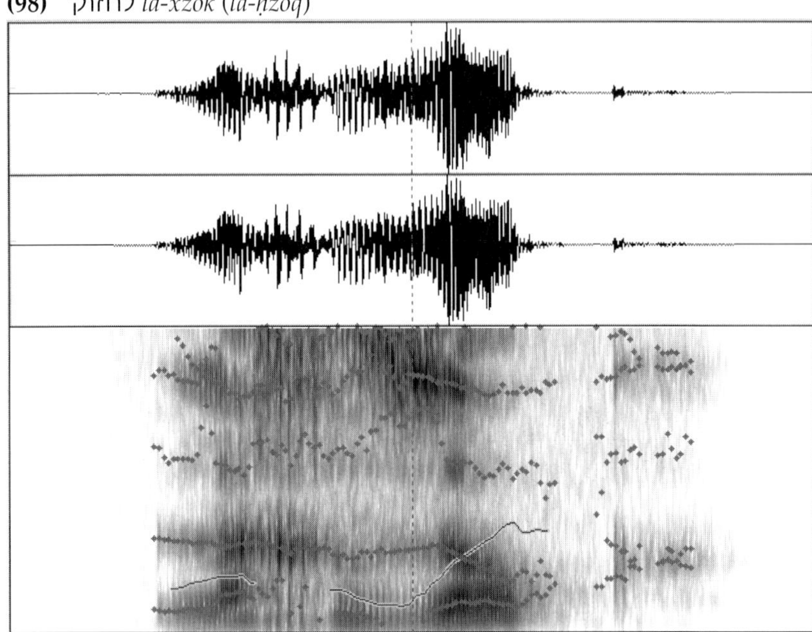

ḥ		*z*

5.5.5.6 The nasals *m* and *n*

(99) החמרה *haxmara* (*haḥmārā*)

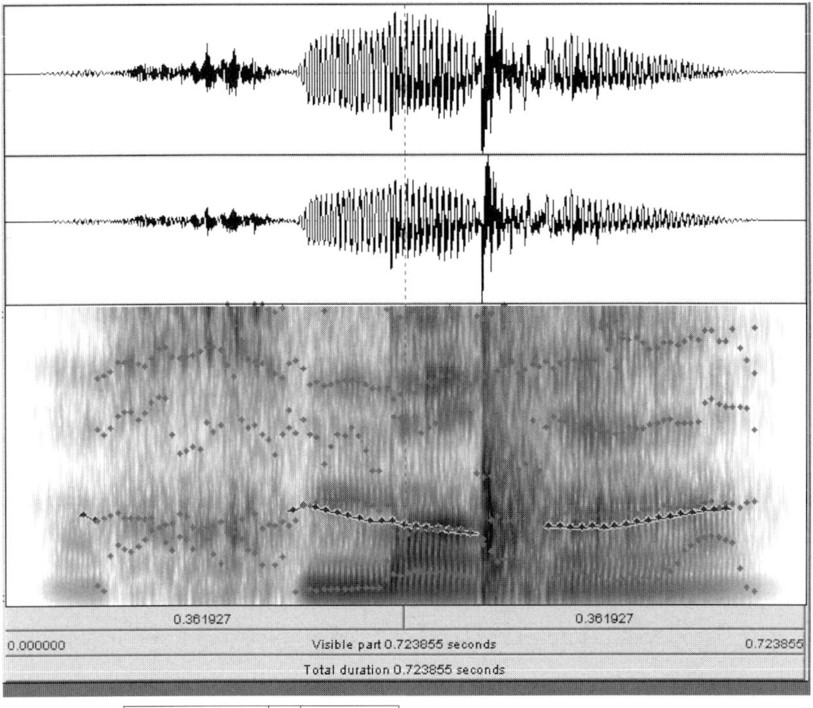

(100) יחנוך *yaxnokh* (*yaḥnōḵ*)

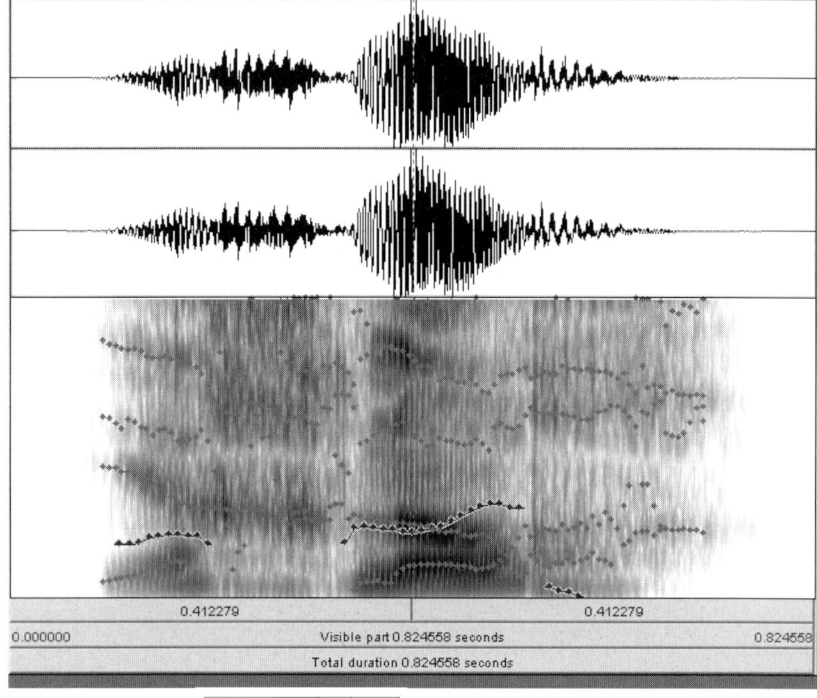

ḥ		*n*

5.5.5.7 The lateral liquid *l*

(101) לחלום *la-xlom* (*la-ḥlōm*)

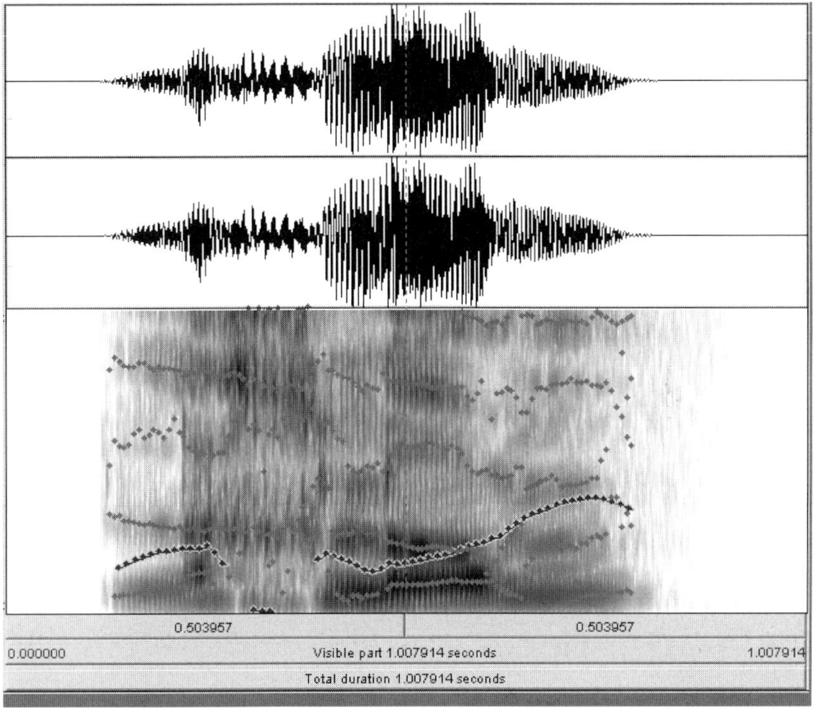

ḥ	*l*

5.5.5.8 The glide *y*

(102) מחיה *mixyu* (*miḥyā*)

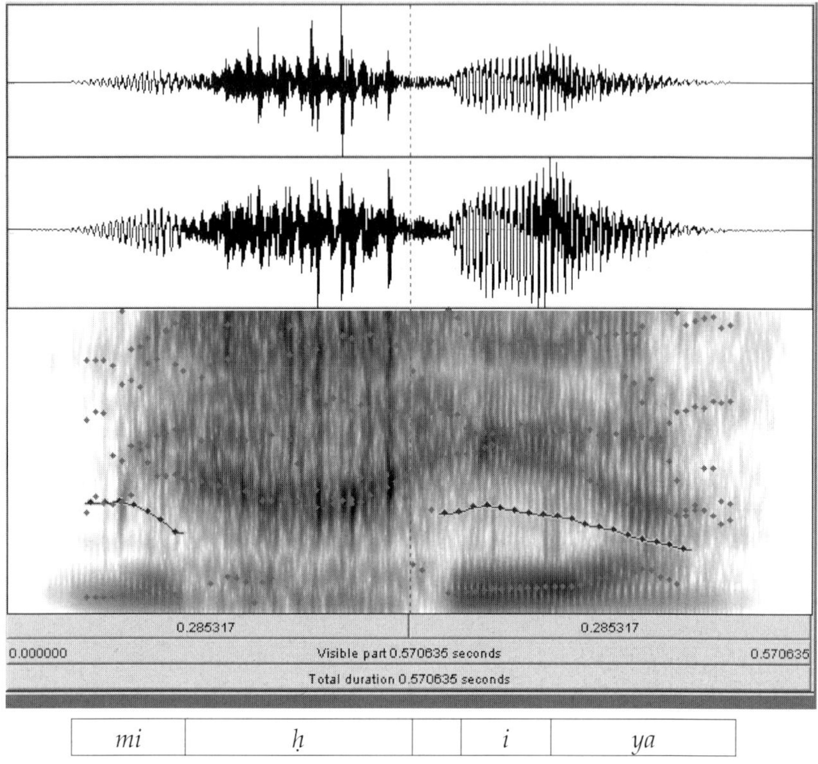

In this case an epenthetic *i* is both audible and visible. Thus, there may be something to the idea mentioned in section 4.1.2.10 above of a phonetically present "*ḥăṭāp̄ i*", but this point needs further investigation.

5.5.5.9 A minimal pair: *ḥ* vs. *ḵ*

In the two examples below can be compared Modern Hebrew *ḥ* and *ḵ*. Both forms are produced by the same informant.

(103) להחזיק *le-haxzik* (*lə-haḥzīq*)

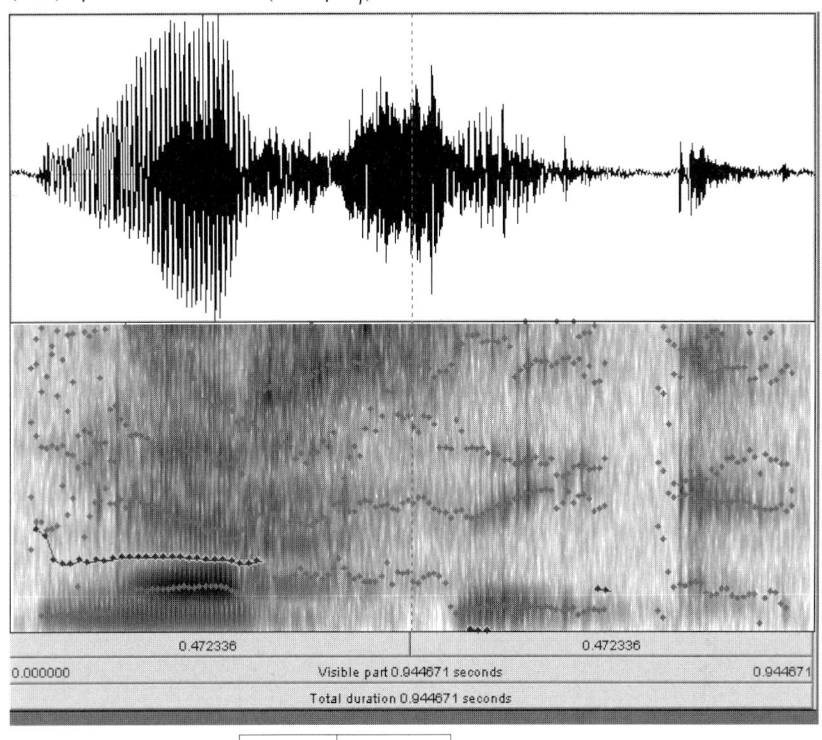

(104) להכזיב *le-hakhziv* (*lə-hak̲zīb̲*)

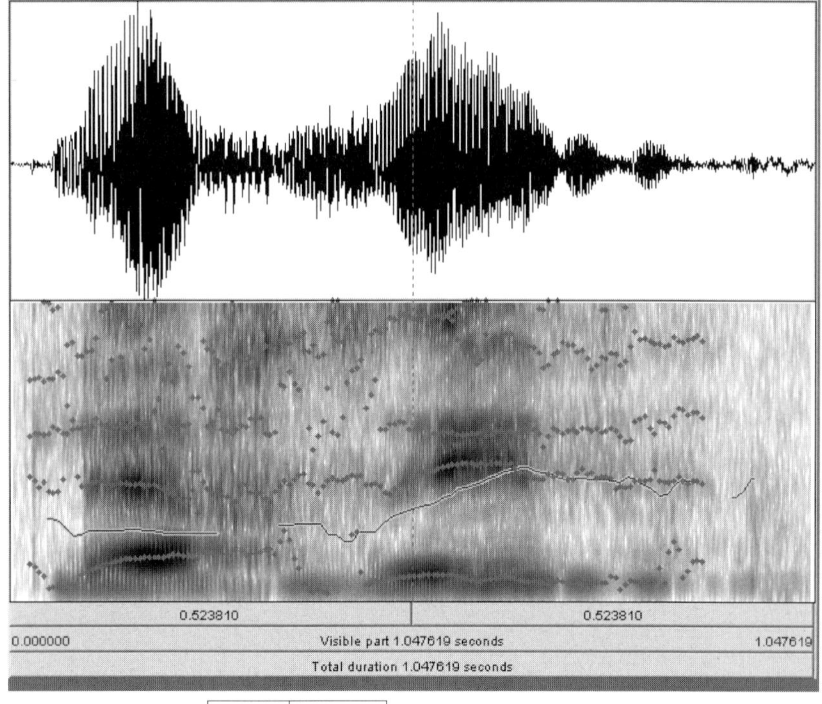

k̲	*z*

5.6 Summary and conclusions

In this chapter we have provided an idea as regards the extent to which spoken Hebrew conforms to the norm when it comes to epenthesis in פ"ח forms in particular, but also in ע"ח forms. Even though our corpus consists of more than 1600 verbal and nominal forms produced by 12 informants it is far from comprehensive enough for us to give meaningful overall statistics. The tendency, though, is that epenthetic vowels are inserted far more seldom in spoken Hebrew than in the norm as appears from four dictionaries of Modern Hebrew.

As regards פ"ח forms, which comprise the majority of the forms in our corpus, our findings suggest that epenthesis is triggered by the same factors as in Biblical Hebrew – except shift of accent forward due to enclitic elements or cantillation phenomena – and dictionaries of Modern Hebrew: the sonority of the second radical, and the presence of a final weak radical.

As for the ע"ח forms, of which there are approximately 300 in our corpus, epenthesis seems to be triggered by other factors, such as word class, since verbal forms exhibit epenthesis significantly more often than nominal forms. A trigger in past forms seems to be feminine gender, which corresponds to the fact that nouns of the type $C_1aC_2(v)C_3a$ exhibit epenthesis significantly more often than other nouns investigated.

When it comes to the phonetic features of *ḥ*, further investigation is needed.

6 Optimality-Theoretic analysis

6.1 Central tenets of Optimality Theory

Many phonetic and phonological observations can be conveniently recast in terms of theories of linguistic preference and natural generative phonology (cf. Hooper 1976), notably in terms of the approach of Vennemann (1983, 1988).[1] Optimality Theory, originally proposed by Prince and Smolensky (1993), offers a formal means to capture the "constraint ranking" that is implicit in the rejection of disallowed forms and the evaluation of competing forms ("candidates") of linguistic surface forms. While Optimality Theory nowadays also witnesses meaningful applications to other realms of grammar, notably syntax, it continues to be most prominent as an explanatory device for linguistic features at the interface of phonology and morphology. Recent linguistic theory has paid much attention to the phonotactics of Arabic dialects, Biblical and Modern Israeli Hebrew, and other Semitic and Afroasiatic languages (notably Ethio-Semitic), especially varieties of Berber.

In Optimality Theory, the set of forms that may reasonably be assumed to be potential surface forms is often referred to as the "richness of the base". One can, in principle, use the same term in reference to the availability of simultaneously occurring forms, some of which may be true alternatives and some of which may be regional variants. The co-occurring forms, or rather the forms that are subject to linguistic evaluation, are called "candidates".

One other central concept in Optimality Theory and elsewhere in linguistic theory is markedness. Broadly speaking, "marked" refers to unusual, rarer, and/or harder-to-pronounce forms, whereas "unmarked" refers to natural, more frequent, and/or easier-to-pronounce forms. The latter state is often called "wellformedness". On the segmental level, for example, velarised stops are considered "marked", whereas plain (non-velarised) stops are considered "unmarked". On the suprasegmen-

1 An attempt to apply this concept to Semitic was made in Edzard 1991. The relevance of the sonority scale for the analysis of morpho-phonological phenomena had, of course, been recognised much earlier (cf., for instance, Speiser 1926).

tal level, for example, the universally "unmarked" syllable structure is CV: onset, nucleus, and no coda; other syllable structures (CVC, CVCC, CCVCC, etc.) are then considered "marked". And even within one and the same syllable type, there may be more or less marked specimens of different quality, depending on the sonority of syllable onset and syllable coda.

Optimality Theory, which always aims at singling out *one* "optimal" form, has the potential to evaluate at least the following morphophonological parameters (cf. McCarthy & Prince 1994: 2):[2] (i) segmental harmony (unmarkedness, itself consisting of various dimensions, some conflicting); (ii) syllabic harmony (having an onset, lacking a coda); (iii) faithfulness (identity between input and output); (iv) alignment (coincidence of edges of morphological and phonological constituents); (v) metrical parsing (satisfying constraints on exhaustivity and alignment of metrical feet); (vi) template satisfaction (meeting shape or constituency requirements imposed on the reduplicated string); (vii) exactness of copying relation; and (viii) identity between the reduplicated string and the base to which it is attached.

While the references to segmental harmony and syllabic harmony are quite straightforward and unproblematic, the reference to faithfulness is interesting insofar as the concept of "underlying representation", i.e., the "input", which Optimality Theory purports to discard, is reintroduced, so to speak, via the backdoor.

It is important to note that in most cases, not all of these parameters can be optimised in any given form. The principle underlying this circumstance is often called the "fallacy of perfection" (cf. also Vennemann 1988: 1f.). For instance, words that are entirely made up of CV syllables – this being the "optimal" syllable structure – may turn out to be lengthy or otherwise clumsy to pronounce.

One can narrow down Optimality Theory to five basic tenets (cf. McCarthy and Prince 1994: 3): (i) universality: U[niversal] G[rammar] provides a set {Con} of constraints that are universal and universally present in all grammars; (ii) violability: constraints are violable; but violation is minimal; (iii) ranking: The constraints of {Con} are ranked on a

2 References are to the e-version (ROA #13-0594).

language-particular basis; the notion of minimal violation is defined in terms of this ranking. A grammar is a ranking of the constraint set; (iv) inclusiveness: the constraint hierarchy evaluates a set of candidate analyses that are admitted by very general considerations of structural well-formedness; (v) parallelism: best-satisfaction of the constraint hierarchy is computed over the whole hierarchy and the whole candidate set. There is no serial derivation. McCarthy and Prince (1994: 4f.) conclude: "The construction of a grammar in Optimality Theory is essentially a matter of determining the proper ranking of the set of constraints {Con}, and to that end the *constraint tableau* is a useful calculational device. A typical constraint tableau, showing the domination of constraint B by constraint A, is the following [our numbering]:

(105) Example of a Constraint Tableau, A >> B

Candidates		A	B
a. **:)**	$cand_1$		*
b.	$cand_2$	* !	

In this tableau, constraints A and B disagree on the two candidates $cand_1$ and $cand_2$, and since the A-obeying $cand_1$ is optimal, constraint A must dominate constraint B. In this and other tableaux, constraints are shown in domination order and violation-marks are indicated by "*". The optimal candidate is called out [in our representation] by a "smiley" ("**:)**"), and fatal constraint violations are signaled by "!". Below these fatal violations, cells are shaded to indicate their irrelevance to determining the outcome of the comparison at hand."

Preservation of faithfulness and preservation of markedness are the two basic competing constraints at the heart of Optimality Theory. Then there are many other language-specific constraints that determine the morpho-phonological "fine-tuning" in the language under observation. While constraints as such are supposed to be universal, their ordering is usually language-specific.

For an in-depth introduction to Optimality Theory interested parties can turn to Kager 1999 and McCarthy 2002. McCarthy (ed.) 2004 is a reader covering the areas of prosody, segmental phonology, and interfaces between various levels of grammar. The Rutgers Optimality Archive (http://roa.rutgers.edu/index.php3.) is an excellent resource for pdf versions of papers in the OT framework. The OT archive can also be searched specifically for languages: as of this writing (autumn 2008), a search yields thirteen papers dealing (inter alia) with Arabic, ten dealing with Modern Hebrew, and one dealing with Berber and Cushitic data (Ethio-Semitic is also attested).

6.2 Applications

6.2.1 Semitic and Afro-Asiatic at large

Let us start with an example from the broader frame of Afro-Asiatic. Alderete (1997) analyses dissimilation phenomena in the Cushitic language Oromo and in Tashlhiyt Berber, among other languages. As a result of a cooccurrence restriction in the latter variety of Berber, which rules out more than one labial in a word, derivational *m*-prefixes are dissimilated (or delabialised) in front of a root already containing a labial (/b, f, m/) (cf. also Edzard 1992 for related processes in Akkadian and Ethio-Semitic). Again, we are looking at two competing constraints:

*PL/LAB$^2_{\text{Stem}}$: Ban any stem with two segments with independent Place specification [labial];

IDENT[PLACE]: Corresponding segments in input and output agree in [space] specification.

Tableau **(106)**, using the reflexive form *nkaddab* 'considered a liar', captures the intrinsic hierarchy of these two constraints, i.e. the circumstance that *PL/LAB$^2_{\text{Stem}}$ dominates IDENT[PLACE]:

(106) Constraint Tableau for delabialisation as a result of dissimilation

Input: m-kaddab	*PL/LAB$^2_{\text{Stem}}$	IDENT[PLACE]
a. :) [n-kaddab]$_{\text{Stem}}$		*
b. [m-kaddab]$_{\text{Stem}}$	*!	

6.2.2 Applications to Arabic dialectology

A highly prominent issue in cyclic phonology, which now also has witnessed an OT treatment, concerns the "underapplication" of syncope in Levantine Arabic dialects, in which minimal pairs such as *fhímna* 'we understood' (Standard Arabic *fahimnā*) vs. *fihímna* 'he understood us' (Standard Arabic *fahima-nā*) arise – in both cases /fihimna/ is considered to be the "underlying representation" or "input". Precisely this minimal pair has also caught the attention of scholars working in the framework of Optimality Theory (cf. Kenstowicz 1996, Kager 1999: 278–293, and Kiparsky 2003: 162–163). Let us first consider a traditional derivation of these forms in terms of a cyclical analysis ("extrinsic rule ordering"), which shows the interaction of stress assignment and vowel syncope viz. the blocking of the latter in the base in front of the object (accusative) suffix (cf. Kager 1999: 281):

(107) Cyclic derivation of mutually opposing surface forms

		we understood	he understood us
Input		$[\text{fihim-na}]_{\text{Subj}}$	$[[\text{fihim-}]\text{na}]_{\text{Acc}}$
	Cycle 1		
Stress		fihím-na	fíhim
	Cycle 2		
Stress		—	fihím-na
Post-cyclic			
	i-Syncope	fhím-na	*application blocked*
	Destressing	*not applicable*	fihím-na
Output		fhímna	fihímna

Within the framework of Optimality Theory, which avoids derivations (and hence intermediary representations) is it possible to capture the emergence of the different output forms by claiming that the unstressed vowel [i] in a verb form with object suffix is protected from deletion if the base of the verb form (without the object suffix) is indeed stressed, as is the case with *fíhim* 'he understood'. (The same holds *mutatis mutandis* for nouns with possessive suffixes.) Technically, this constraint can be formulated as follows:

HEADMAX-BA: Every segment in the prosodic head of the base [i.e., in this case, the first syllable of the word ("base") *fihim*] has a correspondent in the affixed form:

[f i . h i m]
  | |
[[f i . h i m] n a]

The other two necessary constraints in this context are:

NO [i]: /i/ is not allowed in light [open, unstressed] syllables;

MAX-IO: Every segment in the input has a correspondent in the output.

NO [i] is ranked higher (and thus represent more leftward in the tableau) than MAX-IO, since vowel deletion in forms such as *fhímna* occurs at the expense of the constraint MAX-IO. In turn, HEADMAX-BA is ranked higher than NO [i], since vowel deletion is blocked, i.e. i-syncope is "underapplied", whenever the base identity constraint is relevant, as in *fihímna*.

Let us now consider the interaction of these three constraints in the following two tableaux:

(108) Constraint Tableau for *fhímna* 'we understood'

Input: fihim-na/ Base: none	HEADMAX-BA	NO [i]	MAX-IO
a. [fi.hím.na]		*!	
b. :) [fhímna]			*

(109) Constraint Tableau for *fihímna* 'he understood us'

Input: fihim-na/ Base: [fi.him]	HEADMAX-BA	NO [i]	MAX-IO
a. :) [fi.hím.na]		*	
b. [fhímna]	*!		*

In the case of **(108)**, the constraint NO [i] "outranks" the faithfulness constraint requiring that input segments have correspondents in the output. Therefore the candidate [fi.hím.na] incurs a fatal violation. The constraint HEADMAX-BA does not apply in this case, as there is no base. In the case of **(109)**, where there *is* a base ([fi.him]), it is the candidate [fhímna] that incurs a fatal violation, since the highest ranking constraint HEADMAX-BA is not upheld.

Kiparsky (2003: 162f.) deals with the same minimal pair based on his constraint-based elaboration of Lexical Phonology and Morphology and presents pertinent constraint tableaux for the lexical (as opposed to the post-lexical) level of these output forms.

6.2.3 Applications to Tiberian Hebrew and Modern Israeli Hebrew

Bat-El (1996) investigated the functioning of Hebrew blends in terms of OT. Among many other examples, she illustrates the interaction of two constraints when it comes to the formation of bi-syllabic compounds consisting of a noun and an adjective (1996: 302f.). Whereas the canonical pattern follows the natural sequence noun-adjective, e.g., חידק *xaydak* 'bacterium' ("s.th. alive-thin"), the order noun-adjective is reversed in case a disfavoured syllable contact would emerge between the two constituents. Thus, the word for 'loudspeaker' is רמקול *ramkol* ("high-voice""), not *קולרם **kolram*, since the syllable contact "m$k"[3] (falling sonority) is preferred over "l$r" (more or less equal sonority). Formally, this phenomenon can be captured with the following two constraints:

SYLLCONT: The onset of a syllable must be less sonorous than the last segment in the immediately preceding syllable, and the greater the slope in sonority the better.

LINEARITY IO: The sequence of the constituents must follow the unmarked syntactic order (here: noun-adjective).

In the case of *xaydak*, which constitutes a "perfect" form, there is no problem: no constraints are violated. In the case of *ramkol*, however, the

3 As in earlier chapters, "$" marks the syllable boundary (following Vennemann 1988).

interaction of the competing constraints becomes obvious, with the constraint SYLLCONT taking precedence over the constraint LINEARITY IO. The following two tableaux illustrate the evaluation of the respective candidates (with SYLLCONT >> LINEARITY IO):

(110) Constraint Tableau for *xaydak* 'bacterium'

Candidates		SYLLCONT	LINEARITY IO
a. :)	xaydak		
b.	dakxay	* !	*

(111) Constraint Tableau for *ramkol* 'loudspeaker'

Candidates		SYLLCONT	LINEARITY IO
a.	kolram	* !	
b. :)	ramkol		*

A number of recent papers (e.g., Graf 2000, Graf and Ussishkin 2002) analyse stress assignment and nominal reduplication in Modern Hebrew. Adam (2002) analyses, *inter alia*, patterns of spirantisation in Modern Hebrew

In a recent paper, Bat-El analyses morphologically conditioned V – Ø alternation in different registers of Modern Israeli Hebrew. Among other issues, she pays close attention to the concept of the "minimal word" in connection with the verbal paradigm. More specifically, she attempts to account for the different vowel structures in the third person singular m. and f. of the suffix conjugation (disregarding roots *mediae gutturalis*), e.g., זרק *zarak* 'he threw' vs. זרקה *zarka* 'she threw', in a strictly synchronic way. The relevant constraints in this context are the following (Bat-El 2008: 49f.):

Same vowel structure (MAXV^{oo}): no difference in the vowel structure of the two output forms under consideration.

Faithful Syllable Number (FAITHσNO): words in a paradigm sharing the same stem have an identical number of syllables.

No complex sub-syllabic constituent (*COMPLEX): here the prohibition of complex onsets.

As one can see, **FAITHσNO** dominates **MAXV^{oo}**, since maintaining the number of syllables in the two output forms is more important than sticking to the same vowel structure, reflecting the circumstance that Hebrew disfavours sequences of open syllables. In turn, **FAITHσNO** is dominated by the constraint ***COMPLEX**, which selects the optimal output form *zarka*, which does not feature a complex onset.

(112) Constraint Tableau for *zarka* 'she threw'

/zarák/	*COMPLEX	FAITHσNO	MAXV^{oo}
a. [zarak-a]		* !	*
b. [zrak-a]	* !		*
c. :) [zark-a]			*

Furthermore, Bat-El develops the concept of "co-phonologies". It turns out that Hebrew constraint ranking is often dependent on the respective category of a word. Below, we will see, for instance, that participles lexicalised as nouns and certain nouns *tertiae infirmae*, which morphologically overlap with participles, may behave differently than true participles.

Bat-El's (2008: 51) example is the following: The adjective קטן *katan* 'small' (m. sg.), for instance, synchronically features the same vowel distribution and syllable structure as the verb זרק *zarak* 'he threw', yet the feminine singular form turns out to be *ktana*, and not **katna*. Co-phonologies are then set up to account for a different constraint ranking which guarantees the selection of the correct output form. While the abovementioned constraints are still relevant, an additional constraint is needed in order to account for the maintenance of the vowel in the stressed syllable of the matrix form *katán*:

MAX´V^{oo}: prohibition of alternation of a stressed vowel.

The correct feminine singular form emerges then in the following tableau:

(113) Constraint Tableau for *ktana* 'small (f. sg.)'

/katán/		FAITHσNO	MAX´V°°	*COMPLEX	MAXV°°
a.	[katan-a]	* !			
b.	[katn-a]		* ! (á)		*
c. :)	[ktan-a]			*	*

Obviously, the constraint *COMPLEX is ranked lower here, dominated both by the constraint which guarantees the preservation of the stressed vowel in the matrix form and the yet stronger constraint FAITHσNO.[4]

6.3 Analysis of the Masoretic (and Masora-based) data

6.3.1 The constraints / parameters

We will now try to recast the foregoing observations on the Hebrew פ"ח forms in an Optimality-Theoretic framework. At this point, we will treat the Biblical (Masoretic) data and the data that still reflect a "normative-Masoretic" voweling. In this context we will only take "realistic" candidates into consideration. Except for illustration in the first two tableaux, **(115)** and **(116)**, we will not consider hypothetical candidates which have not undergone vowel lowering before /ḥ/, except, of course, the highly marked form יִחְיֶה *yiḥyē* and related forms.

At least the following parameters or constraints appear to be instrumental in this context, arranged here in ascending order from basic to most important (some constraints are conceptually oriented at the inventory provided in Kager 1999: 451f.):

1. LOWERING IO-Pref (the output correspondent of an input vowel in the prefix must be [–high]"): This is the weakest constraint in our Optimality-Theoretic analysis, which stands in direct competition only with "**7.**" (**HARMONY IO-/i/**) in case of the surface form יִחְיֶה *yiḥyē* and related forms, where **LOWERING IO-Pref** is violated (cf. section 4.1.2.10 above).

4 For a traditional treatment of pretonic and antepretonic vowel deletion, cf. Bolozky 1997: 296f.

2. DEP IO (output segments must have input correspondents): This second basic parameter, whose classic application is to outrule epenthetic segments, stipulates that the output forms may not feature any addition to the (synchronic) input form. As only epenthetic *ḥăṭāp̄* vowels play a role in our context, this constraint practically (but, of course, not in principle) stipulates that the number of adjacent light CV syllables be minimal, a principle of great significance in many Semitic languages, notably Akkadian and varieties of Aramaic and modern Arabic. As the guttural /ḥ/ often triggers an epenthetic *ḥăṭap̄ pattāḥ*, *ḥăṭap̄ sẹ̄gōl*, or *ḥăṭap̄ qāmāṣ*, this constraint is regularly violated. In case of a strong C_2 (low sonority), this constraint plays hand in hand with the following constraint "**3a**" (***ḥv̆$^{\$}C_2$[–son]**) ,which also disfavours sequences of CV-syllables.

3. The next group of two parameters is supposed to formally capture the condition for a favourable syllable contact (slope), in tune with the relevant preferance law (cf. again Vennemann 1988: 40). As summarised in section 4.1.3.3.6 above, the sonority scale is not the only factor in determining the optimal output forms (epenthetic *ḥăṭāp̄* or not). Rather, taking all factors into consideration, we came up with the following overall hierarchy, as far as the chances for the insertion of a *ḥăṭāp̄* stand:

(114) Epenthesis hierarchy recapitulated
w, *y* > *l*, *n* > *z*, *r* > *b* (*ḇ*) > *ṭ* > *ś* > *ṣ* > *g*, *š* > *s* > *d*, *k*, *m*, *p*, *q*, *t*

Grosso modo, one could calculate the conditions for a favourable syllable contact as follows:[5] No epenthetic *ḥăṭāp̄*, iff CS (C_2) - CS (C_1 = /ḥ/) ≥ 0 (cf. items **(31)** and **(43)** in sections 3.1.2 and 4.1.2.1), with |ḥ| = 5, but, as already stated, /ṭ/ and /ś/ "behave" more sonorously and /m/ less sonorously as expected, when it comes to the decision on epenthesis.[6] As a constraint technically may not include a condition ("iff"), we therefore suggest the following two constraints (the first of which is a corollary to "**2.**" (**DEP IO**):

5 Examples of calculatory devices for the articulatory slope in a given syllable contact include Bat-El 1996: 303 and Gouskova 2004: 211.

6 For /ṭ/ and /ś/, this has probably historical reasons (voiced and voiced-lateral quality, respectively), for /m/ phonetic reasons (oral cavity).

3a. ***ḥv̆$^{\$}C_2$[–son]** (no syllable contact ḥv̆$^{\$}C_2$[–son]), with C$_2$[–son] ∈ {*ṣ, g, š, m, s, q, d, k, p, t*}[7] and

3b. ***ḥ$^{\$}C_2$[+son]** (no syllable contact ḥ$^{\$}C_2$[+son] – with /ḥ/ as coda of an *unstressed* syllable), with C$_2$[+son] ∈ {*w, y, l, n, z, r, ḇ, ṭ, ś, ṣ, g*}.

As implied above, parameter "**3a.**" colludes with the constraint "**DEP IO**", and stipulates that a sufficiently great difference (≥ 0) between the consonantal strength of C$_2$ and the consonantal strength of /ḥ/ tends to block the insertion of a *ḥăṭāp̄*.

4. RESSPIR (keep [ḇ, ḡ] spirantised; lexicalised feature for C$_2$ ∈ {b, g}): This is an even stronger parameter, which accounts for the circumstance that /b/with certain verbs (roots *ḥbl, ḥbq, ḥbš*) and /g/ in one case (root *ḥgr*) may have been lexicalised in the form of their spirantised variants [ḇ] and [ḡ] at an early stage (assuming the spirantisation pattern in the suffix conjugation as underlying). The Masoretes, not having been aware of this, may in certain cases have introduced a "secondary" *ḥăṭāp̄ pattāḥ* in order to account for the spirantisation in accordance with the *bgdkpt*-rules (cf. section 4.1.2.3 above). Alternatively, one could try here to formalise free variation in terms of "co-phonologies", as becomes necessary, for instance, with the two sets of parallel forms תַּחְבֹּל *taḥbōl* (Ex 22:25) and תַחֲבֹל *taḥăḇōl* (Dt 24:17) on the one hand, and יֶחֶזְקוּ *yeḥzĕqū* (Is 28:22) and יֶחֶזְקוּ *yeḥezqū* (2 Sam 10:11) on the other hand. The difference between these and other pairs can probably not be explained by recourse to prosodic parameters. Technically, the two output forms can be achieved by re-arranging the constraint order (cf. Anttila 1995 and Kager 1999: 404–407).

5. ***ḥ$^{\$}C_2$v̄#** (no ל"ה form – C$_3$ = w/y – without epenthetic *ḥăṭāp̄*): Verbs and nouns of the ל"ה type (*tertiae infirmae*) have a higher tendency to insert a *ḥăṭāp̄* as compared with strong verbs and nouns (with the same C$_2$). This constraint formally captures the likely compensation for the "missing" mora in the last open syllable – again assuming neutral vowel length – of the relevant verbal and nominal forms by an additional mora

7 Obviously, there is some overlap (depending on additional factors) with {*ṣ, g*} in "**3b.**". Also, /m/ is, of course, not [–son], but nevertheless belongs to the set of phonemes, before which *ḥăṭāp̄* vowels never appear (with one exception).

on /ḥ/, as compared with the corresponding strong verb forms (cf. sections 4.2.2.4 and 4.1.3.3.3 above).

6. The next group of three parameters reflects prosodic effects, which can override all the previous constraints. As we have shown above (sections 4.1.2.9 and 4.1.3.3.5), distancing of the main accent through a plural ending or a postclitic element (typically direct or indirect object) tends to trigger epenthetic *ḥăṭāp̄* vowels, even when C_2 is of high consonantal strength, as /q/ in יַחֲקָר־זֹאת *yaḥăqor-zō(ʾ)t̠* (Ps 44:22). We assign this parameter the following label:

6a. *CvḥC$_2$vC$_3$-σ́ (no CvḥC$_2$vC$_3$-structure without epenthetic *ḥăṭāp̄* before a clitic syllable with the feature [+main stress]).

On the other hand, it has been suggested (cf. DeCaen 2003: 43) that the "lack" of epenthesis in the verbal form אֶחְסֶה *ʾeḥsē* is due to the strong pausal accent *ʾat̠nāḥ* on its last syllable. This observation calls for a constraint, which works in the other direction (for a thorough discussion, cf. section 4.1.3.3.5 above). We label this constraint, which runs counter to constraint "**5.**" (***ḥ$^{\$}C_2$v̄**), as follows:

**6b. *ḥv̆$^{\$}C_2$v̄́#** (no ḥv̆$^{\$}$Cv̄́-structure with an epenthetic *ḥăṭāp̄* in case of strong pausal accent on the ultima of a form *tertiae infirmae*).

Pausal forms in the plural of the prefix conjugation retract the accent on the penultima, whereby the vowel reduction typical of these forms is blocked (e.g., יַחְשֹׁבוּ *yaḥšṓb̠ū (P)* instead of יַחְשְׁבוּ *yaḥšəb̠ū* 'they think'). We capture this circumstance by the following constraint:

6c. PAUSACC (pausal accent on the penultima in the plural of the prefix conjugation).

7. HARMONY IO-/i/ (vowel harmony with respect to /i/ amounting to blocking of pre-guttural lowering and *ḥăṭāp̄* epenthesis):[8] This parameter is necessary to assume in order to account for the surface form יִחְיֶה *yiḥyē* and related forms (cf. section 4.1.2.10 above), where vowel lowering and epenthesis is blocked, even though C_2 is maximally sonorous and the verb of the ל״ה type. Therefore, this constraint overrides all the

8 Cf. Kager 1999: 378f, where the constraint HARMONY-IO interestingly is discussed in connection with the constraint LOWERING IO ("any output correspondent of an input vowel must be [–high]").

previous ones. A rationale behind this constraint (marking of the lengthened *i* in the prefix by *gaᶜyā/meṯeḡ*) was proposed in section 4.1.2.10 above (cf. again Khan 1994).

8. PARADIGMLEV (paradigmatic leveling with respect to binyan): This is a parameter set up in conjunction with the previous one. Its function is to account for the fact that an epenthetic *ḥăṭāp̄* never appears in the paᶜal forms of the prefix conjugation belonging to the root *ḥyh*, but always in the hifᶜīl of the suffix conjugation belonging to the same root (no prefix forms are attested in this case).

9. CATCON ("Categorical contrast"): Another constraint has to be posited, a constraint which accounts for the differentiation between otherwise equal surface forms, which belong to different grammatical categories, e.g., "true" participle vs. lexicalised participle (noun) or even a noun belonging to another root – cf. section 4.1.2.7 above. In the case of roots of the type ל"ה, nouns of the structure /maC_1C_2vC_3(v(t))/ overlap morpho-phonologically with hifᶜīl participles, even though no minimal pairs are attested. However, the /maC_1C_2vC_3(v(t))/ nouns (e.g., מַחֲצִית *maḥăṣīṯ*) exhibit a slightly higher tendency to insert epenthetic *ḥăṭāp̄* as compared with the hifᶜīl particples (e.g., מַחְשֶׁה *maḥšē*), whose C_2 is of comparable sonority – cf. section 4.1.2.4 above. Tentatively, we rank this constraint higher than "**3a.**" (***ḥv̆**$^{\$}$**C**$_2$**[–son]**) and "**5.**" (***ḥ**$^{\$}$**C**$_2$**v̄**#) above, even though this ranking does not account for the output forms מַחְתָּה *maḥtā* 'coal shovel' (especially high consonantal strength of C_2) and מִחְיָה *miḥyā* 'preservation of life' (the special case of חיה).

In the special case of verb forms of the shape CvḥC_2v̆C_3v̄ one could operate, following DeCaen 2003: 42, with yet two more constraints, the second of which has been modified by us in order to reflect the data more accurately ("high sonority" instead of "lateral"):

SCHWAEXEMPTION: in forms ending in a vowel of the type CvḥC_2v̆C_3v̄, no *ḥăṭāp̄* vowel can be inserted, irrespective of the consonantal strength of C_2, as the resulting output form would violate the constraints on syllable sequence. (Alternatively, one could argue that the first syllable in CvḥC_2v̆C_3v̄ forms receives a secondary stress (cf. McCarthy 1985: 180ff.) and hence is not susceptible to anaptyxis after its coda.)

HIGHSONORITYEXEMPTION: forms ending in a vowel of the type CvḥC$_2$v̆C$_3$v̄ (tend to) surface as CvḥvC$_2$C$_3$v̄, in case C$_2$ is of especially high sonority (*z* ,*ṭ*, *l*, *n*, or *r*; cf. above sections 4.1.2.5 and 4.1.3.3.2). We have already stated, following Blau 1993: 39, that this case can also be counted as epenthesis.[9]

However, heeding the advice of Bat-El and Bolozky, we decided to proceed with our analysis without these two constraints and to operate only with "**3a.**" (***ḥv̆**$^{\$}$**C$_2$[–son]**) and "**3b.**" (***ḥ**$^{\$}$**C$_2$[+son]**), even though the threshold for CvḥvC$_2$C$_3$v̄ forms is somewhat higher than the threshold for Cvḥv̆C$_2$v̄C$_3$ forms (higher required sonority of C$_2$). In other words: a CvḥvC$_2$C$_3$v̄ plural form always has the singular Cvḥv̆C$_2$v̄C$_3$, but not necessarily *vice versa*.

6.3.2 Analysis of some crucial forms

Let us now consider those forms that are crucial for our discussion in detail. In the following tableaux, the items are arranged in pairs, triplets, and quadruplets that are supposed to illustrate the conflicting parameters (constraints) at work. One has to keep in mind, of course, that the results are not always absolutely determined, but may be subject to a certain degree of variation.

The first pair **(115)** and **(116)** illustrates the different output forms depending simply on the sonority of the second root consonant: while no insertion of a *ḥăṭāp̄* vowel is warranted in **(115)** יַחְתֹּם *yaḥtōm*, such an insertion is plausible in **(116)** יַחֲלֹם *yaḥălōm*, whose second root consonant *l* is much more sonorous than *t*.

9 Fischer & Jastrow (1980: 65) characterise comparable phenomena in Arabic dialects as "Vokalumsprung" (e.g., *yikitbu* instead of *yiktəbu* 'they write').

(115) Constraint Tableau for *yaḥtōm* (Est 8:10)

Input: yiC_1C_2ōC_3	*CvḥC_2vC_3-ṓ[+main stress]	*ḥ$^{\$}C_2$[+son] (no unfortunate syllable contact)	DEP IO (no epenthesis) ≈ *ḥv̆$^{\$}C_2$[–son]	LOWERING IO-Pref (prefix vowel must be [–high])
a. :) יַחְתֹּם	NA			
b. יַחֲתֹּם	NA		* !	
c. יִחְתֹּם	NA			*

(116) Constraint Tableau for *yaḥălōm* (Gen 28:12)

Input: yiC_1C_2ōC_3	*CvḥC_2vC_3-ṓ[+main stress]	*ḥ$^{\$}C_2$[+son] (no unfortunate syllable contact)	DEP IO (no epenthesis) ≈ *ḥv̆$^{\$}C_2$[–son]	LOWERING IO-Pref (prefix vowel must be [–high])
a. יַחְלֹם	NA	* !		
b. :) יַחֲלֹם	NA		*	
c. יִחְלֹם	NA	* !		*

The next pair **(117)** and **(118)** is more tricky, insofar as one and the same second root consonant *b* yields different output forms: while the form **(117)** יַחְבֹּט *yaḥbōṭ* features no epenthetic *ḥăṭāp̄* and hence no spirantisation, the form **(118)** יַחֲבֹל *yaḥăḇōl* does exactly this (the Masoretic system does not allow for a surface form **yaḥḇōl*). In order to account for this difference, we assume a residual transfer of the ([+spirantised]) quality of /b/ in the second case, as argued in section 4.1.2.3 above.

(117) Constraint Tableau for *yaḥbōṭ* (Is 27:12)

Input: yiC_1C_2ōC_3	*CvḥC_2vC_3-ó[+main stress]	RESSPIR (keep [ḇ, ḡ] spirantised)	*ḥ$^{\$}C_2$[+son] (no unfortunate syllable contact)	DEP IO (no epenthesis) ≈ *ḥv̆$^{\$}C_2$[–son]	LOWERING IO-Pref (prefix vowel must be [–high])
a. :) יַחְבֹּט	NA	NA			
b. יַחְבֹט	NA	NA	* !		
c. יַחֲבֹט	NA	NA		* !	

(118) Constraint Tableau for *yaḥăḇōl* (Dt 24:6)

Input: yiC_1C_2ōC_3	*CvḥC_2vC_3-ó[+main stress]	RESSPIR (keep [ḇ, ḡ] spirantised)	*ḥ$^{\$}C_2$[+son] (no unfortunate syllable contact)	DEP IO (no epenthesis) ≈ *ḥv̆$^{\$}C_2$[–son]	LOWERING IO-Pref (prefix vowel must be [–high])
a. יַחְבֹּל		* !			
b. יַחְבֹל			* !		
c. :) יַחֲבֹל				*	

The following pair **(119)** תַּחְבֹּל *taḥbōl* (Ex 22:25) and **(120)** תַּחֲבֹל *taḥăḇōl* (Dt 24:17) most probably reflects free variation, to be technically resolved only by different constraint ranking.[10]

10 Cf. Adam 2002: 162–166 for comparable variation in non-past forms in colloquial registers of Modern Hebrew.

(119) Constraint Tableau for *taḥbōl* (Ex 22:25)

Input: $yiC_1C_2ōC_3$	*CvḥC₂vC₃-ó[+main stress]	*ḥ$C₂[+son] (no unfortunate syllable contact)	DEP IO (no epenthesis) ≈ *ḥv̆$C₂[–son]	RESSPIR (keep [ḇ, ḏ] spirantised)	LOWERING IO-Pref (prefix vowel must be [–high])
a. :) תַחְבֹּל	NA			*	
b. תַחְבֹל	NA	* !			
c. תַחֲבֹּל	NA		* !		

(120) Constraint Tableau for *taḥăḇōl* (Dt 24:17)

Input: $yiC_1C_2ōC_3$	*CvḥC₂vC₃-ó[+main stress]	RESSPIR (keep [ḇ, ḡ] spirantised)	*ḥ$C₂[+son] (no unfortunate syllable contact)	DEP IO (no epenthesis) ≈ *ḥv̆$C₂[–son]	LOWERING IO-Pref (prefix vowel must be [–high])
a. תַחְבֹּל	* ! (?)	* !			
b. תַחְבֹל	* ! (?)		* !		
c. :) תַחֲבֹל				*	

The subsequent quadruplet **(121)**, **(122)**, **(123)**, and **(124)**, which has already puzzled generations of Hebraists (cf. section 4.1.2.10 above), constitutes the crux of our examples, and we can only come up with a tentative solution here. Even though the sonority of the second root consonant in the form **(121)** יִחְיֶה *yiḥyē* is maximal, no epenthesis takes place; at least, such an epenthesis is not reflected in the Masoretic system, which does not allow for a "*ḥăṭāp i*". Phonetically, there may well be an output form like [yiḥĭyē] or [yīḥĭyē], but phonologically, such a form (/yiḥəyē/) does not conform to Tiberian Hebrew phonotactics.[11] Most surprisingly, no vowel lowering takes place before the syllable coda /ḥ/ in this case. Such vowel lowering does occur, however, in the hifʿīl form

11 Cf. again Khan 1994 for the possible marking of the lengthened *i* in the prefix by *gaʿyā / meṯeḡ*.

(123) הֶחֱיָה *heḥĕyā*, which consequently also features an epenthetic *ḥăṭap̄ sẹ̄gōl*. Formally we try to solve this puzzle by arguing that the surface form יִחְיֶה *yiḥyē* is "invisible" to the constraints "**3b.**" (***ḥ**$^{\$}$**C**$_2$**[+son]**) and "**5.**" (***ḥ**$^{\$}$**C**$_2$**v̄**#), since no such thing as a "*ḥăṭāp̄ i*" exists. This "invisibility" is reflected by the position of the constraint "**HARMONY IO-/i/**" – blocking of pre-guttural lowering and epenthesis – as the highest (leftmost) constraint thus far. We are aware, however, that this is not an entirely satisfactory solution. Essentially, we have no explanation for the phenomenon that vowel lowering takes place in the hifʿīl forms **(123)** הֶחֱיָה *heḥĕyā* and **(124)** הַחֲיִתֶם *haḥăyīṯem*, but not in the paʿal form יִחְיֶה *yiḥyē* (and not even in the paʿal form first person singular **(122)** אֶחְיֶה *ʾeḥyē*, where vowel lowering occurs due to the guttural onset /ʾ/ in the first syllable onset). As a formal solution, we therefore posit an even higher constraint "**PARADIGMLEVELING**" that reflects the fact that no attested paʿal form features an epenthetic *ḥăṭāp̄* vowel, whereas all hifʿīl forms do. As no hifʿīl form *yaḥăyē* is attested in the Hebrew Bible, one cannot argue either that a paʿal form *yaḥăyē* would in this case obscure the contrast between a paʿal and a hifʿīl form. For a stative verb such as *ḥyh* the voweling *yeḥĕyē* would be more probable, anyway.

Outi Bat-El (e-mail communication from November 30, 2008) suggests that the the surface form יִחְיֶה *yiḥyē* may be due to a constraint that forbids non-past forms which feature more than one syllable as compared to the respective past form (in this case חָיָה *ḥayā*). She takes the marked mono-syllablic past form חַי *ḥay* as the relevant past form for her argument. According to Gesenius 1910: 218 = §76i, the root *ḥ-y-y* can surface in paʿal (3rd m. sg., past) either as a ל"ה verb (*tertiae infirmae*) (חָיָה *ḥayā*, e.g., Qohelet 6:6) or as an ע"ע verb (*mediae geminatae*) (חַי *ḥay*, e.g., Gen 3:22, just as the adjective חַי *ḥay* 'alive'). However, all other forms belonging to the root *ḥ-y-y*, save the jussive and *way-yiqṭol* forms, look exactly like ל"ה verbs. Therefore, we maintain the structural analogy of חָיָה *ḥayā* to other ל"ה verbs in our treatment.

(121) Constraint Tableau for *yiḥyē* (Dt 8:3)

Input: yiC_1C_2ē	HARMONY IO-/i/ (blocking of pre-guttural lowering and epenthesis)	*ḥv̆$\$C_2$v̄́# [+strong pausal accent]	*ḥ$\$C_2$v̄ (no C_3 = w/y form without epenthesis)	*ḥ$\$C_2$[+son] (no unfortu-nate syllable contact)	DEP IO (no epenthesis) ≈ *ḥv̆$\$C_2$[–son]	LOWERING IO-Pref (prefix vowel must be [–high])
a. :) יִחְיֶה		NA	*	*		*
b. יֶחְיֶה	* !	NA	*	*		
c. יֶחֱיֶה	* !	NA			*	

(122) Constraint Tableau for *ʾeḥyē* (2 K 1:2)

Input: ʾeC_1C_2ē	PARADIGM LEVELING (same pattern in binyan)	HARMONY IO-/i/ (blocking of pre-guttural lowering and epenthesis)	*ḥv̆$\$C_2$v̄́# [+strong pausal accent]	*ḥ$\$C_2$v̄ (no C_3 = w/y form without epenthesis)	*ḥ$\$C_2$[+son] (no unfortu-nate syllable contact)	DEP IO (no epenthesis) ≈ *ḥv̆$\$C_2$[–son]	LOWERING IO-Pref (prefix vowel must be [–high])
a. :) אֶחְיֶה		NA	NA	*	*		
b. אֶחֱיֶה	* !	NA	NA	*		*	

(123) Constraint Tableau for *heḥĕyā* (Jos 14:10)

Input: hiC_1C_2ā	PARADIGM LEVELING (same pattern in binyan)	HARMONY IO-/i/ (blocking of pre-guttural lowering and epenthesis)	*ḥv̆$^{\$}C_2$v̄́# [+strong pausal accent]	*ḥ$^{\$}C_2$v̄ (no C_3 = w/y form without epenthesis)	*ḥ$^{\$}C_2$[+son] (no unfortunate syllable contact)	DEP IO (no epenthesis) ≈ *ḥv̆$^{\$}C_2$[–son]	LOWERING IO-Pref (prefix vowel must be [–high])
a. הִחְיָה	* !		NA	*	*		*
b. הֶחְיָה	* !	*	NA	*	*		
c. :) הֶחֱיָה		*	NA			*	

(124) Constraint Tableau for *haḥăyīṯem* (Jos 2:13)

Input: hiC_1C_2īṯem	PARADIGM LEVELING (same pattern in binyan)	HARMONY IO-/i/ (blocking of pre-guttural lowering and epenthesis)	*ḥv̆$^{\$}C_2$v̄́# [+strong pausal accent]	*ḥ$^{\$}C_2$v̄ (no C_3 = w/y form without epenthesis)	*ḥ$^{\$}C_2$[+son] (no unfortunate syllable contact)	DEP IO (no epenthesis) ≈ *ḥv̆$^{\$}C_2$[–son]	LOWERING IO-Pref (prefix vowel must be [–high])
a. הִחְיִתֶם	* !		NA	*	*		*
b. הַחְיִתֶם	* !	*	NA	*	*		
c. :) הַחֲיִתֶם		*	NA			*	

In the next triplet **(125)**, **(126)**, and **(127)**, we encounter the issue that roots *tertiae infirmae* exhibit a stronger tendency to insert an epenthetic *ḥăṭāp̄* vowel, as compared with strong roots, which – and this is crucial – have a second radical of comparable sonority. The two forms **(125)** יֶחְסָר *yeḥsār* and **(126)** יֶחֱסֶה *yeḥĕsē* may serve as an illustration of the issue at hand. While the first form never receives an epenthetic *ḥăṭāp̄*, the second form regularly does. We account for this circumstance by way of positing the constraint "**5.**" (***ḥC_2v̄#**). However, in the form **(127)** אֶחְסֶה *ʾeḥsē* (Ps 57:2), the latter constraint is overridden by the constraint "**6b.**" (***ḥv̆C_2v̄́#[+strong pausal accent]**), which blocks the insertion of an epenthetic *ḥăṭāp̄* vowel in this case, possibly due to the strong pausal accent *ʾaṯnāḥ* under the last syllable.

(125) Constraint Tableau for *yeḥsār* (Pr 31:11)

Input: yiC₁C₂āC₃	*CvḥC₂vC₃ -ó[+main stress]	*ḥ$C₂v̄ (no C₃ = w/y form without epenthesis)	*ḥ$C₂[+son] (no unfortunate syllable contact)	DEP IO (no epenthesis) ≈ *ḥv̆$C₂[–son]	LOWERING IO-Pref (prefix vowel must be [–high])
a. :) יֶחְסָר	NA	NA			(shaded)
b. יֶחֱסָר	NA	NA		*!	(shaded)

(126) Constraint Tableau for *yeḥĕsē* (Ps 34:9)

Input: yiC₁C₂ē	*ḥv̆$C₂v̄́# [+strong pausal accent]	*ḥ$C₂v̄ (no C₃ = w/y form without epenthesis)	*ḥ$C₂[+son] (no unfortunate syllable contact)	DEP IO (no epenthesis) ≈ *ḥv̆$C₂[–son]	LOWERING IO-Pref (prefix vowel must be [–high])
a. יֶחְסֶה		*!	(shaded)	(shaded)	(shaded)
b. :) יֶחֱסֶה			(shaded)	* (shaded)	(shaded)

(127) Constraint Tableau for *ʾeḥsē* (Ps 57:2)

Input: ʾeC₁C₂ē	*ḥv̆$C₂v́# [+strong pausal accent]	*ḥ$C₂v̄ (no C₃ = w/y form without epenthesis)	*ḥ$C₂[+son] (no unfortunate syllable contact)	DEP IO (no epenthesis) ≈ *ḥv̆$C₂[–son]	LOWERING IO-Pref (prefix vowel must be [–high])
a. :) אֶחְסֶה		*			
b. אֶחֱסֶה	*!			*	

The subsequent pair **(128)** and **(129)** provides another example of the opposition between a straightforward form, in this case **(128)** יַחְשֹׁב *yaḥšōḇ*, and a corresponding form under the impact of the constraint "**6a.**" (***CvḥC_2vC_3-ó[+main stress]**), in this case **(129)** יַחֲשָׁב *yaḥăšōḇ(-)* (Ps 40:18), which properly has to be cited in conjunction with the following *l-ī*, יַחֲשָׁב לִי *yaḥăšōḇ(-)l-ī*, with which it forms a prosodic unit, marked by the poetic accent combination *ʿōlē wə-yōreḏ*.[12] In this case, the constraint "**6a.**" (***CvḥC_2vC_3-ó[+main stress]**) overrides the basic constraint "***ḥv̆$C[–son]**", which otherwise would prevent the insertion of a *ḥăṭāp̄* vowel in this case.

(128) Constraint Tableau for *yaḥšōḇ* (Is 10:7)

Input: yiC₁C₂ōC₃	*Cvḥ$C₂vC₃-ó[+main stress]	*ḥ$C₂[+son] (no unfortunate syllable contact)	DEP IO (no epenthesis) ≈ *ḥv̆$C₂[–son]	LOWERING IO-Pref (prefix vowel must be [–high])
a. :) יַחְשֹׁב	NA			
b. יַחֲשֹׁב	NA		*!	

12 Cf., for instance, Yeivin 1980: 265f.

(129) Constraint Tableau for *yaḥăšōḇ(-)* (Ps 40:18)

Input: $yiC_1C_2oC_3$	*CvḥC$_2$vC$_3$-ó[+main stress]	*ḥC_2$[+son] (no unfortunate syllable contact)	DEP IO (no epenthesis) ≈ *ḥv̆C_2$[−son]	LOWERING IO-Pref (prefix vowel must be [−high])
a. יַחְשָׁב	* !			
b. :) יַחֲשָׁב			*	

The next quadruplet **(130)**, **(131)**, **(132)**, and **(133)** concerns plural forms of the prefix conjugation in which the insertion of an epenthetic *ḥăṭāp̄* vowel is ruled out for phonotactic reasons. Depending on the sonority of C_2, two kinds of output forms emerge: either /$yvC_1C_2əC_2ū$/ in case of a strong C_2 (low sonority) or /$yvC_1vC_2C_3ū$/ in case of a highly sonorous C_2 (cf. Blau 1993: 39); in borderline cases, both forms may co-exist. An example of the first case is **(130)** יַחְגְּרוּ *yaḥgərū*, an example of the second is **(133)** יַחַנְטוּ *yaḥanṭū*, whereas the output forms **(131)** יֶחְזְקוּ *yeḥzəqū* and **(132)** יֶחֶזְקוּ *yeḥezqū* stand for the borderline case (medium sonority of C_2), which has to be handled as free variation. These forms can be treated as **(119)** תַּחְבֹּל *taḥbōl* and **(120)** תַּחֲבֹל *taḥăḇōl* above.

(130) Constraint Tableau for *yaḥgərū* (1 Sam 25:13)

Input: $yiC_1C_2əC_3ū$	PAUSACC (pausal accent on the penultima)	RESSPIR (keep [ḇ, ḡ] spirantised)	*ḥC_2$[+son] (no unfortunate syllable contact)	DEP IO (no epenthesis) ≈ *ḥv̆C_2$[−son]	LOWERING IO-Pref (prefix vowel must be [−high])
a. :) יַחְגְּרוּ	NA	NA			
b. יַחֲגְרוּ	NA	NA		* !	

(131) Constraint Tableau for *yeḥzəqū* (Is 28:22)

Input: $yiC_1C_2əC_3ū$	PAUSACC (pausal accent on the penultima)	$*ḥ^{\$}C_2[+son]$ (no unfortunate syllable contact)	DEP IO (no epenthesis) ≈ $*ḥ\breve{v}^{\$}C_2[-son]$	LOWERING IO-Pref (prefix vowel must be [−high])
a. :) יֶחְזְקוּ	NA	*!		
b. יֶחֱזְקוּ	NA		*	

(132) Constraint Tableau for *yeḥezqū* (2 Sam 10:11)

Input: $yiC_1C_2əC_3ū$	PAUSACC (pausal accent on the penultima)	DEP IO (no epenthesis) ≈ $*ḥ\breve{v}^{\$}C_2[-son]$	$*ḥ^{\$}C_2[+son]$ (no unfortunate syllable contact)	LOWERING IO-Pref (prefix vowel must be [−high])
a. יֶחְזְקוּ	NA	*!		
b. :) יֶחֱזְקוּ	NA		*	

(133) Constraint Tableau for *yaḥanṭū* (Gen 50:26)

Input: $yiC_1C_2əC_3ū$	PAUSACC (pausal accent on the penultima)	$*ḥ^{\$}C_2[+son]$ (no unfortunate syllable contact)	DEP IO (no epenthesis) ≈ $*ḥ\breve{v}^{\$}C_2[-son]$	LOWERING IO-Pref (prefix vowel must be [−high])
a. יַחְנְטוּ	NA	*!		
b. :) יַחַנְטוּ	NA		*	

The subsequent form **(134)** יֶחֱוָרוּ *yeḥĕwā́rū*, whose C_2 is extremely sonorous, can be treated in the same way, as the stress lies on the penultima; thus, the form allows for *ḥăṭāp* epenthesis.[13] In terms of the interacting constraints, the form is structurally comparable to **(116)** יַחֲלֹם *yaḥălōm* above.

13 On the "strong" *w* in the root *ḥwr*, cf. Bergsträsser 1918–1929, vol. 2: 153.

(134) Constraint Tableau for *yeḥĕwā́rū* (Is 29:22)

Input: $yiC_1C_2\acute{\bar{a}}C_3\bar{u}$	PAUSACC (pausal accent on the penultima)	*ḥ$^{\$}C_2$[+son] (no unfortunate syllable contact)	DEP IO (no epenthesis) ≈ *ḥv̆$^{\$}C_2$[–son]	LOWERING IO-Pref (prefix vowel must be [–high])
a. יֶחְוְרוּ	* !	*		
b. יֶחְוָרוּ		* !		
c. :) יֶחֱוָרוּ			*	

Finally, the pair **(135)** and **(136)** as well as item **(137)** illustrate the statistically significant observation that the category of a word can have an impact on its phonological output form. Relevant examples are the minimal pair **(135)** נַחְלָה *naḥlā* 'wounded' (Jer 10:19) and **(136)** נַחֲלָה *naḥălā* 'wound' (Is 17:11) on the one hand,[14] and item **(137)** מַחְשֶׁה *maḥšē* 'soothing' on the other hand. The lexicalised participle נַחֲלָה *naḥălā* prevails over the alternative without epenthetic *ḥăṭāp̄* vowel, without there being a stringent phonological motivation. Technically, we have tried to capture this differentiation by means of the constraint "CATCON", which can, in principle, operate in both directions, but is set up here to reflect the circumstance that "normal" participle forms do not feature epenthesis, as opposed to lexicalised participles and nominal forms with nearly the same structure as participles, which do so.

14 Cf. again Gesenius 1910: 165 = § 63.

(135) Constraint Tableau for *naḥlā* (Jer 10:19)

Input: niC$_1$C$_2$ā	CATCON (categorical contrast: no epenthesis in participle)	*ḥv̆C_2$v̄́# [+strong pausal accent]	*ḥC_2$v̄ (no C$_3$ = w/y form without epenthesis)	*ḥC_2$[+son] (no unfortunate syllable contact)	DEP IO (no epenthesis) ≈ *ḥv̆C_2$[–son]	LOWERING IO-Pref (prefix vowel must be [–high])
a. :) נַחְלָה		NA	*	*		
b. נַחֲלָה	* !	NA			*	

(136) Constraint Tableau for *naḥălā* (Is 17:11)

Input: niC$_1$C$_2$ā	CATCON (categorical contrast: no epenthesis in participle)	*ḥv̆C_2$v̄́# [+strong pausal accent]	*ḥC_2$v̄ (no C$_3$ = w/y form without epenthesis)	*ḥC_2$[+son] (no unfortunate syllable contact)	DEP IO (no epenthesis) ≈ *ḥv̆C_2$[–son]	LOWERING IO-Pref (prefix vowel must be [–high])
a. נַחְלָה	NA	NA	* !	*		
b. :) נַחֲלָה	NA	NA			*	

(137) Constraint Tableau for *maḥšē* (Is 57:11)

Input: $maC_1C_2\bar{e}$	CATCON (categorical contrast: no epenthesis in participle)	*ḥv̆$^{\$}C_2\acute{\bar{v}}$# [+strong pausal accent]	*ḥ$^{\$}C_2\bar{v}$ (no C_3 = w/y form without epenthesis)	*ḥ$^{\$}C_2$[+son] (no unfortunate syllable contact)	DEP IO (no epenthesis) ≈ *ḥv̆$^{\$}C_2$[−son]	LOWERING IO-Pref (prefix vowel must be [−high])
a. :) מַחְשֶׁה		NA	*			
b. מַחֲשֶׁה	* !	NA			*	

7 Conclusions

A seemingly minor issue, the question as to when exactly post-guttural epenthesis takes place in underlyingly closed unstressed syllables with the coda /ḥ/, has grown into a complex study. What started as a puzzle as regards to why לַחְשׁוֹב *la-ḥšōḇ* 'to think' and לַחֲזוֹר *la-ḥăzōr* 'to return' were voweled without and with an epenthetic *ḥăṭāp̄* vowel, respectively, in Bolozky's *501 Hebrew Verbs* (1996/2008), developed into a project on the insertion of epenthetic vowels in verbal *and* nominal forms of the types פ"ח *and* ע"ח, in Biblical Hebrew, as well as in normative *and* spoken Modern Hebrew.

As for the פ"ח forms, we have found out that epenthesis obtains significantly more often in Biblical Hebrew than in normative and spoken Modern Hebrew. In both Biblical and Modern Hebrew the main trigger of epenthesis is the sonority of the second radical. Moreover, forms of the type *tertiae infirmae* are generally involved in epenthesis more often than forms of strong roots. In Biblical Hebrew epenthesis can also be triggered by stress placement, the category of a lemma, and the syntactic position in the verse (context or pause).

When it comes to the ע"ח forms, the triggers are not so much the sonority of the following radical as word class and vowel pattern. Epenthetic vowels are inserted significantly more often in verbal forms than in nouns and adjectives. Past participles of third person singular feminine exhibit epenthesis more often than participles of third person plural, which corresponds to the fact that nouns of the type $C_1aC_2(v)C_3a$ exhibit epenthesis significantly more often than nouns ending on, e.g. *-ut* and *-it*.

Overall, we hope to have made at least the following points in our study:

1) Apparent irregularity in a linguistic system, here on the phonological level, can be resolved within a network of transparent rules, which reflect the interaction of various parameters, both local (language-specific) ones and global (universal) ones. Of special interest is the delimitation of

a linguistic scenario characterised by truly free variation from a linguistic scenario characterised by statistically significant tendencies or even strict preferences of one form over the other.

2) The tension between the norm (to be captured in a normative way) and the corresponding reality (to be captured in a descriptive way) in a linguistic system is by no means just a modern phenomenon, but can, in the case of Hebrew, be traced all the way back to the classical stages of said linguistic system. Here lies an interesting parallel to the diglossic, or better polyglossic situation in Modern Arabic, which cannot be projected back onto a strictly uniform historical scenario either.

3) The sonority scale in conjunction with the relevant preference laws for syllable structure has once again proven to be a powerful explanatory device in phonological theory and emerged as the central argument in the context of our research. Further phonetic parameters may be necessary for an appropriate fine-tuning of the relevant consonantal strength or sonority scales.

4) Optimality Theory yielded a theoretical framework and technical apparatus that forced and enabled us to arrange an array of relevant constraints in order to account for the variety of observable output forms in the Tiberian Hebrew tradition, many forms of which continue to be valid in modern times. All of the parameters "sonority of the second root consonant", "status of the final root slot (strong or weak)", "stress placement", "the category of a lemma", and "the syntactic position in the verse (context or pause)" could be ranked in a meaningful way.

5) The analysis of recorded modern forms in context and isolation confirmed our observations on the Tiberian Hebrew forms at least in principle. When it comes to evaluation of exact phonetic features of intervals including *ḥ* and immediately preceding and following syllables, further investigation is needed. The scholarly software program PRAAT is an excellent means to this end.

Appendices

Appendix 1: Anaptyxis in the Book of Psalms versus the rest of the Hebrew Bible

In section 4.1.3.3.5 we looked into the suggested possibility that contact anaptyxis is triggered or blocked more often in the poetic parts of the Bible than in the prosaic ones. We investigated this hypothesis by using the Book of Psalms as a representative of the poetic books of the Bible. First we singled out the roots represented in the Psalms. For each of these roots we counted the forms with and without anaptyxis in the Psalms on the one hand, and in the other books on the other. Our discussion is based on the data presented in the table below.

In the first column we find all the roots represented in the Book of Psalms. In the second and third column there are two numbers. The first number is the total number of relevant verbal forms, both *a*- and *e*-prefixed, in the book(s) in question. *a*- and *e*-prefixed forms are included in the same number, since we have already established that the prefix vowel is not relevant as far as contact anaptyxis is concerned. The second number is the number of forms in which anaptyxis obtains. The books other than the Psalms in which one or more relevant forms occur are listed in the fourth column. Any comments are placed in the rightmost column, as are the symbols "+" and "–" in cases where the findings go in favour of or against the hypothesis. Whenever the symbol "–" occurs, the book(s) in which the diverging form(s) is/are found is/are also mentioned.

Due to the low number of examples in the Book of Psalms in particular, a presentation of the results in percent is unsuitable.[1]

1 As for the books other than the Psalms, there are five instances of *ḥšh*, in which anaptyxis does not occur. In four of these cases, the form in question is מחשים *maḥšīm*. This form does not occur in the Psalms. Therefore, the numbers may not be representative, and so the symbol "–" might be misleading.

Root	The Psalms	The other books	The books represented	Comments
חגר	2; 0	8; 1	Lev, Judg, 1 Sam, Is	– The anaptyctic form is in Is.
חזה	5; 5	17; 17	Ex, Num, Is, Ez, Job, Prov, Lam, Ct	
חזק	1; 1	124; 123	Gen, Ex, Lev, Dt, Judg, 1 Sam, 2 Sam, 1 K, 2 K, Is, Jer, Ez, Mic, Nah, Zech, Job, Prov, Dan, Neh, 1 Chr, 2 Chr	– The non-anaptyctic form is in Is.
חטא	3; 3	55; 55	Ex, Lev, Num, Dt, 1 Sam, 1 K, 2 K, Is, Jer, Ez, Hos, Job, Qoh, Neh, 2 Chr, Judg	
חטף	2; 1	0		+/– One anaptyctic and one non-anaptyctic form in Ps 10:9.
חיה	6; 0	25; 23	Gen, Ex, Num, Dt, Jos, Judg, 2 Sam, 2 K, Is, Jer, Ez, Hos, Amos, Hab, Zech, Job, Prov, Qoh, Lam, Neh	Anaptyxis never occurs in paʿal, but always in hifʿil (i.e., in Ps there are only paʿal forms).
חלף I	3; 3	14; 14	Gen, Lev, Is, Job	
חלק I	2; 2	5; 5	Prov, Is	
חמד	1; 1	9; 0	Gen, Ex, Dt, Prov	+
חנה	1; 1	99; 99	Ex, Num, Dt, Jos, Judg, 1 Sam, 2 Sam, 1 K, Jer, Job, Ezra, Neh, 1 Chr, 2 Chr	
חנף	1; 1	7; 7	Num, Jer, Mic, Dan	
חסה	7; 5	4; 3	2 Sam, Is, Ruth	(+) The share is high for the other books, too.

Root	The Psalms	The other books	The books represented	Comments
חסר	1; 0	10; 0	Ex, Dt, 1 K, Is, Prov, Ct, Qoh	
חפה	1; 0	0		
חפז	1; 0	2; 0	Job, 1 Sam	
חפץ I	5; 0	14; 0	Dt, Ez, Job, Prov, Ruth, Ct, Qoh, Est	
חפר II	1; 0	5; 0	Is, Job, Prov	
חצה	1; 1	4; 4	Ex, Is, Judg, Job	
חקר	1; 1	8; 0	1 Sam, Ez, Job, Prov, Lam, 1 Chr, 2 Chr, 1 K	+
חרב I	1; 1	24; 22	Is, Hos, Jer, Ez, Job, Amos, 2 K, Nah, Judg, Zeph	– The non-anaptyctic forms are in Is and 2 K.
חרק	1; 1	0		
חרש II	8; 8	32; 32	Gen, Ex, Num, Judg, 1 Sam, 2 Sam, 2 K, Is, Jer, Hab, Zeph, Job, Prov, Est, Neh, Mic	
חשף	1; 1	2; 0	Is, Hg	+
חשב	7; 2	21; 1	Gen, Ex, Num, Neh, 2 Chr, 2 Sam, 1 K, Is, Hos, Job, Prov	+ The third anaptyctic form is in 2 Sam.
חשה	3; 3	12; 7	Is, Neh, Judg, 1 K, 2 K	– (?)
חשך	3; 0	6; 1	Ex, Jer, Job, Qoh, Amos	– The anaptyctic form is in Amos.

Appendix 2:
Nominal forms (incl. n. pr. / n. gent.), prepositions (grammaticalised nouns), and adverbs of the type ע"ח in the Hebrew Bible

ḥăṭāp̄	Gloss	Form
–	n. pr.	אַחְזַי
+	brotherhood	אַחֲוָה
– +	particle expressing desire	אַחְלַי / אַחֲלֵי
–	amethyst (?)	אַחְלָמָה
+	last	אַחֲרוֹן
+	n. pr.	אַחֲרַח
+	after	אַחֲרֵי
+	end, rest	אַחֲרִית
+	creeping locust (aram.) (?)	זַחֲלָא
+	mill	טַחֲנָה
–	together	יַחְדָ(י)ו
–	n. pr.	יַחְזֵרָה
–	n. pr.	יַחְלְאֵל
–	n.pr.	יָחְמַי
–	her cheek	לֶחְיָהּ
–	my bread	לַחְמִי
+	our oppression	לַחֲצֵנוּ
+	n. gent.	מַחֲוִים
+	n. pr. (possibly פ"ח)	מַחֲזִיא(וֹ)ת
–	n. pr.	מַחְלִי
–	n. pr.	מַחְלוֹן
+	next day	מָחֳרָת

ḥăṭāp̄	**Gloss**	**Form**
+	streams of (construct)	נַחֲלֵי
–	water masses (Ps 124:4)	נַחְלָה
+	n. pr.	נַחֲלִיאֵל
+	possession	נַחֲלָה
+	n. pr.	נַחֲמָנִי
–	we (byform of אֲנַחְנוּ)	נַחְנוּ
+	snorting of a horse	נַחֲרָה
+	n. pr.	נַחְשׁוֹן
–	her profit	סַחְרָהּ
–	fear	פַּחְדָּה
+	insolent lie	פַּחֲזוּת
+	bad odour	צַחֲנָה
–	dry areas	צַחְצָחוֹת
+	broad (fem., constr.)	רַחֲבַת
+	uterus (pl.)	רַחֲמִים
–	her uterus	רַחְמָהּ
+	your (f.) uterus	רַחֲמֵיךְ
–	captured female slave	רַחְמָה
+	forgiving	רַחֲמָנִי
–	my washing	רַחְצִי
+	bad behaviour	שַׂחֲטָה
+	n. pr. (place)	שַׁחֲצִים
+	dawn; blackness of hair	שַׁחֲרוּת
–	their (m.) pit	שַׁחְתָּם
–	a patronym	תַּחְכְּמֹנִי
–	name of a bird	תַּחְמָס
–	n. pr. (place)	תַּחְפַּנְחֵס
–	n. pr.	תַּחְפְּנֵס

ḥăṭāp̄	**Gloss**	**Form**
–	armour plate	תַּחְרָא
–	lower / under	תַּחְתּוֹן / תַּחְתִּי

Appendix 3: Verbal forms of the type פ"ח in Modern Hebrew

ḥăṭāp̄ (Even-Shoshan: never *ḥăṭāp̄*, except under root חוה; Lavi and Bantam–Megiddo forms: partially given in assumed analogy)				Verbal forms of the type פ"ח (paᶜal, nifᶜal, hifᶜīl: infinitive, 3. ps. m. sg., participle)	
Bantam–Megiddo	**Even-Shoshan**	**Lavi 2004**	**Bolozky 1996/2008**	**Gloss (usually paᶜal)**	**Verb form**
–	–	–	NA	hide	נחבא
+	–	NA	+	love	לחבוב
+	–	NA	–		יחבוב
–	–	–	NA	knock out	לחבוט
–	–	–	NA		יחבוט
–	–	–	+	beat	לחבול
–	–	–	+		יחבול
–	–	–	–		נחבל
+	–	+	+	embrace (figuratively)	לחבוק
+	–	+	+		יחבוק
+	–	+	+	join (intr.)	לחבור
+	–	+	+		יחבור
NA	–	NA	–		נחבר
+	–	+	NA	bandage	לחבוש
+	–	+	NA		יחבוש
–	–	NA	NA		נחבש
–	–	NA	–	celebrate	לחגוג
–	–	NA	–		יחגוג
NA	–	–	–		נחגג
–	–	–	NA	gird	לחגור

ḥăṭāp̄ (Even-Shoshan: never *ḥăṭāp̄*, except under root חוה; Lavi and Bantam–Megiddo forms: partially given in assumed analogy)				Verbal forms of the type פ"ח (pa^{c}al, nif^{c}al, hif^{c}īl: infinitive, 3. ps. m. sg., participle)	
Bantam–Megiddo	**Even-Shoshan**	**Lavi 2004**	**Bolozky 1996/2008**	**Gloss (usually pa^{c}al)**	**Verb form**
–	–	–	NA		יחגור
–	–	–	NA	cease	לחדול
–	–	–	NA		יֶחדל
–	–	–	–	intrude	לחדור
–	–	–	–		יחדור
–	–	–	–		להחדיר
–	–	–	–		החדיר
–	–	–	–		יחדיר
–	–	–	–		מחדיר
+	–	+	NA	become pale	החוויר
+	–	+	NA		יחוויר
NA	– (+)	+	+	experience	לחוות
NA	–	+	+		יֶחווה
NA	– (+)	NA	+		להחוות
NA	– (+)	NA	+		החווה
NA	–	NA	+		יחווה
NA	–	NA	+		מחווה
+	–	+	NA	see in one's mind	לחזות
+	–	+	NA		יחזה
+	–	+	+	be firm	לחזוק
+	–	+	+		יֶחזק

ḥăṭāp̄ (Even-Shoshan: never *ḥăṭāp̄*, except under root חוה; Lavi and Bantam–Megiddo forms: partially given in assumed analogy)				Verbal forms of the type פ"ח (paʿal, nifʿal, hifʿīl: infinitive, 3. ps. m. sg., participle)	
Bantam–Megiddo	**Even-Shoshan**	**Lavi 2004**	**Bolozky 1996/2008**	**Gloss (usually paʿal)**	**Verb form**
+	–	+	+		להחזיק
+	–	+	+		החזיק
+	–	+	+		יחזיק
+	–	+	+		מחזיק
+	–	+	+	return	לחזור
+	–	+	+		יחזור
+	–	+	+		להחזיר
+	–	+	+		החזיר
+	–	+	+		יחזיר
+	–	+	+		מחזיר
+	–	+	NA	sin	לחטוא
+	–	+	NA		יֶחטא
+	–	+	NA		להחטיא
+	–	+	NA		החטיא
+	–	+	NA		יחטיא
+	–	+	NA		מחטיא
–	–	–	NA	chop wood	לחטוב
–	–	–	NA		יחטוב
–	–	–	NA	tear off	לחטוף
–	–	–	NA		יחטוף
–	–	NA	NA		נחטף

ḥăṭāp (Even-Shoshan: never *ḥăṭāp*, except under root חוה; Lavi and Bantam–Megiddo forms: partially given in assumed analogy)				Verbal forms of the type פ״ח (paᶜal, nifᶜal, hifᶜīl: infinitive, 3. ps. m. sg., participle)	
Bantam–Megiddo	**Even-Shoshan**	**Lavi 2004**	**Bolozky 1996/2008**	**Gloss (usually paᶜal)**	**Verb form**
–	–	–	–	live	לחיות
–	–	–	–		יחיֶה
+	–	+	+		להחיות
+	–	+	+		הֶחיָה
–	–	+ (!)	NA	rub, grate	לחכוך
–	–	– (!)	NA		יחכוך
–	–	–	NA	be wise	לחכום
–	–	–	NA		יֶחכם
–	–	–	NA		להחכים
–	–	–	NBA		החכים
–	–	–	NA		יחכים
–	–	–	NA		מחכים
–	–	–	NA	lease	לחכור
–	–	–	NA		יחכור
–	–	–	NA		להחכיר
–	–	–	NA		החכיר
–	–	–	NA		יחכיר
–	–	–	NA		מחכיר
+	–	+	NA	milk, drain	לחלוב
+	–	+	NA		יחלוב
NA	–	+	NA		להחליב

ḥăṭāp (Even-Shoshan: never *ḥăṭāp*, except under root חוה; Lavi and Bantam–Megiddo forms: partially given in assumed analogy)				Verbal forms of the type פ"ח (pa^cal, nif^cal, hif^cīl: infinitive, 3. ps. m. sg., participle)	
Bantam–Megiddo	**Even-Shoshan**	**Lavi 2004**	**Bolozky 1996/2008**	**Gloss (usually pa^cal)**	**Verb form**
NA	–	+	NA		החליב
NA	–	+	NA		יחליב
NA	–	+	NA		מחליב
+	–	+	NA	become rusty	נחלד
+	–	+	NA		להחליד
+	–	+	NA		החליד
+	–	+	NA		יחליד
+	–	+	NA		מחליד
+	–	+	+	be(come) sick	לחלות
+	–	+	+		יֶחלה
NA	–	NA	+		נחלה
NA	–	+	+		להחלות
NA	–	+	+		החלה
NA	–	+	+		יחלה
NA	–	+	+		מחלה
unmarked	–	–	–	pour (tea etc.); declare impure	לחלוט
unmarked	–	–	–		יחלוט
unmarked	–	–	–	decide	להחליט
unmarked	–	–	–		החליט
unmarked	–	–	–		יחליט
unmarked	–	–	–		מחליט

ḥăṭāp̄ (Even-Shoshan: never *ḥăṭāp̄*, except under root חוה; Lavi and Bantam–Megiddo forms: partially given in assumed analogy)				Verbal forms of the type פ"ח (paᶜal, nifᶜal, hifᶜīl: infinitive, 3. ps. m. sg., participle)	
Bantam–Megiddo	**Even-Shoshan**	**Lavi 2004**	**Bolozky 1996/2008**	**Gloss (usually paᶜal)**	**Verb form**
+	–	+	+	dream, cause to dream; recover	לחלום
+	–	+	+		יחלום
NA	–	NA	+		נחלם
+	–	+	+		להחלים
+	–	+	+		החלים
+	–	+	+		יחלים
+	–	+	+		מחלים
+	–	+	+	pass, change	לחלוף
+	–	+	+		יחלוף
NA	–	+	+		נחלף
+	–	+	+		להחליף
+	–	+	+		החליף
+	–	+	+		יחליף
+	–	+	+		מחליף
+	–	+	+	undress	לחלוץ
+	–	+	+		יחלוץ
+	–	+	+		נחלץ
NA	–	NA	+		להחליץ
NA	–	NA	+		החליץ
NA	–	NA	+		יחליץ
NA	–	NA	+		מחליץ

ḥăṭāp **(Even-Shoshan: never *ḥăṭāp*, except under root חוה; Lavi and Bantam–Megiddo forms: partially given in assumed analogy)**				**Verbal forms of the type פ"ח (paᶜal, nifᶜal, hifᶜīl: infinitive, 3. ps. m. sg., participle)**	
Bantam–Megiddo	**Even-Shoshan**	**Lavi 2004**	**Bolozky 1996/2008**	**Gloss (usually paᶜal)**	**Verb form**
+	–	+	+	divide	לחלוק
+	–	+	+		יחלוק
NA	–	NA	+		נחלק
NA	–	+	NA	be smooth	לחלוק
NA	–	+	NA		יֶחלק
+	–	+	NA		להחליק
+	–	+	NA		החליק
+	–	+	NA		יחליק
+	–	+	NA		מחליק
+	–	+	NA	be(come) weak	לחלוש
+	–	+	NA		יֶחלש
+	–	+	NA		נחלש
+	–	+	NA		להחליש
+	–	+	NA		החליש
+	–	+	NA		יחליש
+	–	+	NA		מחליש
unmarked	–	+	NA	make compliments	להחמיא
unmarked	–	+	NA		החמיא
unmarked	–	+	NA		יחמיא
unmarked	–	+	NA		מחמיא
–	–	–	NA	yearn	לחמוד

ḥăṭāp̄ (Even-Shoshan: never *ḥăṭāp̄*, except under root חוה; Lavi and Bantam–Megiddo forms: partially given in assumed analogy)				Verbal forms of the type פ"ח (paʿal, nifʿal, hifʿīl: infinitive, 3. ps. m. sg., participle)	
Bantam–Megiddo	**Even-Shoshan**	**Lavi 2004**	**Bolozky 1996/2008**	**Gloss (usually paʿal)**	**Verb form**
–	–	–	NA		יחמוד
unmarked	–	+ (part. – !)	NA		נחמד
NA	–	NA	+	get hotter, desirous	נחמם
+	–	–	NA	rob, oppress	לחמוס
+	–	–	NA		יחמוס
unmarked	–	–	NA	become sour	לחמוץ
unmarked	–	–	NA		יֶחמץ
unmarked	–	–	NA		נחמץ
unmarked	–	–	NA		להחמיץ
unmarked	–	+ (!)	NA		החמיץ
unmarked	–	+	NA		יחמיץ
unmarked	–	+	NA		מחמיץ
unmarked	–	+	NA	slip out	לחמוק
unmarked	–	–	NA		יֶחמק
unmarked	–	NA	NA	seethe; cover with asphalt	לחמור
unmarked	–	NA	NA		יֶחמר
unmarked	–	–	NA	make (more) difficult	להחמיר
unmarked	–	–	NA		החמיר
unmarked	–	–	NA		יחמיר
unmarked	–	–	NA		מחמיר
+	–	+	–	camp, park	לחנות

ḥăṭāp̄ (Even-Shoshan: never ḥăṭāp̄, except under root חוה; Lavi and Bantam–Megiddo forms: partially given in assumed analogy)				Verbal forms of the type פ״ח (paʿal, nifʿal, hifʿīl: infinitive, 3. ps. m. sg., participle)	
Bantam–Megiddo	**Even-Shoshan**	**Lavi 2004**	**Bolozky 1996/2008**	**Gloss (usually paʿal)**	**Verb form**
+	–	+	–		יחנה
+	–	+	–		להחנות
+	–	+	–		החנה
+	–	+	–		יחנה
+	–	+	–		מחנה
+	–	+	NA	embalm	לחנוט
+	–	+	NA		יחנוט
+	–	NA	NA		נחנט
+	–	+	+	inaugurate	לחנוך
+	–	+	+		יחנוך
+	–	NA	NA		נחנך
NA	–	–	+	be pardoned	נחנן
+	–	NA	NA	flatter	לחנוף
+	–	NA	NA		יחנוף
+	–	+	NA		להחניף
+	–	+	NA		החניף
+	–	+	NA		יחניף
+	–	+	NA		מחניף
+	–	+	NA	suffocate	לחנוק
+	–	+	NA		יחנוק
+	–	+	NA		נחנק

ḥăṭāp̄ (Even-Shoshan: never ḥăṭāp̄, except under root חוה; Lavi and Bantam–Megiddo forms: partially given in assumed analogy)				**Verbal forms of the type פ"ח (paʿal, nifʿal, hifʿīl: infinitive, 3. ps. m. sg., participle)**	
Bantam–Megiddo	**Even-Shoshan**	**Lavi 2004**	**Bolozky 1996/2008**	**Gloss (usually paʿal)**	**Verb form**
+	–	+	NA		להחניק
+	–	+	NA		החניק
+	–	+	NA		יחניק
+	–	+	NA		מחניק
unmarked	–	+	NA	seek protection	לחסות
unmarked	–	+	NA		יֶחסה
unmarked	–	–	+	save (economise)	לחסוך
unmarked	–	–	–		יחסוך
unmarked	–	NA	–		נחסך
NA	–	NA	+	destroy	לחסול
NA	–	NA	+		יחסול
unmarked	–	–	–	shut off	לחסום
unmarked	–	–	–		יחסום
unmarked	–	NA	NA		נחסם
unmarked	–	NA	NA	store	להחסין
unmarked	–	NA	NA		החסין
unmarked	–	NA	NA		יחסין
unmarked	–	NA	NA		מחסין
unmarked	–	–	–	miss, be deficient	לחסור
unmarked	–	–	–		יֶחסר
NA	–	NA	–		נחסר

ḥăṭāp̄ (Even-Shoshan: never *ḥăṭāp̄*, except under root **חוה**; Lavi and Bantam–Megiddo forms: partially given in assumed analogy)				Verbal forms of the type **פ"ח** (paʿal, nifʿal, hifʿīl: infinitive, 3. ps. m. sg., participle)	
Bantam–Megiddo	**Even-Shoshan**	**Lavi 2004**	**Bolozky 1996/2008**	**Gloss (usually paʿal)**	**Verb form**
unmarked	–	–	–		להחסיר
unmarked	–	–	–		החסיר
unmarked	–	–	–		יחסיר
unmarked	–	–	–		מחסיר
–	–	–	NA	cover	לחפות
–	–	–	NA		יחפה
–	–	NA	NA	hurry up	לחפוז
–	–	NA	NA		יחפוז
–	–	–	NA		נחפז
–	–	–	NA	be in congruence; shampoo	לחפוף
–	–	–	NA		יחפוף
–	–	–	NA	desire, have pleasure	לחפוץ
–	–	–	NA		יחפוץ
–	–	–	–	dig	לחפור
–	–	–	–		יחפור
NA	–	NA	–		נחפר
NA	–	–	NA	bring disgrace over	להחפיר
NA	–	–	NA		החפיר
NA	–	–	NA		יחפיר
NA	–	–	NA		מחפיר
NA	–	NA	–	seek	לחפוש

ḥăṭāp (Even-Shoshan: never ḥăṭāp, except under root חוה; Lavi and Bantam–Megiddo forms: partially given in assumed analogy)				**Verbal forms of the type פ"ח (pa^{c}al, nif^{c}al, hif^{c}īl: infinitive, 3. ps. m. sg., participle)**	
Bantam–Megiddo	**Even-Shoshan**	**Lavi 2004**	**Bolozky 1996/2008**	**Gloss (usually pa^{c}al)**	**Verb form**
NA	–	NA	–		יחפוש
NA	–	NA	–		נחפש
–	–	–	NA	turn up (garments)	לחפות
–	–	–	NA		יחפות
unmarked	–	–	NA	carve stones	לחצוב
unmarked	–	–	NA		יחצוב
unmarked	–	NA	NA		נחצב
+	–	+	+	divide in halves	לחצות
+	–	+	+		יֶחצה
+	–	NA	+		נחצה
NA	–	–	NA	turn outwards	להחצין
NA	–	–	NA		החצין
NA	–	–	NA		יחצין
NA	–	–	NA		מחצין
NA	–	–	NA	be insolent	לחצוף
NA	–	–	NA		יחצוף
NA	–	+	NA		להחציף
NA	–	+	NA		החציף
NA	–	+	NA		יחציף
NA	–	+	NA		מחציף
unmarked	–	–	NA	divide	לחצוץ

ḥăṭāp̄ (Even-Shoshan: never *ḥăṭāp̄*, except under root חוה; Lavi and Bantam–Megiddo forms: partially given in assumed analogy)				Verbal forms of the type פ"ח (pa^cal, nif^cal, hif^cīl: infinitive, 3. ps. m. sg., participle)	
Bantam–Megiddo	**Even-Shoshan**	**Lavi 2004**	**Bolozky 1996/2008**	**Gloss (usually pa^cal)**	**Verb form**
unmarked	–	–	NA		יחצוץ
unmarked	–	–	NA	give a law ("inscribe")	לחקוק
unmarked	–	–	NA		יחקוק
unmarked	–	–	–	investigate	לחקור
unmarked	–	–	–		יחקור
unmarked	–	NA	–		נחקר
NA	–	NA	–		להחקיר
NA	–	NA	–		החקיר
NA	–	NA	–		יחקיר
NA	–	NA	–		מחקיר
+	–	NA	NA	defecate	להחריא
+	–	NA	NA		החריא
+	–	NA	NA		יחריא
+	–	NA	NA		מחריא
+	–	+	NA	be destroyed, desiccate	לחרוב
+	–	+	NA		יֶחרב
+	–	NA	NA		נחרב
+	–	+	NA		להחריב
+	–	+	NA		החריב
+	–	+	NA		יחריב
+	–	+	NA		מחריב

ḥăṭāp̄ (Even-Shoshan: never *ḥăṭāp̄*, except under root חוה; Lavi and Bantam–Megiddo forms: partially given in assumed analogy)				Verbal forms of the type פ"ח (paʿal, nifʿal, hifʿīl: infinitive, 3. ps. m. sg., participle)	
Bantam–Megiddo	**Even-Shoshan**	**Lavi 2004**	**Bolozky 1996/2008**	**Gloss (usually paʿal)**	**Verb form**
unmarked	–	+	NA	break out	לחרוג
unmarked	–	+	NA		יחרוג
+	–	+	NA	tremble, be worried	לחרוד
+	–	+	NA		יֶחרד
+	–	+	NA		נחרד
+	–	NA	NA		להחריד
+	–	NA	NA		החריד
+	–	NA	NA		יחריד
+	–	NA	NA		מחריד
+	–	NA	+	be hot, angry	לחרות
+	–	NA	+		יֶחרה
+	–	NA	+		נחרה
NA	–	+	+		להחרות
NA	–	+	+		החרה
NA	–	+	+		יַחרה
NA	–	+	+		מחרה
+	–	+	NA	put in line, rhyme	לחרוז
+	–	+	NA		יחרוז
+	–	NA	NA		נחרז
+	–	+	+	form on a lathe, engrave	לחרוט
+	–	+	+		יחרוט

ḥăṭāp̄ (Even-Shoshan: never *ḥăṭāp̄*, except under root חוה; Lavi and Bantam–Megiddo forms: partially given in assumed analogy)				Verbal forms of the type פ"ח (paᶜal, nifᶜal, hifᶜīl: infinitive, 3. ps. m. sg., participle)	
Bantam–Megiddo	Even-Shoshan	Lavi 2004	Bolozky 1996/2008	Gloss (usually paᶜal)	Verb form
+	–	NA	NA		נחרט
+	–	+	NA	roast	לחרוך
+	–	+	NA		יחרוך
+	–	NA	NA		נחרך
+	–	+	NA	ban, boycott	להחרים
+	–	+	NA		החרים
+	–	+	NA		יחרים
+	–	+	NA		מחרים
+	–	+	+	(1) vilify; (2) pass the winter	לחרוף
+	–	+	+		יחרוף
+	–	+	NA		יֶחרף 2
+	–	+	+		להחריף
+	–	+	+		החריף
+	–	+	+		יחריף
+	–	+	+		מחריף
+	–	+	NA	scratch in, decide	לחרוץ
+	–	+	NA		יחרוץ
+	–	+	NA		נחרץ
+	–	+	NA	make a rustling sound	לחרוק
+	–	+	NA		יחרוק
NA	–	+	NA	drill, make a hole	לחרור

ḥăṭāp̄ (Even-Shoshan: never *ḥăṭāp̄*, except under root חוה; Lavi and Bantam–Megiddo forms: partially given in assumed analogy)				Verbal forms of the type פ"ח (paʿal, nifʿal, hifʿīl: infinitive, 3. ps. m. sg., participle)	
Bantam–Megiddo	**Even-Shoshan**	**Lavi 2004**	**Bolozky 1996/2008**	**Gloss (usually paʿal)**	**Verb form**
NA	–	+	NA		יחרור
+	–	+	NA	(1) plough; (2) become deaf	לחרוש
+	–	+	NA		יחרוש
+	–	+	NA		יֶחרש 2
+	–	NA	NA		נחרש
+	–	+	NA		להחריש
+	–	+	NA		החריש
+	–	+	NA		יחריש
+	–	+	NA		מחריש
NA	–	+	NA	engrave	לחרות
NA	–	+	NA		יחרות
+	–	NA	NA		נחרת
–	–	–	–	think	לחשוב
–	–	–	–		יחשוב
unmarked	–	NA	–		נחשב
NA	–	–	–		להחשיב
NA	–	–	–		החשיב
NA	–	–	–		יחשיב
NA	–	–	–		מחשיב
unmarked	–	–	–	mistrust	לחשוד
unmarked	–	–	–		יחשוד

ḥăṭāp̄ (Even-Shoshan: never *ḥăṭāp̄*, except under root חוה; Lavi and Bantam–Megiddo forms: partially given in assumed analogy)				Verbal forms of the type פ"ח (paᶜal, nifᶜal, hifᶜīl: infinitive, 3. ps. m. sg., participle)	
Bantam–Megiddo	**Even-Shoshan**	**Lavi 2004**	**Bolozky 1996/2008**	**Gloss (usually paᶜal)**	**Verb form**
unmarked	–	NA	–		נחשד
unmarked	–	–	+		להחשיד
unmarked	–	–	+		החשיד
unmarked	–	–	+		יחשיד
unmarked	–	–	+		מחשיד
+	–	+	NA	be silent	לחשות
+	–	+	NA		יחשה
+	–	+	NA		להחשות
+	–	+	NA		החשה
+	–	+	NA		יחשה
+	–	+	NA		מחשה
unmarked	–	–	NA	be dark	לחשוך
unmarked	–	–	NA		יחשוך
unmarked	–	–	NA		להחשיך
unmarked	–	–	NA		החשיך
unmarked	–	–	NA		יחשיך
unmarked	–	–	NA		מחשיך
unmarked	–	+	NA	be undeveloped	נחשל
unmarked	–	–	–	uncover, strip	לחשׂוף
unmarked	–	–	–		יחשׂוף
unmarked	–	NA	–		נחשׂף

ḥăṭāp̄ (Even-Shoshan: never *ḥăṭāp̄*, except under root חוה; Lavi and Bantam–Megiddo forms: partially given in assumed analogy)				Verbal forms of the type פ"ח (paʿal, nifʿal, hifʿīl: infinitive, 3. ps. m. sg., participle)	
Bantam–Megiddo	**Even-Shoshan**	**Lavi 2004**	**Bolozky 1996/2008**	**Gloss (usually paʿal)**	**Verb form**
unmarked	–	–	NA	have desire	לחשוק
unmarked	–	–	NA		יחשוק
+	–	–	–	be afraid	לחשוש
+	–	–	–		יחשוש
–	–	–	NA	get coal out of the fire	לחתות
–	–	–	NA		יחתה
–	–	–	–	cut off	לחתוך
–	–	–	–		יחתוך
–	–	NA	–		נחתך
–	–	–	–	sign, seal	לחתום
–	–	–	–		יחתום
–	–	NA	–		נחתם
–	–	–	–		להחתים
–	–	–	–		החתים
–	–	–	–		יחתים
–	–	–	–		מחתים
–	–	–	NA	undermine	לחתור
–	–	–	NA		יחתור

Appendix 4:
h-prefixed nominal forms of the type פ"ח in Modern Hebrew

ḥăṭāp̄ ("+" in parentheses indicates that a form with *ḥăṭāp̄* is *also* acceptable)			*h*-prefixed nominal forms of the type פ"ח	
Bantam Megiddo	**Langenscheidt Achiasaf**	**Milon Even-Shoshan**	**Gloss**	**Form**
NA	–	–	hiding	הַחבָאָה
NA	–	–	association	הֶחבֵר
–	–	–	letting enter	הַחדָרָה
NA	–	– (+)	becoming pale	הַחוָורָה
NA	–	– (+)	making visible	הַחזָיָה
NA	–	– (+)	maintenance	הַחזָקָה
NA	–	–	repayment; reflex	הֶחזֵר
NA	–	– (+)	returning	הַחזָרָה
NA	–	– (+)	seduction	הַחטָאָה
+	+	– (+)	revitalisation	הַחיָאָה
NA	–	–	leasing	הַחכָּרָה
unmarked	–	– (+)	decision	הַחלָטָה
unmarked	–	–	absolute	הֶחלֵטִי
unmarked	–	– (+)	recovering	הַחלָמָה
NA	–	– (+)	exchange	הַחלָפָה
NA	–	– (+)	slipping (e.g., on ice)	הַחלָקָה
NA	–	– (+)	becoming sour; missed opportunity	הַחמָצָה
unmarked	–	– (+)	deterioration	הַחמָרָה
NA	+	– (+)	parking	הַחנָיָה
NA	–	– (+)	flattering	הַחנָפָה
NA	–	– (+)	suffocation	הַחנָקָה
unmarked	–	– (+)	storage	הַחסָנָה

ḥăṭāp̄ ("+" in parentheses indicates that a form with *ḥăṭāp̄* is *also* acceptable)			*h*-prefixed nominal forms of the type פ"ח	
Bantam Megiddo	Langenscheidt Achiasaf	Milon Even-Shoshan	Gloss	Form
NA	–	– (+)	subtraction	הַחסָרָה
NA	–	– (+)	extrovertedness	הַחצָנָה
NA	–	– (+)	destruction	הַחרָבָה
NA	–	– (+)	frightening	הַחרָדָה
NA	–	– (+)	seizing; boycott	הַחרָמָה
NA	–	– (+)	(negative) culmination	הַחרָפָה
NA	–	– (+)	becoming deaf	הַחרָשָׁה
NA	–	– (+)	estimation	הַחשָׁבָה
NA	–	– (+)	suspicion	הַחשָׁדָה
NA	–	–	giving to sign	הַחתָמָה

Appendix 5:
m-prefixed nominal forms of the type פ"ח in Modern Hebrew

ḥăṭāp̄ ("+" in parentheses indicates that a form with *ḥăṭāp̄* is *also* acceptable)			*m*-prefixed nominal forms of the type פ"ח	
Bantam Megiddo	**Langenscheidt Achiasaf**	**Milon Even-Shoshan**	**Gloss**	**Form**
+	+	+	hiding place	מַחבֵא
+	+	– (+)	hiding place	מַחבוֹא
+	–	–	prison cell	מַחבוֹש
–	–	–	tennis racket	מַחבֵט
NA	–	–	threshing-machine	מַחבֵטָה
–	–	–	butter-machine	מַחבֵצָה
–	–	–	joint (carpentry)	מַחבָר
–	–	–	joint (machinery)	מַחבֵר
–	–	–	exercise-book	מַחבֶרֶת
+	+	+	frying-pan	מַחבַת
NA	–	–	inhibition	מַחגֵר
–	–	–	pencil-sharpener	מַחדֵד
NA	–	–	omission	מֶחדָל
+	+	– (+)	pointer	מַחווֶה
unmarked	+	– (+)	gesture	מֶחווָה
+	+	– (+)	indicator	מַחווָן
+	+	+	playwright	מַחזאי
+	+	+	play, drama	מַחזֶה
+	+	– (+)	look	מֶחזָה
+	+	– (+)	cycle	מַחזוֹר
+	+	–	periodic	מַחזוֹרי
+	+	– (+)	reflector	מַחזירוֹר
+	+	+	musical	מַחזֶמֶר

ḥăṭāp ("+" in parentheses indicates that a form with *ḥăṭāp* is *also* acceptable)			*m*-prefixed nominal forms of the type פ״ח	
Bantam Megiddo	**Langenscheidt Achiasaf**	**Milon Even-Shoshan**	**Gloss**	**Form**
NA	–	–	held fast	מוּחְזָק
unmarked	+	– (+)	handle	מַחֲזֵק
unmarked	–	–	returned	מוּחְזָר
NA	–	–	back-switch	מַחֲזֵר
NA	+	– (+)	period	מַחֲזוֹרֶת
NA	–	–	slotting machine	מַחְטֵטָה
NA	–	–	razzia	מַחְטוֹפֶת
–	–	–	subsistence	מִחְיָה
–	–	–	informative	מַחְכִּים
–	–	–	lessor	מַחְכִּיר
–	–	–	under lease	מוּחְכָּר
unmarked	–	–	dairy	מַחְלָבָה
unmarked	–	–	rusty	מוּחְלָד
+	+	+	disease	מַחֲלָה
NA	–	–	milking level	מַחְלוֹב
unmarked	–	–	absolute	מוּחְלָט
NA	+	– (+)	disgusting	מַחְלִיא
+	+	– (+)	convalescent	מַחְלִים
NA	+	– (+)	substitute (person)	מַחְלִיף
+	+	– (+)	skates	מַחְלִיקַיִים
NA	–	–	change	מַחְלֵף
NA	–	–	highway-crossing	מֶחְלָף
NA	–	–	changed	מוּחְלָף
unmarked	–	–	plait (of hair)	מַחְלָפָה
unmarked	–	–	cork-screw	מַחְלֵץ

ḥăṭāp̄ ("+" in parentheses indicates that a form with *ḥăṭāp̄* is *also* acceptable)			*m*-prefixed nominal forms of the type פ"ח	
Bantam Megiddo	**Langenscheidt Achiasaf**	**Milon Even-Shoshan**	**Gloss**	**Form**
+	+	– (+)	festive costume	מַחלָצָה
NA	–	–	smoothing machine	מַחלֵק
NA	–	–	smoothened	מוחלָק
NA	–	–	(police) division	מֶחלָק
unmarked	–	–	department	מַחלָקָה
+	+	– (+)	difference of opinion	מַחלוֹקֶת
NA	–	–	departmental	מַחלַקְתי
NA	–	–	weakened	מוחלָש
unmarked	+	– (+)	compliment	מַחמָאָה
+	+	– (+)	butter box	מַחמֵאָה
unmarked	–	–	darling	מַחמָד
NA	–	–	flattering	מַחמיא
NA	–	–	pedantic person	מַחמיר
NA	–	–	loved one (outdated)	מַחמָל
NA	–	–	mixed pickles (sour)	מַחמָץ
NA	–	–	sour dough	מַחמֶצֶת
NA	–	–	made sour; missed	מוחמָץ
NA	–	–	refuge	מַחמָק
NA	+	– (+)	note system (5 lines)	מַחמוֹשֶת
NA	+	+	camping	מַחנָאוּת
+	+	+	camp	מַחנֶה
NA	+	–	suffocating	מַחניק
+	+	– (+)	lack of air	מַחנָק
unmarked	–	– (+)	shelter	מַחסֶה
unmarked	–	–	barrier	מַחסוֹם

ḥăṭāp̄ ("+" in parentheses indicates that a form with *ḥăṭāp̄* is *also* acceptable)			*m*-prefixed nominal forms of the type פ"ח	
Bantam Megiddo	**Langenscheidt Achiasaf**	**Milon Even-Shoshan**	**Gloss**	**Form**
unmarked	–	– (+)	deficiency	מַחסוֹר
unmarked	–	–	storage ("magazine")	מַחסָן
NA	–	–	protected position	מַחפֶה
NA	+	+	protective shoe	מַחפֶה
–	–	–	morally bad	מַחפִיר
–	–	–	dredging-machine	מַחפֵר
–	–	–	mine; digging place	מַחפוֹרֶת
NA	–	–	hewing of stones	מַחצֵב
NA	–	–	mineral	מַחצָב
unmarked	–	– (+)	quarry; stone pit	מַחצָבָה
+	+	– (+)	half	מֶחצָה
+	+	+	half	מַחצִית
unmarked	–	–	mat	מַחצֶלֶת
NA	–	–	extroverted	מוחצָן
NA	–	–	tooth-pick	מַחצֵצָה
–	–	–	research	מֶחקָר
+	+	– (+)	latrine	מַחרָאָה
+	+	– (+)	destructed	מוחרָב
NA	–	–	miḥrāb (in a mosque)	מֶחרָב
NA	–	–	reflex	מֶחרָד
NA	+	– (+)	cheese knife	מַחרוֹץ
+	+	– (+)	row; neck-chain	מַחרוֹזֶת
NA	+	– (+)	turnery	מַחרָטָה
+	+	– (+)	turning-lathe	מַחרֵטָה
+	+	– (+)	destructive	מַחרִיב

ḥăṭāp̄ ("+" in parentheses indicates that a form with *ḥăṭāp̄* is *also* acceptable)			*m*-prefixed nominal forms of the type פ"ח	
Bantam Megiddo	**Langenscheidt Achiasaf**	**Milon Even-Shoshan**	**Gloss**	**Form**
+	+	– (+)	causing fear	מַחריד
+	+	– (+)	deafening	מַחריש
+	+	– (+)	boycotted	מוחרָם
NA	+	– (+)	dessert cup	מחרוֹסֶת
NA	–	–	cut	מֶחרָץ
NA	+	– (+)	bung plane	מַחרֵצָה
NA	+	– (+)	insectarium	מַחרָקָה
+	+	– (+)	plow	מַחרֵשָׁה
–	–	–	computer	מַחשֵׁב
+	+	– (+)	thought	מַחשָׁבָה
NA	–	–	pocket calculator	מַחשְׁבוֹן
NA	+	–	thought-related	מַחשְׁבי
NA	–	–	computer specialist	מַחשבָן
NA	+	– (+)	applied art	מַחשֶׁבֶת
NA	+	– (+)	related to applied art	מַחשַׁבְתי
NA	–	–	computerisation	מִחשוּב
unmarked	–	–	décolleté	מַחשׂוֹף
NA	–	–	darkened	מוחשָׁך
unmarked	–	–	darkness	מַחשָׁך
NA	–	–	darkroom	מַחשֵׁכָה
NA	–	–	trigger	מַחשֵׂף
NA	–	–	hashish den	מַחשָׁשָׁה
–	–	–	coal shovel	מַחתָּה
NA	–	–	horizontal cut	מֶחתָּך
–	–	–	cutting machine	מַחתֵּך

ḥăṭāp̄ ("+" in parentheses indicates that a form with *ḥăṭāp̄* is *also* acceptable)			*m*-prefixed nominal forms of the type פ"ח	
Bantam Megiddo	**Langenscheidt Achiasaf**	**Milon Even-Shoshan**	**Gloss**	**Form**
–	–	–	bread-cutter	מַחתֵכָה
–	–	–	underground path	מַחתֶרת

Appendix 6:
t-prefixed nominal forms of the type פ״ח in Modern Hebrew

ḥăṭāp̄ ("+" in parentheses indicates that a form with *ḥăṭāp̄* is *also* acceptable)			*t*-prefixed nominal forms of the type פ״ח	
Bantam Megiddo	**Langenscheidt Achiasaf**	**Milon Even-Shoshan**	**Gloss**	**Form**
–	–	–	trick	תַחבוּלָה
–	–	–	traffic (connection)	תַחבוּרָה
–	–	–	hobby	תַחבִיב
–	–	–	syntax	תַחבִיר
–	–	–	tactician	תַחבְּלָן
–	–	–	bandage	תַחבוֹשֶׁת
–	–	–	lexical innovation	תַחדִיש
unmarked	+	– (+)	maintenance	תַחזוּקָה
+	+	+	forecast	תַחזִית
NA	+	–	reconstructed model	תַחזוֹרֶת
+	+	– (+)	spreading of a disease	תַחלוּאָה
+	+	– (+)	exchange	תַחלוּפָה
+	+	– (+)	emulsion	תַחלִיב
+	+	– (+)	surrogate	תַחלִיף
unmarked	–	–	oxide	תַחמוֹצֶת
unmarked	–	–	ammunition	תַחמוֹשֶׁת
NA	–	–	silage	תַחמִיץ
NA	+	+	station attendant	תַחנָאִי
+	+	+	station	תַחנָה
+	+	+	supplication	תַחנוּנִים
–	–	–	masquerade	תַחפוֹשֶׂת
NA	+	+	cross-walk	תַחצָה

ḥăṭāp̄ ("+" in parentheses indicates that a form with *ḥăṭāp̄* is *also* acceptable)			*t*-prefixed nominal forms of the type פ״ח	
Bantam Megiddo	**Langenscheidt Achiasaf**	**Milon Even-Shoshan**	**Gloss**	**Form**
unmarked	–	–	investigation	תַחקיר
NA	+	+	peak	תַחרָה
+	+	+	competition	תַחרוּת
unmarked	–	–	etching	תַחריט
unmarked	–	–	lace edging	תַחרים
unmarked	+	– (+)	calculation	תַחשיב
unmarked	NA	–	jigsaw	תַחתיך

Appendix 7:
Verbal and nominal forms of the type ע״ח in Modern Hebrew

ḥăṭāp ("+" in parentheses indicates that a form with *ḥăṭāp* is *also* acceptable)			Relevant verbal and nominal forms of the type ע״ח	
Bantam Megiddo	**Langenscheidt Achiasaf**	**Milon Even-Shoshan**	**Gloss**	**Form**
			unite (oneself)	איחדָה
				איחדוּ
				הִתאַחדָה
				הִתאַחדוּ
			join together	איחתָה
unmarked	–	–	unity	אַחדוּת
+	+	–	brotherhood	אַחוָוה
			grip, hold	אָחזָה
				אָחזוּ
			be held	נֶאֱחזָה
				נֶאֱחזוּ
NA	–	–	maintain (in good condition)	אִחזֵק
NA	–	–		לְאַחזֵק
			congratulate	איחלָה
				איחלוּ
NA	–	–	great! (Arabic)	אַחלָה
NA	NA	+	particle of desire	אַחלֵי/אַחלַי
unmarked	–	–	amethyst	אַחלָמָה
unmarked	–	–	storage	אִחסוּן
unmarked	–	–	store	אִחסֵן
unmarked	–	–		לְאַחסֵן
NA	NA	–	disclose private and discrete matter	אִחצֵן
+	+ (– transcr.)	–	responsible	אַחרָאִי
			be (too) late	אֵחרָה
				אֵחרוּ
NA	NA	–	backpart of a ship	אַחרָה

ḥăṭāp̄ ("+" in parentheses indicates that a form with *ḥăṭāp̄* is *also* acceptable)			Relevant verbal and nominal forms of the type ע״ח	
Bantam Megiddo	**Langenscheidt Achiasaf**	**Milon Even-Shoshan**	**Gloss**	**Form**
+	+	+	last	אַחרוֹן
+	+	+	after	אַחרֵי
+	+ (– transcr.)	–	responsibility	אַחרָיוּת
NA	+	+	end, rest	אַחרִית
			be disgusted	בָּחלָה בָּחלוּ
			investigate	בָּחנָה בָּחנוּ
			choose	בָּחרָה בָּחרוּ
			be elected	נִבְחרָה נִבְחרוּ
+	+	+	youth; choosiness	בַּחרוּת
NA	+	+	choosy	בַּחרָן
			stir	בָּחשָׁה בָּחשׁוּ
NA	+	+	cooking spoon	בַּחשָׁה
NA	NA	+	(up)stirring person	בַּחשָׁן
			smile	גִיחכָה גִיחכוּ
NA	+	–	jester	גַחכָן
+	–	–	glow-worm	גַחלִילִית
NA	+	+	carbuncle (tumour)	גַחלִית
NA	+	– (+)	peculiarity	גַחמָה
+	NA	– (+)	arsonist	גַחמוֹן
NA	NA	– (+)	stubborn	גַחמָן
NA	NA	– (+)	stubbornness	גַחמָנוּת
NA	NA	– (+)	stubborn	גַחמָנִי

ḥăṭāp ("+" in parentheses indicates that a form with *ḥăṭāp* is *also* acceptable)			Relevant verbal and nominal forms of the type ע״ח	
Bantam Megiddo	**Langenscheidt Achiasaf**	**Milon Even-Shoshan**	**Gloss**	**Form**
			bow over	גָחנָה
				גָחנוּ
			push, adjourn	דָחתָה
			to suppress (psych.)	הִדְחתָה
unmarked	–	–	scarecrow	דַחליל
			press	דָחסָה
				דָחסוּ
			push	דָחפָה
				דָחפוּ
			push (oneself)	נִדְחפָה
			forward	נִדְחפוּ
NA	+(– transcr.)	–	impulsive	דַחפוֹני
–	–	–	bulldozer	דַחפּוֹר
NA	+ (– transcr.)	NA	impulsive person	דַחפָן
			push	דָחקָה
				דָחקוּ
			push (oneself)	נִדְחקָה
			forward	נִדְחקוּ
NA	+ (– transcr.)	+	pressure	דַחקוּת
			creep	זָחלָה
				זָחלוּ
NA	+	+	creeping	זַחלי
unmarked	–	–	light tank	זַחל״ם
NA	–	–	opportunist	זַחלָן
NA	NA	–	opportunism	זַחלָנוּת
NA	NA	–	opportunistic	זַחלָני
NA	NA	–	boasting person	זַחתָן

ḥăṭāp ("+" in parentheses indicates that a form with *ḥăṭāp* is *also* acceptable)			Relevant verbal and nominal forms of the type ע"ח	
Bantam Megiddo	**Langenscheidt Achiasaf**	**Milon Even-Shoshan**	**Gloss**	**Form**
			grind, mill	טָחנָה
				טָחנוּ
+	+	+	mill	טַחנָה
NA	NA	–	one who always has to make an effort	טַחרָן
			devote	ייחדָה
				ייחדוּ
			isolate oneself	הִתיַחדָה
				הִתיַחדוּ
NA	NA	–	simultaneous	יַחדָוִוי
unmarked	–	–	together	יַחדָ(י)ו
			hope (outdated form)	ייחלָה
				ייחלוּ
			be sexually excited	יָחמָה
				יָחמוּ
NA	+	+	sexual excitement	יַחמָה
NA	NA	–	horny person	יַחמָני
unmarked	–	–	alcelaphus bubalis (zool.)	יַחמוּר
NA	–	–	helleborus (bot.)	יַחנוּן

ḥăṭāp̄ ("+" in parentheses indicates that a form with *ḥăṭāp̄* is *also* acceptable)			Relevant verbal and nominal forms of the type ע"ח	
Bantam Megiddo	**Langenscheidt Achiasaf**	**Milon Even-Shoshan**	**Gloss**	**Form**
			ascribe	ייחסָה
				ייחסוּ
			relate to	הִתיַחסָה
				הִתיַחסוּ
+	+	+	case (gramm.)	יַחסָה
NA	NA	–	relation	יְחסָה
+	+	+	relativity	יַחסוּת
+	+	+	relative	יַחסי
NA	+	+	relativism	יַחסיוּת
+	–	–	of noble offspring	יַחסָן
NA	–	–	arrogance	יַחסָנוּת
NA	–	–	arrogant	יַחסָני
				(יַחֲסֵי)
NA	NA	+	barefootedness	יַחפָה
NA	–	–	barefoot person	יַחפָן
NA	–	–	PR-consultant	יַחצ"ן
			conceal	כיחדָה
				כיחדוּ
			be devoured	נִכחדָה
				נִכחדוּ
			spit	כָחתָה
NA	–	–	clear(ing of) one's throat	כִחכוּח
unmarked	–	–		כִחכַח
unmarked	–	–		לְכַחכֵח
			put on mascara	כָחלָה
				כָחלוּ
NA	NA	–	darkish	כַחלוּל
NA	–	–	bluish	כַחלוּלי
NA	NA	–	cyanosis	כַחלוֹן
NA	NA	–	darkness	כַחלוּת

ḥăṭāp̄ ("+" in parentheses indicates that a form with *ḥăṭāp̄* is *also* acceptable)			Relevant verbal and nominal forms of the type ע״ח	
Bantam Megiddo	**Langenscheidt Achiasaf**	**Milon Even-Shoshan**	**Gloss**	**Form**
			lose weight	כָחשָה
				כָחשוּ
			deny	כיחשָה
				כיחשוּ
			to distance oneself	הִתכַחשָה
				הִתכַחשוּ
NA	NA	–	apostasy	כַחשוֹן
NA	NA	–		כַחשוּת
NA	NA	–	one who denies wrongdoing	כַחשָן
			moisten	ליחחָה
				ליחחוּ
NA	–	–	cheek	לֶחיָה
			lick	לַחכָה
				לַחכוּ
NA	–	–	moistening	לִחלוּח
unmarked	–	–	somewhat moist	לַחלוּחי
unmarked	–	–	moisten	לִחלַח
unmarked	–	–		לְלַחלֵח
			fight	לָחמָה
				לָחמוּ
				נִלחמָה
				נִלחמוּ
unmarked	–	–	way of fighting	לוֹחמָה
NA	NA	–	my bread; bread-like	(לַחמי)
NA	–	–	thin bread crust	לַחמית
unmarked	–	–	roll (of bread)	לַחמָניה

ḥăṭāp ("+" in parentheses indicates that a form with *ḥăṭāp* is *also* acceptable)			Relevant verbal and nominal forms of the type ע"ח	
Bantam Megiddo	**Langenscheidt Achiasaf**	**Milon Even-Shoshan**	**Gloss**	**Form**
			press	לָחצָה
				לָחצוּ
			be under pressure	נִלחצָה
				נִלחצוּ
NA	NA	+	hand-muscle trainer	לַחצית
NA	NA	+	oppression	לַחצָן
NA	NA	–	push-botton	לַחצָן
unmarked	–	–	little push-button	לַחצָנית
			whisper (v.)	לָחשָה
				לָחשוּ
				הִתלַחשָה
				הִתלַחשוּ
NA	+ (– transcr.)	–	whisper (n.)	לַחשוּש
unmarked	–	–	prompter (souffleur)	לַחשָן
NA	–	–	inspiration	לַחשָנוּת
NA	–	–	whisper	לִחשֵש
			clap (one's hands)	מָחאָה
				מָחאוּ
NA	+	– (+)	claqueur	מַחאָן
			wipe out; protest	מָחתָה
			transfer money	הִמחתָה
			specialise	הִתמַחתָה
			dissolve	מיחתָה
NA	+	+	thin like a needle	מַחטי
NA	NA	–	needle-like	מַחטָני
			forgive	מָחלָה
				מָחלוּ
			squish	מָחצָה
				מָחצוּ

ḥăṭāp ("+" in parentheses indicates that a form with *ḥăṭāp* is *also* acceptable)			Relevant verbal and nominal forms of the type ע"ח	
Bantam Megiddo	**Langenscheidt Achiasaf**	**Milon Even-Shoshan**	**Gloss**	**Form**
			erase	מָחקָה
				מָחקוּ
NA	NA	– (+)	eraser	מַחקָן
+	+	+	next day	מָחֳרָת
+	+	+	two days after	מָחֳרָתַיים
NA	NA	–	acronym: "young fighter" (military)	נַחלאי
			acquire possession	נָחלָה
				נָחלוּ
			settle	הִתנַחלָה
				הִתנַחלוּ
+	+	+	estate, inheritance	נַחלָה
NA	NA	–	water masses (Ps 124:4)	נַחְלָה
			repent	נִחמָה
				נִחמוּ
			comfort, console	ניחמָה
				ניחמוּ
			console oneself	הִתְנַחמָה
				הִתְנַחמוּ
NA	NA	–	we (byform of אֲנַחְנוּ)	נַחנוּ
NA	NA	–	with emphasis	נַחצי
			snore	נָחרָה
				נָחרוּ
+	+	+	snoring	נַחרָה
NA	NA	–	light snoring	נַחרוּר
NA	–	–	snoring person	נַחרָן
unmarked	–	–	big wave	נַחשוֹל

ḥăṭāp ("+" in parentheses indicates that a form with *ḥăṭāp* is *also* acceptable)			Relevant verbal and nominal forms of the type ע"ח	
Bantam Megiddo	**Langenscheidt Achiasaf**	**Milon Even-Shoshan**	**Gloss**	**Form**
NA	–	–	anhinga rufa (zool.)	נַחשוֹן
NA	–	–	pioneer spirit	נַחשוֹנוּת
unmarked	–	–	audacious	נַחשוֹנִי
NA	+ (– transcr.)	–	soothsayer	נַחשָׁן
unmarked	–	–	baker (outdated) (Akk. *nuḫatimmu*)	נַחתוֹם
NA	–	–	bakery	נַחתוֹמָר
			descend, land	נָחתָה
				נָחתוּ
NA	–	–	quiet, moderate	נַחתָן
NA	NA	–	moderation	נַחתָנוּת
			pull hard	סָחבָה
				סָחבוּ
			be pulled	נִסחבָה
				נִסחבוּ
NA	NA	– (+)	puller	סַחבָן
NA	NA	–	"your fellow" (= "I") (Arabic)	סַחבָּק
			press, blackmail	סָחטָה
				סָחטוּ
unmarked	–	–	blackmailer	סַחטָן
NA	NA	–	blackmail	סַחטָנוּת
NA	NA	–	engaged in blackmail	סַחטָנִי
unmarked	–	–	orchid	סַחלָב
NA	–	–	almondmilk-drink	סַחלֵב
			erode	סָחפָה
				סָחפוּ
			be eroded	הִסְתַחפָה
				הִסְתַחפוּ

$\underset{.}{h}\breve{a}\underset{.}{t}\bar{a}\bar{p}$ ("+" in parentheses indicates that a form with $\underset{.}{h}\breve{a}\underset{.}{t}\bar{a}\bar{p}$ is *also* acceptable)			**Relevant verbal and nominal forms of the type ע״ח**	
Bantam Megiddo	**Langenscheidt Achiasaf**	**Milon Even-Shoshan**	**Gloss**	**Form**
			trade	סָחֲרָה
				סָחֲרוּ
			trade bills	סִיחֲרָה
				סִיחֲרוּ
				(סַחֲרֵי)
NA	NA	– (+)	trader	סַחֲרָן
unmarked	–	–	spinning top	סִחְרוּר
unmarked	–	–	spin	סִחְרֵר
unmarked	–	–		לְסַחְרֵר
NA	NA	–	to your health, too (Arabic: "2 healths")	סַחְתֵּן
			be afraid	פָּחֲדָה
				פָּחֲדוּ
			be intimidated	נִפְחֲדָה
				נִפְחֲדוּ
			fear (v.)	פִּיחֲדָה
				פִּיחֲדוּ
NA	NA	–	fear (n.)	פַּחֲדָה
unmarked	–	–	anxious person	פַּחֲדָן
unmarked	–	–	fearfulness	פַּחֲדָנוּת
NA	–	–	fearful	פַּחֲדָנִי
			act thoughtlessly	פָּחֲזָה
				פָּחֲזוּ
NA	NA	+	thoughtlessness	פַּחֲזָה
+	+	+	thoughtless acting	פַּחֲזוּת
NA	+	– (+)	thoughtless person	פַּחֲזָן
NA	+	– (+)	thoughtlessness	פַּחֲזָנוּת
NA	+	– (+)	thoughtless	פַּחֲזָנִי
unmarked	–	–	stuff (animals)	פִּחְלוּץ
unmarked	–	–		פִּחְלֵץ
unmarked	–	–		לְפַחְלֵץ

ḥăṭāp̄ ("+" in parentheses indicates that a form with *ḥăṭāp̄* is *also* acceptable)			Relevant verbal and nominal forms of the type ע"ח	
Bantam Megiddo	**Langenscheidt Achiasaf**	**Milon Even-Shoshan**	**Gloss**	**Form**
			burn charcoal	פיחמָה
				פיחמוּ
unmarked	–	–	carbonate	פַּחמָה
unmarked	–	–	carbonisation	פִּחמוּן
		–	a lung disease	פַּחמוֹן
unmarked	–	–	carbonic	פַּחמִי
unmarked	–	–	carbo-hydrate	פַּחמֵימָה
unmarked	–	–	hydro-carbon	פַּחמֵימָן
unmarked	–	–	carbon	פַּחמָן
unmarked	–	–	carbonise	פִּחמֵן
unmarked	–	–		לְפַחְמֵן
unmarked	–	–	containing carbon	פַּחמָנִי
+	NA	+		פַּחמֵי אֶבֶן
			press flat	פָּחסָה
				פָּחסוּ
NA	NA	–	steaming (of a train)	פִּחפּוּח
NA	NA	–		פַּחפּוּחָה
			diminish	פָּחתָה
				פָּחתוּ
			devaluate (currency)	פיחתָה
				פיחתוּ
NA	NA	–	of low character	פַּחתִי
NA	NA	+	clairvoyance (compound)	צַחזוּת
			be clean	צָחחָה
				צָחחוּ
			stink	צָחנָה
				צָחנוּ
+	+	+	bad odour	צַחנָה
NA	NA	+	bad-smelling person	צַחנָן

ḥăṭāp ("+" in parentheses indicates that a form with *ḥăṭāp* is *also* acceptable)			Relevant verbal and nominal forms of the type ע"ח	
Bantam Megiddo	**Langenscheidt Achiasaf**	**Milon Even-Shoshan**	**Gloss**	**Form**
unmarked	–	–	clean, polish	צִחצוּח
unmarked	–	–		צִחצֵח
unmarked	–	–		לְצַחצֵח
NA	NA	–	superclean	צַחצַח
NA	NA	–	uncultured person	צַ'חצַ'ח
NA	NA	+	platform	צַחפָּה
NA	NA	–	whitish	צַחרוּרִי
NA	NA	+	"whiteness"	צַחרוּת
			laugh	צָחקָה
				צָחקוּ
+	NA	+	laughter	צַחקָה
unmarked	–	–	giggling	צִחקוּק
unmarked	–	–	giggle	צִחקֵק
unmarked	–	–		לְצַחקֵק
unmarked	NA	– (+)	laughing person	צַחקָן
NA	+ (– transcr.)	– (+)	laughter	צַחקָנוּת
NA	+ (– transcr.)	– (+)	laughing	צַחקָנִי
NA	–	–	anthemis (bot.)	קַחווָן
			become broader	רָחבָה
				רָחבוּ
			be broad	נִרחבָה
				נִרחבוּ
NA	NA	+	breadth	רַחבוּת
NA	NA	+		(רַחבֵי)
NA	NA	+	broad person	רַחבָן

ḥăṭāp̄ ("+" in parentheses indicates that a form with *ḥăṭāp̄* is *also* acceptable)			Relevant verbal and nominal forms of the type ע״ח	
Bantam Megiddo	**Langenscheidt Achiasaf**	**Milon Even-Shoshan**	**Gloss**	**Form**
			have pity	ריחמָה
				ריחמוּ
+	+	+	pity	רַחמים
+	+ (– transcr.)	– (+)	forgiving person	רַחמָן
+	+ (– transcr.)	– (+)		רַחמָנא
+	+ (– transcr.)	– (+)	forgivingness	רַחמָוּת
NA	+ (– transcr.)	– (+)	forgiving	רַחמָני
NA	NA	+		רַחמֵי שָׁמַיים
			be suspended	רָחפָה
				רָחפוּ
				ריחפָה
				ריחפוּ
unmarked	+ (– transcr.)	–	suspended	רַחפָני
NA	NA	–	slight movement	רִחפּוּף
NA	NA	–	move slightly	רִחפֵּף
NA	NA	–		לְרַחפֵּף
			wash	רָחצָה
				רָחצוּ
			take a shower	הִתרַחצָה
				הִתרַחצוּ
unmarked	–	–	bath	רַחצָה
NA	NA	–	bathing person	רַחצָן

ḥăṭāp̄ ("+" in parentheses indicates that a form with *ḥăṭāp̄* is *also* acceptable)			Relevant verbal and nominal forms of the type ע״ח	
Bantam Megiddo	**Langenscheidt Achiasaf**	**Milon Even-Shoshan**	**Gloss**	**Form**
			be distant	רָחקָה
				רָחקוּ
			remove	ריחקָה
				ריחקוּ
			distance oneself	הִתרַחקָה
				הִתרַחקוּ
NA	NA	+	distance	רַחקוּת
NA	NA	–	one who distances oneself	רַחקָן
unmarked	–	–	smell, sniff	רִחרוּח
unmarked	–	–		רִחרֵח
unmarked	–	–		לְרַחרֵח
NA	–	–	overcurious person	רַחרְחָן
			whisper (v.);	רָחשָׁה
			be plentiful	רָחשׁוּ
			happen	הִתרַחשָׁה
				הִתרַחשׁוּ
NA	NA	+	whisper	רַחשׁוֹן
NA	NA	– (+)	whisper	רַחשׁוּשׁ
NA	NA	+		(רַחשֵׁי)
NA	NA	–	exercise to change a syntactic pattern?	שִׁחבּוּר
NA	NA	–		שִׁחבֵּר
NA	NA	–		לְשַׁחבֵּר
			bribe	שָׁחדָה
				שָׁחדוּ
				שיחדָה
				שיחדוּ
			accept a bribe	נֵשְׁתַחדָה
				נֵשְׁתַחדוּ

ḥăṭāp ("+" in parentheses indicates that a form with *ḥăṭāp* is *also* acceptable)			Relevant verbal and nominal forms of the type ע״ח	
Bantam Megiddo	**Langenscheidt Achiasaf**	**Milon Even-Shoshan**	**Gloss**	**Form**
			swim	שָׂחִתָה
unmarked	–	–	swimmer	שַׂחְיָן
unmarked	NA	–	swimming sport	שַׂחְיָנוּת
NA	NA	+	prostrate oneself	שָׁחָה
+	+	+		הִשְׁתַּחֲוָה
NA	NA	–	warm thing or person (Aramaic)	שַׁחֲוָן
NA	+	–	minister, duke	שַׁחֲוָר
unmarked	–	–	reconstruction	שִׁחְזוּר
unmarked	–	–	reconstruct	שִׁחְזֵר
unmarked	–	–		לְשַׁחְזֵר
NA	NA	–	be reconstructed	הִשְׁתַּחְזֵר
NA	NA	–	one who likes dialogues	שַׂחֲוָן
			slaughter	שָׁחֲטָה
				שָׁחֲטוּ
NA	NA	– (+)	moral corruption	שַׁחֲטָה
			sneek oneself in	הִשְׁתַּחֲלָה
				הִשְׁתַּחֲלוּ
+	+	+	ovaries	שַׁחֲלָה
NA	NA	+	a certain plant (lepidium)	שַׁחֲלַיִים
unmarked	–	–	change back	שִׁחְלֵף
unmarked	–	–		לְשַׁחְלֵף
NA	–	– (+)	brownish	שַׁחֲמוּמִי
NA	NA	–		שַׁחֲמָנִי
unmarked	–	–	chess	שַׁחְמָט
		–	chess playing	שַׁחְמְטָאוּת
NA	NA	–	marinated fodder (compound)	שַׁחֲמִיץ

ḥăṭāp ("+" in parentheses indicates that a form with *ḥăṭāp* is *also* acceptable)			Relevant verbal and nominal forms of the type ע״ח	
Bantam Megiddo	**Langenscheidt Achiasaf**	**Milon Even-Shoshan**	**Gloss**	**Form**
			pine away	שָחפָה
				שָחפוּ
			get tuberculosis	נִשְחפָה
				נִשְחפוּ
	+ (– transcr.)	–	person smitten with tuberculosis	שַחפָן
+	NA	–	smitten with tuberculosis	שַחפָני
NA	+	+	sea swallow (sterna)	שַחפית
			be proud	שָחצָה
				שָחצוּ
NA	NA	–	pride	שַחצָה
NA	NA	+		שַחצוּת
NA	+ (– transcr.)	– (+)	boasting (n.)	שַחצית
+	+	– (+)	boasting person	שַחצָן
+	+	– (+)	boasting behaviour	שַחצָנוּת
+	+	– (+)	boasting	שַחצָני
NA	–	–	behave arrogantly	הִשתַחצֵן
			play (v.)	שׂיחקָה
				שׂיחקוּ
NA	NA	–	play (n.)	שַׂחקָה
NA	NA	–		שַׂחקוּנָה
+	+ (– transcr.)	– (+)	actor	שַׂחקָן
+	+ (– transcr.)	– (+)	acting	שַׂחקָנוּת
NA	+ (– transcr.)	– (+)	actress	שַׂחקָנית
			rub, grind	שָׂחקָה
				שָׂחקוּ
			be ground	נִשׂחקָה
				נִשׂחקוּ
			seek (outdated)	שָחרָה
				שָחרוּ

ḥăṭāp̄ ("+" in parentheses indicates that a form with *ḥăṭāp̄* is *also* acceptable)			Relevant verbal and nominal forms of the type ע"ח	
Bantam Megiddo	**Langenscheidt Achiasaf**	**Milon Even-Shoshan**	**Gloss**	**Form**
unmarked	–	–	liberation	שִחרוּר
unmarked	–	–	liberate	שִחרֵר
unmarked	–	–		לְשַחרֵר
NA	+ (– transcr.)	– (+)	blackbird	שַחרוּר
NA	NA	– (+)	blackness	שַחרוּרית
+	+	+	youth; blackness	שַחרוּת
+	+	+	morning time, matinee	שַחרית
NA	NA	–	"Fernsprecher" (compound)	שַחרָחוֹק
			spoil, delete	שיחתָה
				שיחתוּ
NA	NA	– (+)	spoiler	שַחתָן
			plug in	תָחבָה
				תחבוּ
unmarked	–	–	invent a ruse	תִחבֵל
unmarked	–	–		לְתַחבֵּל
unmarked	–	–	ruseful person	תַחבְלָן
unmarked	–	–	rusefulness	תַחבְלָנוּת
NA	–	–	ruseful	תַחבְלָני
unmarked	–	–	maintain in good order	תִחזֵק
unmarked	–	–		לְתַחזֵק
unmarked	–	–	reconstruction	תִחזוּר
unmarked	–	–	reconstruct	תִחזֵר
unmarked	–	–		לְתַחְזֵר
			loosen the ground ("Boden auflockern")	תָחחָה
				תָחחוּ
unmarked	–	–	intellectual rafinesse	תִחכוּם
unmarked	–	–	emulsify	תִחלֵב
unmarked	–	–		לְתַחלֵב

ḥăṭāp ("+" in parentheses indicates that a form with *ḥăṭāp* is *also* acceptable)			Relevant verbal and nominal forms of the type ע"ח	
Bantam Megiddo	**Langenscheidt Achiasaf**	**Milon Even-Shoshan**	**Gloss**	**Form**
NA	–	–	replacing	תִחלוּף
			confine, delineate	תָחמָה
				תָחמוּ
unmarked	–	–	make sour	תִחמֵץ
unmarked	–	–		לְתַחמֵץ
unmarked	–	–	provide with ammunition	תִחמֵש
unmarked	–	–		לְתַחמֵש
unmarked	NA	–	dress up (in masquerade)	תִחפֵשׂ
unmarked	NA	–		לְתַחְפֵשׂ
NA	–	–	investigate the results of a test	תִחקֵר
NA	–	–		לְתַחקֵר
NA	–	–	lace; point	תַחרָה
			be in competition	תִיחרָה
				תִיחרוּ
+	NA	+	compete	תִחרָה
+	NA	+		יתַחרֶה
+ (analogy)	NA	+		לְתַחרֶה
NA	–	–	calculate	תִחשֵב
NA	–	–		לְתַחשֵב
NA	–	–	calculation	תִחשוּב
unmarked	–	–	lower	תַחתוֹן
unmarked	–	–	pants (underwear)	תַחתוֹנים
unmarked	–	–	petticoat, slip	תַחתוֹנית
unmarked	–	–	lower	תַחתי
unmarked	–	–	saucer	תַחתית
NA	NA	–	noise	תִחתוּח

Appendix 8:
Selected modern test forms in context

בשנה הבאה, הוא יחגוג את יום העצמאות בארץ עם כל המשפחה שלו. אישתו לא רוצה לחגוג את יום העצמאות כל הזמן בחוץ לארץ.

אם מישהו יחזיק במעקה הרקוב ויפול מן המדרגות, יהיו לנו צרות צרורות.

קשה לדעת כמה זמן ניתן עוד יהיה להחזיק בשטחים המוחזקים.

מיכאל יחזור מחר; אני צריך להחזיר לו את המחשב ששאלתי ממנו.

רינה לא החזירה לו את הטבעת, ובצדק.

אני מחכה להחזר ממס הכנסה. כל שנה מוחזרים לי אלף או אלפיים דולר בצורה זו.

אנחנו צריכים לחיות בביטחון; אנחנו פוחדים שלא נחיה בביטחון בתחום-העיר הזאת.

הרופא הצליח להחיות את הפצועים בבית החולים החדש.

אני מקווה שלא אחלה לפני החופשה; יש לי תוכניות מעניינות לקייץ, אז אני לא רוצה לחלות.

הציבור הגיב בזעם על ההחלטה, וההסתדרות הכללית של העובדים החליטה לקיים סידרה של שביתות.

בלילה הבא תחלום את אותו חלום מבהיל אם לא תירגע עכשיו.

השחקנית הזאת מחליפה בעלים כל שנה-שנתיים. בעלה האחרון "הוחלף" לפני שישה חדשים.

גם אזרח מן הסביבה נחלץ לעזרת הנפגעים.

גם המומחים נחלקים אודות הפוליטיקה של הממשלה.

שר החינוך והתרבות יחנוך ביום שני את המכון החדש. זהו המכון השלישי שנחנך השנה.

אנחנו מקווים שנוכל סוף סוף לחסוך קצת לרכישת דירה.

כמו כן, מכיוון שהחסיר מספר שעות בחינוך גופני, חיסר לו המורה לספורט יותר נקודות מכפי שציפה.

המפקד הורה לחייליו לחפור שוחות ולהתחפר בהן. עד לשעת הצהריים נחפרו כל השוחות.

החשוד נחקר שעות ארוכות בידי המשטרה. החוקרים ממשיכים לחקור אותו היום בערב.

רגלי העץ של השלחן נחרטות במחרטה; לאחר מכן חורט עליהן האומן פיתוחים שונים.

היחסים בין שתי המדינות הלכו והחריפו מיום ליום. החרפת היחסים הגיעה לשיאה לאחר שמדינת א׳ התקיפה את מדינת ב׳.

חיים נחשב למומחה החשוב בארץ בכלכלה; שר האוצר מחשיב מאוד את דעתו, וכמעט מתחשב בהמלצותיו.

לטענת המשטרה, החשוד נתפס בנסיבות מחשידות; הוא נחשד בניסיון לפרוץ לבית מגורים.

הם חוששים לחשוף את העור לשמש.

רשת גדולה של סוחרי סמים נחשפה לאחרונה.

אפריים נחתך הבוקר בזמן הגילוח.

עורכי הדין החתימו את לקוחותיהם על החוזה.

References

Abu-Mansour, Mahasen H. 2003. "Epenthesis in Makkan Arabic: unsyllabified consonants vs. degenerate syllables", in: Bernard Comrie and Mushira Eid (eds.). *Perspectives on Arabic Linguistics III. Papers from the Annual Symposium on Arabic Linguistics,* 173–154. Amsterdam: J. Benjamins.

Adam, Galit. 2002. *From Variable to Optimal Grammar: Evidence from Language Acquisition and Language Change.* Doctoral dissertation, Tel Aviv University.

Al-Ani, Salman. 2008. "Phonetics", in: Kees Versteegh et al. (eds.). *Encyclopedia of Arabic Language and Linguistics.* Volume III. Lat–Pu, 593–603. Leiden: Brill.

Alderete, John. 1997. "Dissimilation as local conjunction", in: Kiyomi Kusumoto (ed.). *Proceedings of the North East Linguistic Society* 27: 17–32. Amherst, MA: GLSA Publications.

Angoujard, Jean-Pierre. 1986. "Les hiérarchies prosodiques en arabe", *Revue québécoise de linguistique* 16/1: 1–38.

Angoujard, Jean-Pierre. 1997. *Théorie de la syllabe.* Paris: CNRS.

Anttila, Arto. 1995. *Deriving Variation from Grammar: a study of Finnish genitives.* Ms., Stanford University. [Rutgers Optimality Archive #ROA–63-0000, http://roa.rutgers.edu/index.php3]

Bantam-Megiddo 1975 = *The New Bantam-Megiddo Hebrew & English Dictionary.* By Dr. Reuven Sivan and Edward A. Levenston. New York et al.: Bantam Books.

Bat-El, Outi. 1995. "On the apparent ambiguity of the schwa symbol in Tiberian Hebrew", *Langues Orientales Anciennes Philologie et Linguistique* 5–6: 79–96.

Bat-El, Outi. 1996. "Selecting the best of the worst: The grammar of Hebrew blends", *Phonology* 13: 283–328.

Bat-El, Outi. 2008. "Morphologically conditioned V–Ø alternation in Hebrew: Distinction among nouns, adjectives & participles, and verbs", in: Sharon Armon-Lotem, Gabi Danon, and Susan Rothstein (eds.). *Current Issues in Generative Hebrew Linguistics,* 27–60. Amsterdam: J. Benjamins.

Bauer & Leander 1922 = Bauer, Hans and Leander, Pontus. 1922. *Historische Grammatik der hebräischen Sprache des Alten Testaments. Erster Band: Einleitung. Schriftlehre. Laut- und Formenlehre.* Halle: Max Niemeyer.

Beer & Meyer 1952–1955 = Beer, Georg and Meyer, Rudolf. 1952–1955. *Hebräische Grammatik. Erster Band. Schrift-, Laut- und Formenlehre I. Zweiter Band. Formenlehre II, Syntax und Flexionstabellen.* Berlin: Walter de Gruyter.

Ben-David, Israel. 1994/1995. "Two comments on morphology" (in Hebrew), *Lĕšonénu* 58/4: 297–307.

Ben-Horin, Gad and Bolozky, Shmuel. 1972. "Hebrew *b, p, k* – rule opacity or data opacity", *Hebrew Computational Linguistics* 5: 24–35.

Bennett, Patrick. 1998. *Comparative Semitic Linguistics. A Manual.* Eisenbrauns: Winona Lake.

Benua, Laura. 1997. *Transderivational Identity. Phonological Relations between Words.* Doctoral dissertation, University of Massachusetts at Amherst. [also published: 2000. New York, NY: Garland]

Bergsträsser, Gotthelf. 1918–1929. *Hebräische Grammatik.* Leipzig: J.C Hinrichs'sche Buchhandlung.

Berman, Ruth. 1997. "Modern Hebrew", in: Robert Hetzron (ed.). *The Semitic Languages*, 312–333. London: Routledge.

Biblia Hebraica Stuttgartensia. 1997 (5th edition). Stuttgart: Deutsche Bibelgesellschaft.

Blake, Frank R. 1926. "The Hebrew ḫatephs", in: Cyrus Adler and Aaron Ember (eds.). *Oriental Studies Published in Commemoration of the Fortieth Anniversary of Paul Haupt*, 329–343. Baltimore: The Johns Hopkins Press and Leipzig: J.C. Hinrichs'sche Buchhandlung.

Blanc, Haim. 1970. "The Arabic dialect of the Negev Bedouins", *Proceedings of the Israel Academy of Sciences and Humanity* 4: 112–150.

Blau, Joshua. 1990. "On the multilayered structure of Biblical Hebrew in the light of Modern Hebrew" (in Hebrew), *Lĕšonénu* 54: 103–114.

Blau, Joshua. 1993 (2nd amended ed.). *A Grammar of Biblical Hebrew.* Wiesbaden: Harrassowitz.

Bolozky, Shmuel. 1996 (1st ed.)/2008 (2nd ed.). *501 Hebrew Verbs.* Hauppauge, NY: Barron's Educational Series.

Bolozky, Shmuel. 1997. "Israeli Hebrew Phonology", in: Alan S. Kaye (ed.). *Phonologies of Asia and Africa*, vol. 1, 287–311. Winona Lake: Eisenbrauns.

Bolozky, Shmuel. 1999. *Measuring Word Productivity. The Case of Israeli Hebrew.* Leiden: Brill.

Bolozky, Shmuel. 2006. "A note on initial consonantal clusters in Israeli Hebrew", *Hebrew Studies* 47: 227–235.

Bolozky, Shmuel. 2008. "The limits of describing the morpho-phonology of Israeli Hebrew with the Masoretic system." Handout to the Roundtable *Current Issues in Hebrew Morpho-Phonology*, Oslo, October 27, 2008.

Brockelmann, Carl. 1908. *Grundriß der vergleichenden Grammatik der semitischen Sprachen. I. Laut- und Formenlehre.* Berlin: Reuther & Reichard. [reprint: 1999. Hildesheim: Olms]

Brønno, Einar. 1970. *Die Aussprache der hebräischen Laryngale nach Zeugnissen des Hieronymus.* Aarhus: Universitetsforlaget.

Buccellati, Giorgio. 1997. "Akkadian and Amorite phonology", in: Alan S. Kaye (ed.). *Phonologies of Asia and Africa*, vol. 1, 3–38. Winona Lake: Eisenbrauns.

Bürki, Audrey, Fougeron, Cécile, and Gendrot, Cédric, 2007. "On the categorical nature of the process involved in *schwa* elision in French". [http://www.unige.ch/fapse/psycholinguistique/equipe/buerki/burki_et_al_interspeech2007.pdf]

Chomsky, Noam. 1995. *The Minimalist Program.* Cambridge, Mass.: MIT Press.

Churchyard, Henry. 1999. *Topics in Tiberian Hebrew Metrical Phonology and Prosodics.* Doctoral dissertation, University of Texas at Austin.

Clements, George N. 1990. "The role of the sonority cycle in core syllabification", in: John Kingston and Mary E. Beckman (eds). *Papers in Laboratory Phonology I: Between the Grammar and Physics of Speech*, 282-333. Cambridge: Cambridge University Press.

Coetzee, Andries W. 1997. "Syllabification and epenthesis in Tiberian Hebrew: perspectives from Optimality Theory", *Journal for Semitics* 9: 87–128.

Coetzee, Andries W. 1999. *Tiberian Hebrew Phonology: focusing on consonant clusters.* Assen: Van Gorcum.

Coffin, Edna and Bolozky, Shmuel. 2005. *A Reference Grammar of Modern Hebrew.* Cambridge: Cambridge University Press.

Crystal, David. 1989. *A Dictionary of Linguistics and Phonetics.* Oxford: Basil Blackwell.

DeCaen, Vincent. 2003. "Hebrew sonority and Tiberian contact anaptyxis: the case of verbs *primae gutturalis*", *Journal of Semitic Studies* 48/1: 35–46.

de Jong, Rudolf. 2007. "Gahawa-Syndrome", in: Kees Versteegh et al. (eds.). *Encyclopedia of Arabic Language and Linguistics.* Volume II. Eg–Lan, 151–153. Leiden: Brill.

Edzard, Lutz. 1991. "Semitic phonology and preference laws for syllable structure", in: Alan S. Kaye (ed.). *Semitic Studies in Honor of Wolf Leslau on the Occasion of His Eighty-Fifth Birthday, November 14th, 1991*, vol. 1: 397–410. Wiesbaden: Harrassowitz.

Edzard, Lutz. 1992. "The Obligatory Contour Principle and Dissimilation in Afroasiatic", *Journal of Afroasiatic Languages* 3: 151–171.

Edzard, Lutz. 2008. "Optimality and Arabic", in: Kees Versteegh et al. (eds.). *Encyclopedia of Arabic Language and Linguistics.* Volume III. Lat–Pu, 491–499. Leiden: Brill.

Eldar, Ilan. 1980–1981. "*Hidāyat al-Qāri* (the longer Arabic version): a specimen text, critically edited, with Hebrew translation, commentary and introduction" (in Hebrew), *Lĕšonénu* 45: 233–259.

Even-Shoshan, Avraham. 1990. *Konkordantsya xadasha: le-Tora, Neviim u-Khetuvim: otsar leshon ha-Mikra – Ivrit va-Aramit: shorashim, milim, shemot pratiyim, tserufim ve-nirdafim* (קונקורדנציה חדשה: לתורה, נביאים וכתובים: אוצר לשון המקרא־־עברית וארמית: שרשים, מלים, שמות פרטיים, צרופים ונרדפים). Jerusalem: Kiryat Sefer.

Even-Shoshan 2003 = Even-Shoshan, Avraham. 2003. *Milon Even-Shoshan. Mechudash u-me'udkan li-shnot ha-'alpayim.* Israel [no place and publisher].

Faust, Noam. 2006. *The Fate of the Historical Gutturals in Modern Hebrew.* MA Thesis, Tel Aviv University.

Fischer, Wolfdietrich and Jastrow, Otto (eds.) 1980. *Handbuch der arabischen Dialekte.* Wiesbaden: Harrassowitz.

Garr, W. Randall. 1989. "The *seghol* and segholation in Hebrew", *Journal of Near Eastern Studies* 48: 109–116.

Geers, Friedrich Wilhelm. 1945. "The treatment of emphatics in Akkadian", *Journal of Near Eastern Studies* 4: 65–67.

Gesenius 1910 = *Gesenius' Hebrew Grammar as edited by the late E. Kautzsch.* Second English edition revised in accordance with the 28th German edition (1909) by A.E. Cowley. Oxford: Clarendon Press.

Gesenius 1995 = *Wilhelm Gesenius' Hebräisches und Aramäisches Handwörterbuch über das Alte Testament.* 18th ed. 2. Lieferung ד-י. Berlin: Springer Verlag.

Ginsberg, H. Louis. 1929–1930. "Studies on the Biblical Hebrew Verb – III Phonetic studies", *American Journal of Semitic Languages and Literatures* 46: 127–137.

Glinert, Lewis. 1989. *The Grammar of Modern Hebrew.* Cambridge: Cambridge University Press.

Goerwitz, Richard L. 1996. "The Jewish scripts", in Peter D. Daniels and William Bright (eds.). *The World's Writing Systems*, 487–498. New York/Oxford: Oxford University Press.

Gouskova, Maria. 2004. "Relational hierarchies in Optimality Theory: the case of syllable contact", *Phonology* 21: 201–250.

Graf, Dafna and Ussishkin, Adam. 2002. "Emergent iambs: stress in modern Hebrew", *Lingua* 13/3: 239–270. [Rutgers Optimality Archive #ROA-446-0701, http://roa.rutgers.edu/index.php3]

Grassmann, Hermann. 1863. "Über das ursprüngliche vorhandensein von wurzeln deren anlaut und auslaut eine aspirate enthielt", *Zeitschrift für vergleichende Sprachforschung auf dem Gebiete der indogermanischen Sprachen* 12: 110–138.

Greenberg, Joseph. 1950. "The patterning of root morphemes in Semitic", *Word* 6: 162–181.

Greenstein, Edward. 1984. "The phonology of Akkadian syllable structure", *Afroasiatic Linguistics* 9/1: 1–71.

Harris, Zellig. 1941. "The linguistic structure of Hebrew", *Journal of the American Oriental Society* 61: 143–167.

Hasselbach, Rebecca and Huehnergard, John. 2008. "Northwest Semitic Languages", in Kees Versteegh et al. (eds.). *Encyclopedia of Arabic Language and Linguistics.* Volume III. Lat–Pu, 408–422. Leiden: Brill.

Hoberman, Robert D. 1989. "Initial consonant clusters in Hebrew and Aramaic", *Journal of Near Eastern Studies* 48/1: 25–29.

Hooper, Joan Bybee. 1976. *An Introduction to Natural Generative Phonology.* New York: Academic Press.

Huehnergard, John. 2000. *A Grammar of Akkadian.* Winona Lake: Eisenbrauns.

Huehnergard, John. 2003. "Akkadian *ḫ* and West Semitic **ḥ*", in Leonid Kogan (ed.). *Orientalia: Paper of the Oriental Institute* 3 [Alexander Militarev Volume], 102–119. Moscow: Russian State University for the Humanities.

Idsardi, William J. 1998. "Tiberian Hebrew spirantization and phonological derivations", *Linguistic Inquiry* 29/1: 37–73.

Jespersen, Otto. 1897–1899. *Fonetik. En systematisk fremstilling af læren om sproglyd.* Copenhagen: Det Schubotheske Forlag.

Jespersen, Otto. 1904 [4th ed. 1926; unchanged since 2nd ed. 1912]. *Lehrbuch der Phonetik.* Leipzig: B.G. Teubner.

Joüon, Paul and Muraoka, Takamitsu. 1993. *A Grammar of Biblical Hebrew. Part One: Orthography and Phonetics. Part Two: Morphology.* Rome: Editrice Pontificio Istituto Biblico.

Kager, René. 1999. *Optimality Theory.* Cambridge: Cambridge University Press.

Kahle, Paul. 1902. *Der masoretische Text des Alten Testaments. Nach der Überlieferung der babylonischen Juden.* Leipzig: J. C. Hinrichs. [reprint: 1966. Hildesheim: Olms]

Kahle, Paul. 1959 (2nd ed.). *The Cairo Geniza.* Oxford: Blackwell.

Kapeliuk, Olga. 1997. "Tav ve-dalet rafot be-'aramit xadasha", *Masorot* 9–11: 527–544.

Kenstowicz, Michael. 1996. "Base-identity and uniform exponence: Alternatives to cyclicity", in: Jacques Durand and Bernard Laks (eds.). *Current Trends in Phonology: Models and Methods*, 363–393. Salford: European Studies Research Institute.

Khan, Geoffrey. 1987. "Vowel length and syllable structure in the Tiberian tradition of Biblical Hebrew", *Journal of Semitic Studies* 32: 32–82.

Khan, Geoffrey. 1994. "The pronunciation of the verbs היה and חיה in the Tiberian tradition of Biblical Hebrew", in: Gideon Goldenberg and Shlomo Raz (eds.). *Semitic and Cushitic Studies*, 133–144. Wiesbaden: Harrassowitz.

Khan, Geoffrey. 1997. "Tiberian Hebrew phonology", in: Alan S. Kaye (ed.). *Phonologies of Asia and Africa*, vol. 1, 85–102. Winona Lake: Eisenbrauns.

Kiparsky, Paul. 2003. "Syllables and moras in Arabic", in: Caroline Féry and Ruben van der Vijver (eds.). *The Syllable in Optimality Theory*, 147–182. Cambridge: Cambridge University Press.

Koehler & Baumgartner 1994 = Koehler, Ludwig and Baumgartner, Walter. 1994. *The Hebrew and Aramaic Lexicon of the Old Testament, subsequently revised by Walter Baumgartner and Johann Jakob Stamm*, translated and edited under the supervision of M.E.J. Richardson, vol. I: א - ח. Leiden etc.: Brill.

Kristoffersen, Gjert. 2000. *The Phonology of Norwegian.* Oxford: Oxford University Press.

Kutscher, Eduard Yechezkel. 1982. *A History of the Hebrew Language.* Jerusalem: Magnes Press.

Lambdin, Thomas O. 1978. *Introduction to Classical Ethiopic (Ge^{c}ez).* Scholars Press: Missoula.

LaSor, William Sanford. 1956. "Secondary opening of syllables originally closed with gutturals (in Hebrew)", *Journal of Near Eastern Studies* 15: 246–250.

Lavi 2004/Langenscheidt – Achiasaf 2004 = Lavi, Yaacov. 2004. *Handwörterbuch Hebräisch-Deutsch*. Berlin et al.: Langenscheidt – Tel Aviv: Achiasaf.

Lipiński, Edward. 2001 (2nd ed.). *Semitic Languages. Outline of a Comparative Grammar.* Louvain: Peeters.

Lisowsky, Gerhard. 1993. (3rd ed.). *Konkordanz zum hebräischen Alten Testament.* Stuttgart: Deutsche Bibelgesellschaft.

Lowenstamm, Jean and Kaye, Jonathan. 1985. "Compensatory lengthening in Tiberian Hebrew", in: Leo Wetzels and Engin Sezer (eds.). *Studies in Compensatory Lengthening*, 97–132. Dordrecht: Foris Publications.

Malone, Joseph. 1993. *Tiberian Hebrew Phonology.* Winona Lake: Eisenbrauns.

McCarthy, John J. 1985. *Formal Problems in Semitic Phonology and Morphology.* New York: Garland Publishing.

McCarthy, John. 1986. "OCP effects: gemination and antigemination", *Linguistic Inquiry* 17/2: 207–263.

McCarthy, John J. 1991. "Semitic gutturals and distinctive feature theory", in: Bernard Comrie and Mushira Eid (eds.). *Perspectives on Arabic Linguistics III. Papers from the Annual Symposium on Arabic Linguistics*, 63–92. Amsterdam: J. Benjamins.

McCarthy, John J. 1994. "The phonetics and phonology of Semitic pharyngeals", in: Patricia Keating (ed.). *Papers in Laboratory Phonology III: Phonological Structure and Phonetic Form*, 191–233. Cambridge: Cambridge University Press.

McCarthy, John J. 2003. "Sympathy, cumulativity, and the Duke-of-York gambit", in: Caroline Féry and Ruben van de Vijver, (eds.). *The Syllable in Optimality Theory*, 23–76. Cambridge: Cambridge University Press.

McCarthy, John J. 2004 (ed.). *Optimality Theory in Phonology. A Reader.* Malden etc.: Blackwell Publishing.

McCarthy, John J. 2005. "Optimal paradigms", in: Laura Downing, Tracy Alan Hall, and Renate Raffelsiefen (eds.). *Paradigms in Phonological Theory*, 170–210. Oxford: Oxford University Press.

McCarthy, John J. and Prince, Alan. 1994. "The emergence of the unmarked. Optimality in prosodic morphology", in: Mercè Gonzàlez (ed.). *Proceedings of the North East Linguistic Society 24*, 333–379. Amherst, MA: GLSA Publications. [Rutgers Optimality Archive #ROA-13-0594, http://roa.rutgers.edu/index.php3]

McCarthy, John J. and Prince, Alan. 1995. "Prosodic morphology", in: John A. Goldsmith (ed.). *The Handbook of Phonological Theory*, 318–366. Oxford: Blackwell.

Morag, Shlomo. 1962. *The Vocalization Systems of Arabic, Hebrew, and Aramaic.* s'Gravenhage: Mouton & Co.

Murray, Robert and Vennemann, Theo. 1982. "Syllable contact change in Germanic, Greek, and Sidamo", *Klagenfurter Beiträge zur Sprachwissenschaft* 8: 333–356.

Nöldeke, Theodor. 1898. *Kurzgefaßte syrische Grammatik.* Leipzig: T.O. Weigel. [reprint: 1966. Darmstadt: Wissenschaftliche Buchgesellschaft]

Nöldeke, Theodor. 1912. "Inkonsequenzen in der hebräischen Punktuation", *Zeitschrift für Assyriologie* 26: 1–15.

Ohala, John J. 1992. "Alternatives to the sonority hierarchy for explaining segmental sequencial constraints", in: Michael Ziolkowski, Manuela Noske, and Karen Deaton (eds.). *Papers from the 26th Regional Meeting of the Chicago Linguistic Society,* vol. 2, 319–338. Chicago: Chicago Linguistic Society.

Oxford: Levy, Ya'acov. *Hebrew-English English-Hebrew Dictionary.* Kernerman – Lonnie Kahn.

Parker, Steve. 2002. *Quantifying the Sonority Hierarchy.* Doctoral disseration, University of Massachusetts at Amherst.

Pons Moll, Clàudia. 2008. "The sonority scale: categorical or gradient?", poster presented at the CUNY Conference on the Syllable, January 17th – 19th, 2008. [http://www.cunyphonologyforum.net/SYLLABSTRACTS/PonsPoster.pdf]

Prince, Alan and Smolensky, Paul. 1993. *Optimality Theory: Constraint Interaction in Generative Grammar.* New Brunswick, NJ: Rutgers University Center for Cognitive Science. [Rutgers Optimality Archive #ROA–13-0594, http://roa. rutgers. edu/index.php3]

Rabin, Chaim. 1960. "The development of Proto-Semitic *a*", *Tarbiz* 30: 99–111.

Rappaport, Malka. 1981. "On the phonology of gutturals in Biblical Hebrew", in: Hagit Borer and Youssef Aoun (eds.). *Theoretical Issues in the Grammar of Semitic Languages* (*MIT Working Papers in Linguistics* 3), 101–120.

Rendsburg, Gary. 1997. "Ancient Hebrew phonology", in: Alan S. Kaye (ed.). *Phonologies of Asia and Africa,* vol. 1, 65–83. Winona Lake: Eisenbrauns.

Rose, Sharon and Walker, Rachel. 2004 "A typology of consonant agreement as correspondence", *Language* 80: 475–531.

Ružička, Rudolf. 1954. "La question de l'existence du *ġ* dans les langues sémitiques en général et dans la langue ugaritique en particulier", *Archív Orientální* 22: 176–237.

Sáenz-Badillos, Angel. 1983. *A History of the Hebrew Language.* Cambridge: Cambridge University Press.

Schwarzwald, Ora R. 2001. *Modern Hebrew.* Munich: LINCOM EUROPA.

Segal, Moses Hirsch. 1958. *A Grammar of Mishnaic Hebrew.* Oxford: Clarendon Press.

Sievers, Eduard. 1901a. *Grundzüge der Phonetik.* Leipzig: Breitkopf & Härtel.

Sievers, Eduard. 1901b. "Metrische Studien I. Studien zur hebräischen Metrik. Erster Teil: Untersuchungen", *Abhandlungen der philologisch-historischen Classe der Königlich-Sächsischen Gesellschaft der Wissenschaften* 21: 1–400.

Speiser, Ephraim A. 1926. "Secondary developments in Semitic phonology", *The American Journal of Semitic Languages* 42/3: 145–169.

Steiner, Richard. 1977. *The Case for Fricative-Laterals in Proto-Semitic.* New Haven: American Oriental Society.

Tropper, Josef. 1995. "Akkadisch *nuḫḫutu* und die Repräsentierung des Phonems /ḥ/ im Akkadischen", *Zeitschrift für Assyriologie* 85: 58–66.

Vennemann, Theo. 1986. *Neuere Entwicklungen in der Phonologie.* Berlin: Mouton de Gruyter.

Vennemann, Theo. 1988. *Preference Laws for Syllable Structure and the Explanation of Sound Change.* Berlin: Mouton de Gruyter.

Waltke, Bruce and O'Connor, M. 1990. *An Introduction to Biblical Hebrew Syntax.* Winona Lake: Eisenbrauns.

Wehr, Hans. 1979. *A Dictionary of Modern Written Arabic.* Edited by J. Milton Cowan. 4th edition, considerably enlarged and amended by the author. Wiesbaden: Harrassowitz.

Wetzstein, János Gottfried. 1868. "Sprachliches aus den Zeltlagern der syrischen Wüste", *Zeitschrift der Deutschen Morgenländischen Gesellschaft* 22: 69–194.

Wevers, John William. 1970. "*Ḥeth* in classical Hebrew", in: John William Wevers and Donald B. Redford (eds.). *Essays on the Ancient Semitic World*, 101–112. Toronto: University of Toronto Press.

Yeivin, Israel. 1980. *Introduction to the Tiberian Masora* (*Mavo la-masora ha-ṭavranit*), translated and edited by E.J. Revell. Chico, CA: Scholars Press.

Yeivin, Israel. 1985. *The Hebrew Language Tradition as Reflected in the Babylonian Vocalization* (in Hebrew). Jerusalem: The Academy of the Hebrew Language.

Index of subjects

Index of Hebrew Bible passages

Index of authors